The Arab-Israeli Conflict

S0-CHE-263

RENEWALS 458-4574
DATE DUE

WITHDRAWN
UTSA Libraries

Volume No. 28 in the Series
Norwegian Foreign Policy Studies

The Arab-Israeli Conflict

*Psychological Obstacles
to Peace*

By DANIEL HERADSTVEIT

Universitetsforlaget

Oslo · Bergen · Tromsø

© The Norwegian Research Council for
Science and the Humanities 1979
(Norges almenvitenskapelige forskningsråd)
Section: B.48.44.005T

Cover design: Oddvar Wold

ISBN 82-00-01822-9

Printed in Norway by
Tangen-Trykk, Drammen

Distribution offices:

NORWAY
Universitetsforlaget
P.O. Box 2977 Tøyen
Oslo 6

UNITED KINGDOM
Global Book Resources Ltd.
109 Great Russell Street
London WC1B 3Nd

UNITED STATES and CANADA
Columbia University Press
136 South Broadway
Irvington-on-Hudson
New York 10533

Library
University of Texas
at San Antonio

Acknowledgments

During the many years of work on this study, I have been exceedingly fortunate to have the guidance and assistance of an outstanding scholar, Alexander L. George of Stanford University. His tremendously constructive influence on my research can scarcely be adequately aknowledged.

I am also grateful to a large number of other people and institutions. The fellowship support provided by the Ford Foundation allowing me to go to Stanford and Harvard Universities proved to be of particular importance.

Robert D. Putnam gave me useful suggestions on the problems of interviewing elites, and Ole R. Holsti gave me outstanding advice in developing the coding scheme for the study.

Also, I want especially to acknowledge the assistance of Knut Midgaard, Charles Stabell, G. Matthew Bonham, Michael J. Shapiro and Thomas G. Hart, who, along with the others I have mentioned, have read through entire drafts and offered constructive criticism.

Finally, I am indebted to my colleagues at the Norwegian Institute of International Affairs, and particularly John Sanness, who received my ideas and new approaches with openness and enthusiasm.

A special thanks also goes to my research assistant, Ove Narvesen, who proved to be a most vital asset in the research effort.

Contents

CHAPTER I

Introduction

Nobody seems to question seriously the high likelihood of another war between Arabs and Israelis. For the people in the Middle East there is thus the very real possibility that war may again become part of their daily lives. This alone is sufficient cause for concern.

For us all, however, there is also the threat the conflict represents to world peace. The deep involvement of the superpowers, as well as the gradual development of nuclear weapons, reminds us that the possibility of a world war or a nuclear war originating in the Middle East is somewhat more than a hypothetical scenario.

These concerns have been an important source of continued motivation for a research effort on the Middle East conflict at the Norwegian Institute of International Affairs.

Since its inception in 1969, this effort has produced a number of discrete studies, of which the present monograph is the most recent. Although the focus and conceptual framework have evolved, there are several common themes pervading the different studies — beyond the constant focus of attention on this specific conflict. The most significant has been an emphasis on identifying and understanding the stumbling blocks in the way to peace as opposed to focusing on the causes of the conflict; an emphasis on defining processes that might bring about an amelioration in the relations between the conflicting parties as opposed to the processes that produced the conflict in the first place.

Changes in the direction of the research effort, on the other hand, can broadly be accounted for by the strengthening of an aspiration to elaborate on theories and methods that might be relevant to international conflict resolution and international conflicts in general. This concern has naturally led to an increasing sharpening of concepts and focus.

The choice of psychological lenses can in part be attributed to the use of interviews with elites in the conflict area as the main source of data throughout the research effort. Partly the perspective was suggested by the results of the earlier studies. The psychological perspective embraced in this study — implicit in its focus on what we have labeled the cognitive invariants in the conflict situation — is the result.

Understanding the concept 'cognitive invariants' is important in order to understand this investigation. Instead of attempting to define the term directly, it is useful to do it first indirectly by indicating how the concern for the issues embraced by the concept emerged over time in our research effort. At this point it suffices to note that cognitive invariants are the stable and basic orientations of actors that are operational particularly in novel and highly uncertain situations, where less basic cognitive components seem inappropriate and inadequate.

Earlier studies used both a unitary, rational actor perspective (Heradstveit, 1973) and a bargaining perspective (Heradstveit, 1974). The *goals* and *strategies,* as well as the *resources* broadly defined, of the different actors were assessed. The bargaining perspective focused attention on the possible impact of differences in the actors' *definition of the conflict situation.* Certain characteristics of the situation were seen as important constraints on processes that might lead toward open negotiations and bargaining with a view to a conflict settlement. Of particular significance were the differences in meanings ascribed to various aspects of the situation by the participants in the conflict.

The studies suggested that *competing interpretations within* as well as *across* elites might be a major stumbling block in any move toward a settlement. For example, we found that there appeared to exist a systematic variation concerning beliefs about the real motives of the opponent on both sides in the conflict.

In short, these earlier studies suggested questions such as: why is it that some recommend conciliatory moves while others do not? Is this in part because of systematic differences in beliefs? What are the beliefs that together form the whole which defines the actors' interpretation, diagnosis, and prescription vis-à-vis the conflict situation? More specifically, what characterizes the beliefs and thinking of those favorable to conciliatory moves and those who are not?

The focus on the concept of cognitive invariants can thus be seen as an attempt to formulate a more general version of the specific questions suggested by the earlier studies. However, the focus is not an end in itself. In order both to define the concept of cognitive invariants and in order to further motivate our investigation, it is useful to consider the three interrelated issues of *what* aspect of behavior the invariants are hypothesized to affect, *how* the invariants are hypothesized to affect behavior, and under *what conditions* these effects are hypothesized to be most important.

The cognitive invariants of an individual are defined as the basic and stable beliefs of the actor. The concept is obviously *relative*. However, it is meant to exclude beliefs that are quite concrete and situation-specific — and therefore not relevant across situations or only valid in a limited context. The concept excludes beliefs that vary as the situation changes. It is meant to focus attention on beliefs that are sufficiently abstract to have a relatively wide range of application. The invariants are seen as potentially important factors in all phases and for all aspects of the actor's cognitive activities.

From a decision-making perspective, the invariants might influence the individual's interpretation of events, and thus the individual's identification of when there is a need or opportunity for making a choice: the individual's choice and use of information, the individual's definition of what constitutes realistic alternative courses of action, and what values are considered in a choice between alternative courses of action.

From a negotiating and bargaining perspective, the invariants might influence the actor's definition of both the objectives and alternative courses of action available to the opponent; and the actor's perception of the likely consequences of alternative combinations of his own and his opponent's actions.

We hypothesize that the cognitive invariants of the actors will lead them to view different characteristics of the problem as salient for the decision. The invariants will explain different diagnostic propensities, which lead to different choice propensities or preferred policies in the conflict.

The effects of cognitive invariants are assumed to be most pronounced in novel situations and in situations with large degrees of uncertainty. In this case, the situation is hypothesized to provide little or no guidance to the actor. The actor is therefore forced to fall back on his basic beliefs.

In routine and highly certain contexts, on the other hand, the logic of the situation — as it is perceived through more situation-specific beliefs — will dominate one's actions.

Most foreign policy problems are characterized by uncertainty, and this is certainly true of the Arab-Israeli conflict. Initiating policies of conciliation is perceived as risky; there is a lack of adequate information about the situation; and it is difficult to determine the likely outcome of different courses of action.

'Cognitive invariants' is a concept that is not necessarily linked to international conflict situations. It is meant to capture a general characteristic of the individual's information-processing and decision-making behavior. What is needed is a concept that delineates the beliefs particularly relevant to the cognitive domain of international conflicts. The work of Alexander L. George on operational codes has provided the basis for such a delineation.

Simply stated the concept of the operational code is a comprehensive and interrelated set of questions on the nature of political life broadly defined. We hypothesize that the questions sample the beliefs that might form the key invariants in the cognitive domain of international conflicts.

Thus, although cognitive invariants are both a more general and somewhat broader concept, operational code beliefs and cognitive invariants can be viewed as synonymous when we restrict our attention to the context of international conflict situations. This study will therefore hereafter mainly use the concept 'operational code beliefs'.

One of the distinguishing characteristics of the study is its application of the operational code approach. The study seeks to contribute to the research on this approach in a number of ways.

First of all we are dealing with a relatively large sample of elites as opposed to one political 'celebrity' or a severely restricted sample. The operational code studies to date have been for the most part case studies of individuals. The large sample allows us to investigate key assumptions in the operational code approach such as the centrality, stability, and consistency of the belief-dimensions included.

It is also the first time the Operational Code approach has been applied to a contemporary foreign policy problem of great importance. The simultaneous interviewing with actors on both sides of a major ongoing international conflict allows us to investigate the possibly interlocked nature of beliefs in international conflict.

It also adds a new dimension of operational code studies, in that it provides a highly visible and specific conflict domain on which to study the operational code as opposed to dealing with an actor's more general perceptions of international affairs.

The use of interview data as opposed to content analysis of public speeches, documents, letters, etc. linked with the projection of the operational code into a specific conflict, has led to the extension of the operationalization of the operational code construct in that an alternative coding scheme has been developed.

Limitations of the study

The cognitive approach is open to several objections. There is no consensus about what are the most relevant independent variables in explaining foreign policy behavior. It is difficult to isolate the effect of any one variable. However, it should not be necessary to know exactly which variables have the most explanatory power in order to justify their study. We do not claim that cognitive variables are the most powerful variables in accounting for policies in the Arab-Israeli conflict, but they are certainly relevant ones. Our very limited knowledge of what actually determines foreign policy behavior may explain the constant search for better methodologies. But perhaps there are only alternative methodologies, each better suited to the analysis of a particular problem.

In addition there is the fact that few findings within psychology are not debatable, and competing explanations are offered for most phenomena. Yet few dispute that psychology can offer political scientists theoretical insight. Both disciplines deal with human behavior, so it should be possible to extract those elements, assumptions, and postulated relationships that seem to be reasonably well-founded, and to sort out those theoretical formulations that make sense for the political issue at hand. The task becomes the critical one of transforming abstract theory into meaningful questions and hypotheses on foreign policy behavior.

This study focuses narrowly on cognitive preconditions for a settlement rather than on all the various conditions that might be required to bring about a 'settlement'. We recognize that policies or specific choices made in any given situation will be the result of an interaction between the beliefs held by the individual and the characteristics of the situation, and that both these aspects have to be dealt with in explaining outcomes.

We will not be able to predict behavior solely on the basis of knowledge and understanding of the cognitive invariants.

As already stated, we intend to examine the cognitive constraints on the way elites in the conflict define the problem and decide how to respond. It is important that the reader realizes the general limits of a cognitive approach.

Politics is a pluralistic game, where variables other than cognitive ones account for decisions and outcomes. There are situational and institutional, economic, technological, etc., constraints on decision-making behavior, and it would be unreasonable to take a simplistic view of what actually determines this process. In addition, sabotage or lack of efficiency in carrying out a decision, as well as environmental changes, may undermine the decisional intent.

This study deals primarily with beliefs and not behavior, even though it is a central concern of the study to examine the relationship of these beliefs to policy choices.

The concern with the actors' definition of the situation is not something that is not of interest to other approaches on international relations. In decision-making or bargaining this will be central — approaches do overlap. It is more a question of where the emphasis is.

Dealing with the cognitive invariants is limited when it comes to explaining outcomes — what happens. It is clearly less ambitious in what it wants to explain than a bargaining approach or the analysis of specific decisions. At the same time it is more general than both a bargaining or a decision-making perspective in that it is relevant to the explanation of the outcomes of bargaining processes or the outcome of decision-making processes as well, or for that matter information search.

We can only arrive at some conclusions about how these factors will probably constrain elite members in their choices. We hypothesize that disagreements on policies in the conflict can often be related to some fundamental beliefs (cognitive invariants) about the opponent, for example. But knowledge about these beliefs will not necessarily enable us to predict decisions in a decision-making group; even though knowledge of the participants' beliefs about the opponent may enable us to predict the disagreement within the group. This may sound like a contradiction, but note that the issue being discussed here may have no direct bearing upon the participants' images of the opponent — yet these beliefs may be the basis for hidden assumptions forming the premises upon which the disagreement rests. Knowing the operational code of a given elite member we may be able to predict that he is likely to choose option A of three alternatives options A, B, and C. He may, nevertheless, agree to option C because of situational and institutional constraints, thus behaving in a way that is inconsistent with his cognitive invariants.

Another possible limitation of the study has been the concern for methodological and theoretical questions linked to a cognitive approach in the study of conflict.

It has been our purpose to contribute to improvement in conceptual tools and empirical methods, as well as the theoretical basis for a cognitive approach in the study of conflict.

We do hope we have struck a sensible balance between, on the one hand, the concern for improvement in theory as well as empirical methods and, on the other hand, our concern with the substance of the problem: How can the long-lasting conflict between Arabs and Israelis be brought to an end through a negotiated settlement?

Organization of the study

In chapter II the analytical framework is described, as well as the cognitive theory used as an aid in investigating the validity of the operational code approach, including cognitive consistency theory as well as attribution theory.

In chapter III the methodological issues of the data collection are discussed. The particular problems encountered in interviewing persons on a highly sensitive international conflict required both imagination and procedures not readily available in textbooks on methods.

As a consequence we have found it justified to discuss our experiences at length both for the purpose of giving the reader a chance to judge the validity of our data and in order to pass on our particular experiences to those of our colleagues who may engage in similar research.

In chapters IV and V we investigate the stability of beliefs. In chapter IV we explain by the use of attribution theory how parties to a conflict can deal with unexpected developments without changing beliefs, and how the explanation of events tends to follow systematic patterns predicted by the theory. In the subsequent chapter an intertemporal measure of belief stability is used. A descriptive analysis of beliefs at different time periods is investigated. Having conducted interviews at different points in time, we have data that give us some leverage at least to say something about this. But the conclusions here are more in the form of hypotheses, since the data base does not allow us to generalize (lack of a representative sample).

In chapter VI and VII consistency within as well as across the components of the operational code belief system is investigated. And finally we look at the discriminatory value of the operational code to choice propensities in the conflict.

The last chapter examines how much we can say about the problem of conflict resolution on the basis of the results in the previous chapters. What does this cognitive perspective tell us about the problem of resolution of the conflict? What has the cognitive approach identified as the essential issues, and what are the key problems for conflict resolution? What we can say about this will be tempered by some of the limits of the operational code approach. What are the weakness and possible sources of error of this approach to the study of conflict? The study will not resolve the question whether other variables are important, because we have not looked at these other variables. But we will ask the question whether the cognitive approach gives us new and fruitful ideas of how to look at the problem, and whether the operational code is a useful framework to apply to the study of conflict.

Added to this is a discussion of how much the study contributes to methods and theory in research on international conflict.

CHAPTER II

The Conceptual Framework

The operational code approach

Some of our first attempts at applying a cognitive perspective in the study of conflict resolution in the Arab-Israeli conflict dealt with specific beliefs and were concerned with black/white thinking in the conflict.[1] Even though the research did provide additional insight into the psychological mechanisms of what has been called 'the inherent bad faith model', it did not tell us very much about the problem of conflict resolution. What we really needed was an analytical framework to examine the *relationship* between beliefs, as well as a more direct link to policies conducted by the parties involved.

In the search for an analytical framework that could aid us in making some progress in this respect, we turned to Alexander L. George's refinement of the operational code construct as a framework for further analysis.[2] The construct was originally put forward in some early works of Nathan Leites.[3]

George defines the operational code as

> a prism or filter that influences the actor's perception and diagnosis of political situations, and that provides norms and standards to guide and channelize his choices of action in specific situations. The function of an operational code belief system in decision-making, then, is to provide the actor with 'diagnostic propensities' and 'choice propensities'.[4]

Note that in his definition George talks about a *system* of beliefs. The operational code assumes that there are certain forms of interdependence among the beliefs constituting the code. In other words, it looks not only at the content of separate beliefs, but also at the *relationship* among the beliefs.

Rather than viewing beliefs as a random collection, the operational code approach tries to capture the rules for actions as these are constrained and governed by beliefs. The code deals with how we relate our knowledge of the world (knowledge here also includes values) to action, and what rules for action we believe in.

The operational code as dealt with in the works of Alexander L. George and later Ole R. Holsti and others[5] offers a useful starting point for the analysis of beliefs in the Arab-Israeli conflict. It points out the value of looking at beliefs as a system, of examining the centrality of different beliefs within this system, and offers theory and hypotheses as to how these beliefs may determine information-processing and political choice.

The 'decision' rules or 'heuristics' outlined in the operational code do not necessarily conform to 'rational action'. An operational code assumes that beliefs are linked in the cognitive structure of political elites with a certain order and stability which make it possible to analyze beliefs as belonging to a system. We are therefore not dealing with specific beliefs and specific choices, but with belief sets belonging to a system of beliefs and choice propensities. We are not looking at the correlation between *specific* beliefs and *specific* choices.

Key issues: Centrality, stability, and consistency

The operational code states that the content of some central belief dimensions will have a strong resemblance to certain types of approaches to political action. The main concern of the operational code is then to search for these crucial or central belief dimensions.

The notion of centrality refers to the degree to which other beliefs in the belief system are dependent on the belief in question. Knowledge of a central belief enables us to say a lot about other beliefs, and changes in a central belief will lead to a number of other changes.[6]

Therefore the identification of central beliefs becomes an objective of the study.

On an intuitive basis, we did have some notions about what beliefs could be relevant and central to the problem of conflict resolution, but the operational code points out the relative centrality of different beliefs as a significant problem and offers a guideline on how to approach the issue. The operational code sets up questions that focus on fundamental issues of political life and what should be the appropriate strategy. The views or premises revealed in answer to these questions comprise the beliefs assumed to be central regarding the relationship between knowledge and political action. The code sets up a number of 'master beliefs' likely to be of great impact across situations. The code does not comprise the total set of beliefs of the individual, but only those that are believed to be significant to political action. Thus, the operational code provides a guide for devising a comprehensive set of beliefs relevant and central to political action across situations — beliefs considered most relevant when response is calculated vis-à-vis the opponent in an international conflict. The set of 'master beliefs' is assumed to have an impact on the way information is processed, options are formulated and evaluated, and action taken.

The rationale of the operational code approach is to deal with a few manageable categories that will presumably extract the essential elements of the person's political belief-system. Knowing these belief dimensions, we will be able to say a lot about this person's inclinations in making a political choice.

In the operational code approach abstract categories are developed for classifying a whole set of beliefs. The concept of centrality refers to the relative position of idea-elements in a more comprehensive set of beliefs conceived of as a system. The operational code makes some assumptions on centrality before starting the data collection. The construct offers at the outset a number of categories. The categories listed limit the data collection, in that it is implied that these are the belief dimensions that we should look for.[7]

Once the belief dimensions listed in the construct have been charted, the issue of centrality will not be dropped. The search for centrality continues. With the aid of cognitive theory we will examine the stability and consistency of the beliefs included in the operational code belief system. The theory postulates that the most consistent and stable beliefs are also the most central ones.[8] The purpose of this exercise is eventually to come up with a new construct that will provide a simpler and better guide to charting beliefs central to political life. This will be done in the last chapter, in which we discuss the implications of the results.

Stability

The stability of beliefs is important. The operational code beliefs rapidly lose their value as predictors if the cross-situational consistency of the beliefs is weak. We shall therefore make an assessment of the stability of the beliefs, both by a descriptive analysis of how beliefs have developed over time in the Arab-Israeli conflict and by investigating how parties to conflict deal with their causal analysis of events (attributional tendencies). With the aid of recent developments in cognitive theory on attribution,[9] we shall make a systematic investigation of this.

Since cognitive theory proposes that stable beliefs are at the same time the most central beliefs, an assessment of stability is therefore at the same time an assessment of centrality.

Consistency

In analyzing the beliefs as belonging to a system, an important question arises: what beliefs seem to go together? It is not difficult to trace 'logical' linkages between the beliefs. How this operates on the cognitive level is a far more complicated question. In this analysis we are concerned with the cognitive linkages. If we discover that two beliefs seem to go together across a number of persons, it does not necessarily mean that these two beliefs are linked together in a 'system' in each person's beliefs; it cannot be presumed that when one belief changes, other beliefs in the code will also change. However, we will take it as a strong indicator of a system linkage in the person's set of beliefs.

Cognitive theory proposes that consistency works more strongly on central beliefs than on more peripheral beliefs. We therefore expect consistency to apply to a higher extent to the more fundamental cognitive orientations as opposed to the less central or peripheral beliefs, which we will expect to be more inconsistent. Consistency can thus serve as an aid in assessing centrality. The belief dimensions that are most consistent in their structure will also tend to be the most central ones. This stems from the fact that central beliefs, being used most frequently as an organizing tool in the individual's information-processing, tend to be *simple* in structure and have a high degree of consistency.[10]

The operational code defines consistency as connectedness or linkages between idea-elements in the operational code beliefs conceived of as a system. But rather than have pre-conceived notions of how these linkages function, we are going to investigate this. We may say that we have a more exploratory approach toward consistency, rather than taking consistency as given. In view of the controversy among social psychologists on how consistency operates, this seems reasonable.[11]

It may also be an important task of political research to 'borrow' from social psychology, to test even widely held assumptions in the field, because we are transferring the theory to settings that social psychologists typically do not deal with. An operational code analysis allows this.

While it is important that the beliefs themselves remain stable across situations, their centrality varies from one situation to another. The relevance or centrality of different beliefs in the code may change with different types of situations in international relations. The centrality of 'the image of the opponent', for example, may be more central in a conflict situation than in cooperative situations. In short, the operational code lacks a more specific theory or typology of situations to identify the types of beliefs most relevant in particular situations. It is a question of not only what beliefs will be evoked in a given situation, but also how central they are to each situation. This analysis will be limited to a situation of intense international conflict.

A test of the importance in practice of the operational code beliefs would be to chart the beliefs of the individuals whose behavior we want to predict, and then look at their behavior. This introduces another limitation to the study, in that we have no direct test of the pragmatic validity of the construct. We are not in a position to do this with the type of data we have. The respondents were asked to voice their positions on issues central to the Arab-Israeli conflict.

In this way, we obtained their policy statements. This is not the same as overt behavior and could be compared to what some cognitive psychologists call 'behavioral intentions'.[12]

The basic psychological mechanisms

Cognitive psychology concerns itself with attitudes and ideas. These are 'mentalistic' concepts.

The main issues in cognitive psychology are how beliefs relate to one another, how and to what extent they mediate behavior and, finally, under what conditions they change.[13] We generate beliefs about ourselves and the world through experience. In cognitive theory, 'belief' is defined as:

> If a man perceives some relationship between two things or between some thing and a characteristic of it, he is said to hold a belief.[14]

We give meaning to our environment through beliefs.

It follows from the previous discussion of the operational code that centrality is an important concept in our study. The notion of centrality in cognitive theory refers to the degree to which other beliefs in the belief system are dependent on the belief in question. If we change a central belief, it is expected that other beliefs will change. The centrality of a belief depends on how it is reinforced (proven to be correct to the individual).[15] All beliefs are not held with the same degree of confidence. The amount of information stored under a given belief, and how often it is used as an organizing concept, varies.

We may thus discover 'basic beliefs' on which the other beliefs rest.[16]

The beliefs most resistant to change are the most central ones.[17] Cognitive theory states that we are conservative in that we tend to change as little as possible. Change in one belief requires changes in some other beliefs within the system. The beliefs most likely to change are the weakest beliefs, or those less central in the system, while the strongest beliefs, or those most central in the system, will remain more resistant to change.[18]

Most of our beliefs are not based on a single experience, but result from generalizations of experience over time, during which we also apply experiences to a broader set of phenomena. We store the experience in our brain by abstraction and generalize it by applying it to a broader set of cases than that with which we have direct experience.

From a complicated social interaction we draw out the essential features of the situation.

Cognitive theorists not only argue that we generalize from a limited set of experiences, but also that this is a necessary process. Every event is unique, but it would be impossible for us to deal with reality if we were to treat every event as unique. (Bem calls this a 'thinking device'.[19])

Through generalizing we also acquire stereotypes. We deal with people on the basis of our limited experiences, on the basis of beliefs that ultimately rest on central beliefs. The formation of stereotypes provides yardsticks with which we organize our experiences.[20]

Such yardsticks in the Arab-Israeli conflict provide the participants with a convenient tool for interpreting the movements of the opponent. The beliefs are simple in their structure, frequently used, and are shared by a large number of people. The cognitive inference mechanism works to keep the structure of beliefs — particularly central beliefs — as simple as possible.

An example of a central belief on the Israeli side is that the Arabs want to destroy Israel; a similar master belief on the Arab side is that Israel is expansionist. Since many other beliefs are linked to central notions of this kind, a change in the content of a central belief would mean that the elite members would have to change other beliefs as well.

Stability and Change

Cognitive theory states that beliefs (especially central beliefs) remain relatively stable over time.[21] The more stable a belief, the more valuable it becomes as a variable for prediction. The usefulness of the operational code construct relies on the stability of beliefs. An inherent mechanism in the individual 'works against' change, so minimal change will be expected. Cognitive theorists have outlined in great detail the rules governing this process.[22] Since it would be disfunctional for change to take place each time inconsistencies occur, resistance to change in beliefs is highly functional. A single instance of inconsistency is usually not enough to force a person to reconsider his beliefs. If this should occur, the individual would have to reconsider other beliefs linked to that belief. One should be cautious in labeling the resistance to change as 'irrational' and the like.[23]

Cognitive theory claims that minimal cognitive adjustments will take place with change in environmental or situational factors.[24]

How can stability in beliefs be explained?

We now turn to how parties to the conflict make their causal analysis, how they explain events, and how they draw inferences from these events. We ask how the parties to a conflict arrive at answers to the question *why* something happens. For example, how does one party in a conflict explain what caused the behavior of the opponent when the opponent behaved in a way that contradicted his earlier theory about how the opponent behaves?

Causality as a main rule governing the formation of the belief systems has been emphasized by many.

> Our method of representing beliefs of decision-makers reflects the proposition that decision-makers tend to believe that international events are related causally and thus try to infer causal relationships underlying these events and the actions of other nations, even when there is little or no evidence of causal nature.[25]

When we try to explain events, we may say that we act as 'intuitive' scientists.[26] We try to explain the behavior of others. But we also try to explain our own behavior. Why did I behave as I did? As 'intuitive' scientists we try to come up with the best explanation possible. In most cases our judgement is not based on one single observation but on several.[27]

The individual does not only observe behavior, but takes into consideration the 'circumstances in which it occurs'.[28] These are what Bem calls the 'controlling variables' of the behavior. Observation of behavior in addition to 'controlling variables' is the basis on which the individual arrives at what cognitive psychologists typically call 'the definition of the situation'. To the extent that the behavior is free from 'controlling variables', the individual will impute the causes of behavior to the actor. Even though Bem does not discuss it explicitly, 'controlling variables' must be meant to refer only to those that the individual perceives.[29]

But how does self-perception differ from interpersonal perception? This difference is important in our study. Bem mentions four ways in which self-perception may differ from interpersonal perception:

a) The private stimuli play a role — even though this varies with the situation — and these private stimuli are, of course, not directly available to the observer.
b) Our experiences of the past that determine the meaning attached to what is perceived (observed) are not available in the same way to the 'stranger'.
c) The protection of self-esteem and defense against threat. This may distort self-attributions in various ways.
d) Features of the situation are differentially salient to yourself and the observer. There seems to be a difference of focus in attention between the actor and the observer. The actor's attention may be more focused toward situational cues, while to the observer, the actor's behavior is more salient.[30]

These sources of 'imperfection' will concern us here. What are the types of causal analysis involved in the Arab-Israeli conflict which maintain beliefs that may impede resolution of the conflict? Are there any errors and biases in the way in which information is processed? Is there a systematic distortion when Arabs and Israelis explain the way the enemy behaves, and, equally important, the way they behave themselves?

Attribution theory

To aid us in this analysis we shall turn to attribution theory. Attribution theory specifies the conditions under which behavior is seen as caused by the person performing the action, or by environmental influences and constraints. Attributions or causal explanations for behavior and outcomes are characterized in terms of an internal/external or dispositional/situational dichotomy.[31]

Internal property: abilities, traits or motives
External property: environmental pressures and constraints

Attribution theory deals with the likelihood of alternative causal factors as explanations of observed behavior.[32]

When the causes of behavior and outcomes are being explained, 'logical' thinking processes are of course involved. For example, when we observe a consistent behavior of an actor under different conditions and at different times, we are most likely to explain that behavior as caused by some internal traits of the actor. Such 'logical' causal analysis is also involved when we observe an actor whose behavior we perceive as differing from that of other actors. In such cases environmental influences and constraints are not sufficient to explain his behavior, and internal attributions will be made. Or in situations where we perceive alternative courses of action available to the actor, his particular choice will most likely be attributed to internal traits. Perceived freedom of choice may sometimes explain the causal analysis made. Other postulates about this kind of logical schema for attributional analysis could be listed, but it is unnecessary to discuss this in detail, since it is causal analysis, containing biases and distortions, that is of interest to our study.[33]

The parties to the conflict will be interested in structuring 'reality', so that they can respond most appropriately to this 'reality'.[34] They are active information seekers and want to know as much as possible about what happens, and *why* it happens. They certainly do not want distorted facts, but facts relevant to their contingent interaction with the enemy, so that the optimal choices can be made. Nevertheless, attribution theory points to information-processing biases that may act as cognitive constraints on what could be seen as the most logical or rational way of making inferences from the enemy's behavior and our own behavior.[35]

The parties to the conflict *want control* of their environment.[36] Therefore they want their assumptions and general theories on the conflict to be valid. Sources of bias can have serious repercussions. Any distortions that we find in the way elite members in the conflict process information may potentially also have serious implications for resolution of the conflict.

We are asking whether the techniques the elites use for collecting, processing, and interpreting the data are adequate. In examining why something happens we claim that there are systematic distortions involved in the analysis. This leads us to the aspect of attribution theory which postulates that there will be a systematic bias in the attribution process. It is claimed by attribution theories that even though we act as 'intuitive' scientists in the search for explanations of what is happening in our environment, we nevertheless do not proceed exactly 'scientifically'. Our attributional tendencies have a bias, called by the theorists the *fundamental attribution error*.[37]

The hypothesis, as put forward by Jones and Nisbett,[38] claims that in making our inferences about behavior there is a *tendency* to over-emphasize situational variables (the circumstances in which it occurs) when explaining our own behavior, while when observing the behavior of others, there is a tendency to over-emphasize dispositional (internal characteristics of the actor) variables.[39] We do not draw statistical inferences because we analyze the behavior of others differently from how we analyze our own behavior. Actors are likely

24

to attribute their own behavioral choices to situational factors and constraints, while observers attribute the same choices to the actor's stable abilities, attitudes, and personality traits.

Behavior is thus seen by the observer to be a manifestation of the actor and seen by the actor to be a response to the situation.

The tendency to infer dispositional causes is *enhanced when the observer dislikes the actor who performs the blameworthy act*.[40] The degree of involvement in the observed action also influences the attribution process. The higher the degree of involvement the greater the chance of attributional bias. Where the observer is also an actor, he is likely to exaggerate the uniqueness and emphasize the dispositional origins of the responses of others to his own actions. He assumes his own actions to be perfectly standard, unexceptional, and unprovocative.[41]

The one extreme degree of involvement is the mutual contingency interaction and the other extreme is passive observation.[42] The Middle East conflict will be viewed as an instance of the former. The conflict is seen by the elite members as an interaction process where the actions of the other side directly affect their own side and vice versa. This situation should increase the likelihood of attributional bias.

In the study we will investigate whether the causal analysis of the parties to the conflict conforms to the pattern attribution theory would predict. The extent to which this is the case makes changes in beliefs in the conflict difficult and accounts for their relative stability. Beliefs about an object may be held across situations, just as beliefs about a certain type of situation may be held across beliefs about objects.[43] Beliefs about the enemy, for example, may be held across changing beliefs about the power relationships in the conflict. But it is also possible to imagine a change in beliefs about the enemy while beliefs about the power relationships remain the same. But the most stable beliefs would generally be those with reference to internal propensities of the actors, e. g. 'Jews are good businessmen' or 'Arabs are irrational'.[44]

The extent to which parties to a conflict are dispositional in their analysis of the apparent behavior may make their subsequent beliefs very hard to change.

But in addition to investigating hypotheses from attribution theory that deals with cognitive processes, we will make a descriptive analysis of change. To make such a descriptive analysis we will have to know our point of departure.

Theoretically, the problem is quite easy to state: A belief system at time (T_1) is transformed into another state at time (T_2). In the meantime, various events have intervened. The difficulty arises because identification of cumulative processes over time, which do seem to play an important role in belief change,[45] may be difficult to record or measure. These are incremental changes over large time periods.

In the Middle East, wars may be a testing ground for established beliefs. The June war in 1967 and the October war in 1973 may be examples of such 'reality tests'. A war then becomes an experience that may lead to readjustments of beliefs, but these readjustments may not necessarily lead to more conciliatory beliefs. Wars of this type can be characterized as dramatic events, which sometimes lead to drastic changes in beliefs. But there is also the possibility that wars may be taken as a confirmation of pre-established beliefs. We will make an assessment of the stability of beliefs before and after the October war in 1973.

The usual pattern will be that central beliefs will remain relatively stable over time while less central beliefs may undergo a higher change rate. We can also find important individual differences in resistance to change. At the same time, belief systems are not static, but are in a dynamic relationship to their environment.

Much research has been devoted to determining under what conditions the weakest link in the belief system may change, while less has been devoted to the conditions under which the strongest links in the belief system change. Research on the effect of communication and persuasion, for example, has mainly concerned change in the weakest links or incremental changes.[46]

Cognitive theory states that a single incremental change sets in motion a cumulative change, since the original change leads one to seek further information, which again leads to further change, and so on.

We are only concerned with the stability of any one of the 'master beliefs' constituting the operational code. Central beliefs are resistant to change — and if they do change, there are far-reaching repercussions for the belief system. Which beliefs must be changed in order to promote conflict resolution, and which beliefs are likely to change, are some of the questions we will discuss.

Types of Change

To further illustrate our approach, we shall clarify the types of change we are concerned with. The research to date has been concentrated on how cognitions control behavioral responses. As previously stated, there is an interrelationship between cognition and behavior. Change in beliefs will usually be related to behavioral changes and vice versa.

Inconsistency between overt behavior and beliefs can lead to changes in behavior, cognitions, or both.[47] But the response to a given stimulus may first take the form of behavior, followed by the cognitive

26

response. In other words, the cognitive response becomes the third chain in the link (I, Stimuli — II, behavioral response — III, cognitive response). But this can be taken as a learning experience, whereby the cognitive readjustments or new beliefs become determinants for subsequent action. These newly formed beliefs will in turn determine how new information is being interpreted. Subsequent behavior is then calculated on the basis of these newly established beliefs. Thus we look at the October war as a dramatic intervening event from which we hypothesize that some changes in beliefs have taken place. However, we shall not be able to explain how these change processes have been triggered, because we do not have sufficient time series data to investigate processes of change.[48]

Cognitive theory tells us that the meaning we give the environment is of major importance for how we act. This assumption must be modified somewhat to account for the possibility that the stimuli may trigger the action directly. Afterwards the individual will attribute meaning to the action (why I behaved as I did). In instances like this, beliefs do not control behavior, and as a consequence, behavior cannot be predicted on the basis of beliefs.[49]

We are also open to the possibility that the environment places constraints on behavior that alter behavior but not necessarily beliefs. For example, Soviet policies in the Middle East have taken many twists and turns without the 'master beliefs' in the operational code being changed. This sort of 'adaptive' behavior is distinct from those behavioral changes with which the operational code is concerned. Tactics may change very quickly, but they are based on the same premises, i.e., one's set of operational code beliefs which permits, indeed encourages, *adaptive* behavior. These are situation-specific changes in behavior, but not necessarily changes in the central beliefs on which we focus.

Previous studies on operational code beliefs reveal that these beliefs vary considerably in the extent to which they facilitate flexible, adaptive behavior.[50] In international conflicts like the Middle East conflict, one may too easily assume at the outset that beliefs of the elites are rigid. The opposite may also be a problem in international relations — assuming that beliefs are flexible to the point of losing the ability to act sufficiently firmly.

There may be significant behavioral changes (adaptive changes) which do not trigger cognitive changes. 'Hawks' suddenly behaving in a compromising fashion may be attributed to a change in central beliefs about the opponent, but may also be attributed to situational constraints. Behavioral change does not always lead to cognitive change.[51]

Consistency theory

Up to this point we have dealt with stability of beliefs, which is one of the more important assumptions in the operational code approach.

Attribution theory does not, however, tell us anything about the way we link beliefs. But we have chosen to deal with the operational code beliefs as a system, which means that we assume that the beliefs are connected internally. To deal with the assumption on linkages we will draw on *consistency theory*.[52] This theory or notion within cognitive theory deals with how we relate beliefs and the relationship of beliefs to behavior. As a matter of fact, much of cognitive psychology has been based on the notion that we need to see reality as being consistent (balanced). From this basic idea was derived the theory of cognitive dissonance, which has produced an enormous amount of research.[53]

The consistency notion or principle refers to the idea that human beings strive toward consistency between beliefs that are seen as relevant and toward consistency between beliefs and behavior. In explaining why this is the case, cognitive theory claims that learning depends on perceived regularities and patterns in our environment, which impel consistencies in our beliefs. Our preference for balanced states makes us remember balanced states better than imbalanced ones.[54]

Cognitive theorists hold that much of our learning is a search for regularity in causality. We find lawfulness in events. Each interaction is, of course, unique, but for the mind it is necessary to make events similar or minimally different. The person's idea-elements are consistent, because this represents the most efficient way of processing information. The organization of ideas along rules of consistency enables a person to interpret his environment without too much pain. The individual will strive toward consistency within his cognitive system and also between this cognitive system and his behavior.[55]

We therefore assume that consistency affects the storing of our past experience (the formation of beliefs), our information-processing, and our behavior. To determine inconsistency, the total set of *relevant* beliefs (in the eyes of the individual) has to be considered. What on the surface appears quite inconsistent (what the individual says, for example) may be quite consistent when we look at the reasoning underlying the beliefs expressed: this is called *hidden consistency*.[56]

Cognitions can be either relevant or irrelevant to each other (belonging to the unit). For consistency to be operational between two given beliefs or beliefs and behavior, the individual must see or feel them as *relevant* to each other. If they are relevant and inconsistent, they will produce tension or strain; this situation can be dealt with in a number of ways, with change of beliefs being one of the ways in which consistency is restored. Experiments in the field of dissonance theory indicate that we do tolerate inconsistent cognitions without experiencing dissonance.[57]

It is only after we have passed a certain 'threshold' that we experience dissonance. It is generally agreed that we do have a lot of 'inconsistency' that we are not even aware of. We may have inconsistent unconscious beliefs, but the need for consistency becomes more operational when the beliefs are 'activated'.[58] The amount of inconsistency has to reach a certain threshold to produce change. Imbalance does not always create stress or tension toward consistency. The controversial issue is how much inconsistency do we tolerate before making adjustments.

A main concern of our research is to learn which beliefs seem to constitute a unit or a system, or which clusters of beliefs are linked together. The answer to this question determines to a high degree the predictive power of consistency. A high degree of relatedness of the beliefs we have measured will increase their predictive value, assuming this general notion of consistency-striving.

Cognitive theory does not specify or clarify which beliefs will be seen as 'relevant'. This therefore has to be explored by examining our data. No one seems to deny that we are governed by some consistency principle, but how and to what extent is open to argument. While we take the need for consistency for granted, the research issue is the degree to which it applies, and how it applies, to our data.

Even though there is a general agreement that there is a consistency principle involved in the way cognitions are organized and between these cognitions and behavior, we do also tolerate inconsistency.

Relevance — Consistency

The notion of consistency assumes certain relationships between beliefs. If the individual does not view beliefs as related, there can be no striving for consistency. These relationships need not be constant, but may differ with different situations.[59] Our beliefs are not a random collection of individual beliefs, but a system with constraints to which beliefs are connected. Beliefs are linked in various ways to each other, and change in one linkage may require changes in others.[60] The extent to which we relate or link beliefs is controversial.

In the case of the Middle East conflict, it is probable that beliefs tend to be highly related. There is a 'collective' thinking around the issues where conformity also strongly operates. If this assumption is correct, consistency should operate rather strongly. Furthermore, differences exist where some individuals have their belief systems organized in a more coherent way than others. Differences may also appear according to the type of problem being considered.

Are beliefs linked into extensive systems, or do we find beliefs linked into small units? The answer is clearly not yes or no. Among other things, it seems to depend on the problem.

Converse finds a rather sharp distinction between how the 'public' organizes its political beliefs and how the 'elites' do, because 'elites' are much more consistent than the 'public'. We find, according to Converse, more extensive belief systems among elites, while we move steadily into smaller units as we move 'down' in society.[61] While as a rule this is probably true for the issue areas in Converse's investigation, he makes the mistake of generalizing. While elites are likely to have greater self-consciousness, articulateness, and discussion ability than 'the public' as to the content and validity of politically relevant beliefs, this might not hold true in other areas. If Converse had asked for beliefs central to elites as well as to 'the public', it is far from certain that he would have found this sharp distinction. However, Converse's findings illustrate the important general point that the need for consistency becomes more operational when beliefs in the given problem area are frequently 'activated'. We are most consistent in the areas in which we are experts or our thinking is often challenged.

In the Arab-Israeli conflict, the political elites express their beliefs constantly and must defend or account for changes. Therefore we expect the need for consistency to be operational. We also expect consistency to be more operational for *narrow portions* of the operational code belief system.

The need for consistency does not fall a prey to rules of formal logic. The notion 'consistency' is meant to operate not in a logical but in a psychological sense.

The issue is how parties to the conflict combine beliefs cognitively. How does one idea-element lead to another psychologically? We may call this the psychology of inference or 'psycho-logic'. What matters is that the individual experiences certain ideas as connected on a *subjective* level. What matters is how and to what extent the individual *feels* that beliefs belong together.

Obviously there is considerable overlap with 'logical thinking'. This may be most usefully demonstrated by representing the thought processes in the form of a syllogism.[62]

But while formal logic tends to be two-valued, individuals typically discriminate between a number of gradations along such dimensions as likelihood or desirability.[63] The internal coherence of an individual system in the Arab-Israeli conflict will tend to be governed by various constraints, such as wishful thinking or other non-rational needs. This in turn will cause consistency to deviate from 'logical' rules. For example, in our previous study, when asking questions about the likelihood that guerrillas in Jordan would be defeated by King Hussein, we noted systematic differences in the way the respondents arrived at their probability estimate. Those who saw a defeat as desirable would upgrade the likelihood of defeat, while those seeing defeat as undesirable would downgrade the likelihood of defeat.

The way Converse deals with consistency comes close to the way we operationalize the notion of consistency in our study. Converse defines consistency both in a static and in a dynamic case. Statically, . . . 'the success we would have in predicting, given initial knowledge, that an individual holds a specified attitude, that he holds certain further ideas and attitudes'.[64]

In the dynamic case, as: 'the probability that a change in the perceived status (truth, desirability and so forth) of one idea-element would psychologically require from the point of view of the actor, some compensating change(s) in the status of idea-elements elsewhere in the configuration.'[65]

We will investigate how beliefs in the Arab-Israeli conflict are constrained. Given, for example, that we know the beliefs held by a given elite member about the image of the opponent, how successfully can we predict his self-image or image of change?

In our study we will only investigate linkages in a static sense. A dynamic way of investigating consistency would be to see what change in a belief would produce changes in other beliefs. This we do not have a sufficient data base to assess.

CHAPTER III

Method: Interviewing Elites in International Conflict

Introduction

Access to data and measurement problems are common, in varying degrees, to all the social sciences. We will not attempt to treat these problems on a general level, but will discuss them as we have confronted them in this study. Since relatively few studies in political science have conducted interviews with representatives of both sides in an international conflict, our experiences and the specific problems we encountered may be of particular interest. The purpose of this discussion thus is twofold: to make clear the limitations of our data, and to share experiences that might be useful for researchers doing similar projects. The discussion will mainly center around two problems: the *validity* of the answers given to our questions, and the *representativeness* of the respondents.

We recognize that the problems are serious. Much time was devoted to this. The quality of the interviewing procedure is essential for obtaining good results. When considering the objectives of the study, we thought that interviewing would be the best data collection strategy.

We expected to ascertain beliefs not readily found in documents, but nevertheless important to the research problem. For example, it is quite common to play down disagreements on policies in the newspapers which confidential interviews may reveal.

We regarded the comparative aspect of the study as essential. The comparative aspect becomes important when dealing with conflict resolution. One definite advantage of interviewing is the possibility of simultaneous data collection, as well as the possibility of posing the same questions on both sides. It offered a good starting point for comparative analysis of beliefs.

Response validity

The interviews were conducted in Egypt, Jordan, Lebanon and Syria in 1970. In 1972 *further* interviews were conducted in Israel. In this first round we used informal directed interviews. Types of questions asked are listed in the appendix. In 1974 and 1976 we conducted interviews in the same countries, except Syria in 1974, and except Syria and Lebanon in 1976, using a standardized interview schedule with open-ended answers. The first round of interviews (70—72) served as a pilot study.

For all the years 70—72—74—76 the interviewing was carried out in April and May, and the respondents from all samples are listed in the appendix.

Measuring belief systems directly is simply impossible. We are dealing with internal subjective states that are not directly measurable.[1] Some beliefs may also simply be difficult to verbalize. Other beliefs might be hidden to the individual. This is a general problem in measuring belief systems, which we will not deal with any further. But when interviewing, there is also the possibility that interviewees may deliberately mislead the interviewer — give instrumental answers. They will not tell us what they 'really' think, and if this is the case the data may not be valid.

Any group in an international conflict will tend to define the situation to its own advantage — or what it thinks is to its own advantage. In a sensitive conflict like the Middle East conflict, the possibility of expressing opinions believed to be useful to one's own side in the conflict may be present in the interview situation. If the interviewee deliberately tries to mislead the interviewer into something that the interviewee does not believe, then we get invalid beliefs expressed. Since instrumentality of this type seems to come frequently to the mind in discussions on interviewing in the Middle East, a further elaboration on this seems to be in order.

The issue stated simply is: Does the interviewee say what he thinks or does he try to convey an opinion that he believes will be useful to his side in the conflict or to himself? If the latter is the case, the respondents express themselves in ways that conflict with our interests. The problem may be of two kinds: 1) Does the respondent expect to gain by stating certain beliefs on some issues (of course, this problem may differ from question to question) that deviate from his 'true beliefs'? 2) Does he see a risk in being frank (sanctions)? The problem is to create a situation where the respondents will generate a verbal behavior that adequately reflects their beliefs (validity), and that these beliefs will be accurately repeated both in the note-taking and the coding of the data (reliability). In other words, by deciding how to conduct the interview, we are, to a certain extent, able to manipulate those variables that may influence the verbal behavior of the interviewee. Some of the variables are given, like the interview situation, but others can be dealt with in various ways, so as to increase the validity of the answers. An example of this is to reduce the possibility that the interviewee would fear sanctions for being frank. Before starting the interview we underlined the anonymity of the interview and the note-taking. Nothing the respondent said could be traced back to him. In this way we tried to neutralize possible fears of sanctions that the interviewee might have had.

When Yassir Arafat speaks in the UN, the influence on the verbal behavior is probably somewhat different from, let's say, a personal conversation with Arafat in a refugee camp in Amman. What he says may or may not be the same. The interview situation is given, but still the answers may depend on how the interviewee will define the interview situation. A respondent in a conflict area is likely to consider the motives of the interviewer, and he will also try to make an assessment of how his own needs can be adapted to the interview. A respondent may try to defend action that he suspects the interviewer disapproves of. He may try to present both himself and the party to the conflict he sympathizes with in a more favorable light, making energetic efforts in trying to persuade that his conflict party has 'history' or 'right' on its side, etc. But how the interviewee will do this is also dependent on how the interviewer presents himself.[2]

Interviewers

An influential factor in any interview situation is the interviewees perception of *who* is doing the interviewing. Much of the debate on interviewing is centered on minimizing the negative function of the interviewer — namely not to influence the respondent in a way that will produce biases. An important source of bias in the Middle East is probably introduced if the respondent perceives the interviewer as representing certain positions in the conflict. This may lead the respondent to give either biased answers served to please the interviewer or answers that are polemics against those views he imputes to the interviewer.

Saying that one is neutral does not eliminate this bias, because some will perceive neutrality as opposition. It is also possible that Arabs perceived this differently from Israelis, or that there was also a variation within elites. An alternative to the 'neutral outsider' approach would have been to try to appear as a 'subjective insider' of both groups in the conflict. It may very well be that giving the respondent the impression that we were on his side in the conflict would have led to more goodwill than saying that we made an effort to present all points of view. This would not have conformed with rules of ethics from our point of view. We would not say one thing in Cairo and another thing in Tel Aviv. Also, the 'subjective insider' approach does not eliminate the problem of bias.

It was also obvious from our experience that 'neutrality' was immediately and widely accepted. It seemed to appeal to their sense of 'fairness'. In no cases did interviewers report that any interviewee argued against this position. As a matter of fact it seemed to please most of them. Remarks like, 'We're happy to hear that', or, 'There is really need for objective information about this problem', were quite frequent. We did manage, we believe, to a considerable extent to appear as 'neutral observers' to the respondents, a fact that in many cases may have been a prerequisite for getting interviews. The Norwegian sponsorship of the study added credibility to this claim.

Our position as researchers on conflict was also helpful. Our impression was that this stimulated openness and frankness. It was often expressed that serious research on the conflict was necessary. It probably also reduced expectancies of rewards and sanctions, since there was no immediate effect from what was told to us. Instrumental thinking should therefore be reduced.

Interviewees

When the possibilities of invalid answers are being evaluated, it is important to take into account *whom* you are interviewing, not only the presentation of oneself. Some people are quite sensitive to various kinds of influence. It is easy in interview situations to manipulate their answers. They may, for example, express what they feel is the 'right' thing to say. The possibility of invalid answers increases with these types of respondents.

Politically active elites do not generally fall into this category. Research has shown that we find a relatively high degree of consistency between what political activists say in an interview and what they will say and do in other situations.[3] The respondents we have are political activists.

Here we also have to differentiate among the respondents along roles. When a general director of the Foreign Ministry in Israel grants an interview, instrumentality may be strong. A university professor, on the other hand, may simply want to give as fair a presentation as possible.

Degree of involvement in the issue may be influential. We are asking about an issue in which the respondents are deeply involved. The respondent's involvement probably does not only increase the possibility of instrumental answers, but reduces the possibility that the respondent will give answers to 'please' the interviewer. The issue is so important to him that he will express his opinion despite his feeling that it may run counter to the interviewer's personal opinions.

In addition to considerations of who is interviewing whom, the type of question asked plays a crucial role. Is it reasonable to think that the interviewee has much to gain by not expressing his 'true' beliefs? This may differ from question to question. The sensitivity of the issue must be taken into account. When sensitivity is high, the respondent will simply refuse to answer or give a highly misleading answer. But there is not one single question that we asked that could be considered highly sensitive. Most of the questions demand purely descriptive answers, where it is difficult to see how the respondents should have anything to gain by not telling what they believe. Moreover, the respondents do not know our coding scheme.

So far we have only discussed the possible biases introduced into the interview situation by the respondent wanting to influence the interviewer (extrinsic motivation).[4]

But, there is another major source of motivation in an interview: the opportunity to speak out freely about a subject that occupies and interests the interviewee (intrinsic motivation).[5] The interview is a two-way process between the respondent and the interviewer. In this process, probably too much discussion has been focused on the respondent's possible wish to influence the interviewer. On the other hand, it is important to reduce biases in the answers by systematically charting those variables that may have a negative influence and see what can be done to reduce them. However, given the interaction process, it is also important that the interviewer is able to direct and control the interaction process, so as to attain the basic objectives of the interviewer — namely to influence and stimulate the respondent to talk on those subjects he is asked about. Motivating the respondent to talk is important, or else he will give more incomplete answers and more poorly thought through answers. It is our experience that intrinsic motivation operates much more strongly than extrinsic motivation. All interviewers reported this. There is therefore an inherent danger in not giving the intrinsic motivation enough thought and exclusively focusing on extrinsic motivation.[6]

The respondent should be motivated — he should feel that there is some reward in just talking to the interviewer. To what extent one succeeds with this depends, of course, very much upon the interviewer.

Of the two basic sources of motivation assumed by us to be present in the interview situation — the desire to influence and the gratification (reward) that the respondent feels from speaking freely about the topic to an outsider in the conflict, we feel, on the basis of our experience, that the latter source of motivation is the most important by far.

Structure of interview

The informal interview technique we used in our first round (1970/72) is fraught with the danger of posing leading questions and coming up with subjective and distorted perceptions of what was said. Therefore, the results depended primarily on the interviewer's skill and acumen.[7] A standardized interview schedule reduces, but does not necessarily eliminate, the danger of subjective influence that will produce bias.

Some of the questions we posed may be viewed as leading questions, as, for example: In what way and how much is your side dependent on the superpowers? It may be argued that the question is 'leading' by making an assumption that there is a relationship of dependency. If posed 'correctly' the question should have been: Is your state dependent on the superpowers? (If so, in what ways?)

If we chose to conform to these rules, the interview would have been longer and some important questions omitted.

Also, on the basis of our earlier experience, we do not consider this question or any other in the interview 'leading'. We have to consider that these are questions posed to elite persons of some sophistication. In the elite we can, supported by our previous data, safely assume that some kind of dependency to the superpowers is taken for granted.

Using the informal, unstructured, interview in our first study gave us the advantage of 'adjusting' the questions to different situations and different respondents. There are some obvious advantages from this type of procedure and some definite disadvantages.

Our method, both of sampling and questioning in our first round of interviews, is similar to that used by Bonham and Shapiro in their study of foreign policy-making in Finland and Austria.[8] On the basis of the experience of our first round of interviews, we found that we had gained enough insight into the universe of responses and the typical way respondents would use and understand language to employ a standardized interview schedule.

Our pilot study facilitated the task of sorting out the most relevant aspects of our inquiry. We had a better idea of what to ask about. This last point is also important, we feel, because many good interviews worked out at research institutions somehow lose touch with reality, and one ends up asking only vaguely relevant questions and getting quizzical looks from bewildered respondents.

This, in addition to a more focused theoretical design, made it easier to come up with what questions to ask.

Nevertheless, it was a difficult task to formulate meaningful questions that could be posed to both sides. They had to be readily understood by both parties and understood in the same way, which

also represented a problem. The questions are posed across natio-
nalities, a situation that makes the formulation of the questions an
important issue. It may be argued that the simple language employed
in the questions suffers from lack of precision. Considering what we
want to measure, i.e. the elite's general beliefs about itself and the
opponent, etc., this is probably not the case. Again our pilot study
turned out to be valuable, because it gave us a good indication of
which language the respondents would use. In this way we could
'gear' the language in the questions so that it would be understood
in the same way by everyone.

It would have been advantageous to conduct the interviews in the
native language rather than in English. We could not do so as we
did not know Hebrew or Arabic. It would have been possible to
'hire' interviewers who were familiar with the languages; however,
we saw it as important to have trained political scientists who were
intimately linked to our project to conduct the interviews. An optimal
situation would be if those political scientists linked to the project
spoke the languages in question. When this is not the case, it is debatable to what extent better data would be obtained by hiring outside interviewers.

In addition to the experience we could draw on from our pilot
study, we conducted pre-tests (six) of the interview schedule while
in Oslo, before the second round, with Arabs and Israelis living
there, an exercise that proved quite useful. We made some important
revisions of the questions on the basis of these pre-tests. We had the
chance to get together and discuss the experiences as a group —
something we could not do in the Middle East. Our pilot study, as
well as these pre-tests, probably explains why none of the interviewers
reported any serious problems with the questions when conducting
the second and third rounds of interviews.

It is important to note that the interviewers were not selected at
random. They were qualified persons familiar with the research issues
and trained to be neutral in the interview situation. The personal
qualities of the interviewer are of course always important, but in this
case they are crucial, considering the importance of the neutral outsider role and the subjective elements of note-taking.[9]

Another important issue was *open versus closed questions*. Kahn
and Cannel argue that the decision should be based on the following
considerations:

1. The interview objectives.
2. The respondents' level of information on the interview topic.
3. The degree of structure which characterizes respondent opinions
   on the topic.

4. The ease with which the material can be communicated.
5. The interviewer's knowledge and insight into the respondent's situation.[10]

Not only knowledge of the universe of answers, but also the data that we are interested in should account for how we decide between open and closed questions. Certain interview data such as investigations of policy positions are more readily suitable to closed questions. Closed questions are not well suited *for measuring general perceptions and beliefs where the structure of thinking is important.* Finally, the type of interviewees has to be considered. Elites are far less receptive to closed questions.[11]

The questionnaire method with closed answers is now well developed and is a cheap and mechanical way of getting data,[12] but there seems to be a growing scepticism attached to this kind of data gathering within elites.[13]

We concluded that open questions would be more appropriate, even more so considering that one of the main objectives of the study was to establish the structure of belief systems. Then it is advantageous to let the respondent have the chance to talk freely.

Another alternative would have been to use both open and closed answers. It may be argued that for some questions, the type of response was well enough known in advance to justify closed answers. In retrospect, this criticism seems valid.

Our serious drawback with open questions is that it adds the very demanding task of coding the answers afterwards.

When we used a standardized interview schedule with open-ended questions, this did not mean that the interviewer could talk as freely as he wanted. Follow-up questions were not allowed, except on a few questions where we had agreed that if the respondent refused to answer, a follow-up question could be posed. However, it was the same follow-up question for all the interviewers. In other words, the interviewers were not allowed any choice to pose questions that they found appropriate. Thus, open-ended questions did not imply a free-wheeling discussion. This technique is an intermediary between the informal, semi-structured one used in the first round and the formal, structured, and closed one used in many surveys.

In our second and third rounds we exclusively used note-taking (edited notes). We did not find that a tape recorder was a good instrument for getting people to express themselves frankly in a sensitive conflict-area. Note-taking inevitably reduces reliability. To minimize these errors it was decided that after each interview, time had to be allocated for the interviewer to go back to the hotel and work over the notes from the interview while they were still fresh in his mind. On both sides, we had more than one interviewer, which should allow us to measure interviewer effect where note-taking is one of the variables.

The respondent was given an indication of the types of questions to be asked, but nobody was given the questions ahead of time.

Representativeness

Our list of respondents could undoubtedly have been better. There were obstacles in getting the respondents one would ideally have wanted. Difficulties with defining what constitutes the universe and gaining access to its members are formidable. These obstacles, on the other hand, should not limit research in the area, but should suggest caution in the treatment of the data. Because of these problems we have been quite conservative in the application of statistical methods.

In our case the characteristics of the universe are unknown. For this reason alone, it would be impossible to get a 'representative' sample. We were looking for members of elites who were active in shaping the policies in the conflict. So far, no well-defined, universally applicable criteria have been developed for determining political activists.[14] Even if we had a good definition of the relevant elite groups, it would still not be possible to specify the persons who should be included in the theoretical universe. The lack of statistical material would require that we carry out costly research, including a significant amount of field work in the area, simply to delineate the theoretical universe. Also, a random sample would mean travelling from city to city and, of course, make the whole project exceed both temporal and financial resources.

Our solution could be to investigate a specific elite group, like elected representatives to parliaments. Given the different political systems in the Middle East, this would not make sense from a comparative point of view. It would have become a case where methodology becomes more important than contributing to the issues at stake. As LaPiere points out:

> it would seem far more worthwhile to make a shrewd guess regarding that which is essential than to accurately measure that which is likely to prove quite irrelevant.[15]

Ideally, the data should mirror the characteristics of the universe. But the sample's requirements must also be evaluated in relation to the objectives of the study. We are not conducting Gallup Polls where differences in percentages are critical. Comparisons that are sensitive to frequency distributions of the universe will therefore not be made.

The type of problem posed must not be sensitive to having a so-called representative sample. The tabular results are presented as *descriptive summaries* of the results. We do not in any way generalize from this 'sample' to a universe. A non-random, non-representative sample requires us to use the data cautiously. We have no statistical evidence to prove that the perceptions we have covered are representative of the elites. We think, however, given the sampling procedures employed, that the likelihood of having covered the range of *influential* views on the Arab-Israeli conflict is very high. What we cannot say anything about is the *frequency distribution* of these views within the respondents' universes.

We have covered a wide spectrum of elite perceptions. We have avoided charting beliefs clearly belonging to marginally important, highly idiosyncratic groups. Given our research purpose, we are only interested in those patterns of beliefs in the mainstream of thought in the area, i.e. the major variants of elite opinion in each country.

More important to note is that what we want to investigate is not dependent on having a representative sample. The bulk of the analysis deals with *attribution processes* and relationships among beliefs in *individual* respondents.[16] To find out how individuals make causal analysis samples does not make much difference. Also when one is attempting to establish the structure of belief systems, a representative sample is not required. Given these objectives, the data base may very well serve our needs. It need not be considered a 'sample' in the statistical sense.

To look at attribution and consistency, there is no need for a representative sample. Over-representation of certain groups or lack of representation of others does not necessarily lead to any distortion of results on attribution and consistency.

Given the objectives in mind, the requirements of the sample will be less demanding. Of course, we do not claim to have a 'perfect' sample. As in the case of most studies in the social sciences we have a smaller sample than we should like. And it should be added that one part of the analysis is also quite sensitive to the frequency distribution in the universe. This is the descriptive analysis of stability of beliefs. The results here should therefore only be regarded as hypothesis.

An effort to validate the results was done by letting experts on the conflict in the area itself read through our first round of interviews, where answers were listed verbally. From these we received very favorable comments, and none of them could think of any important beliefs that we had left out. Additional samples from 1974 and 1976 increase the confidence in the results, where sampling procedures ensured a wider coverage of elite persons.

Procedure for selecting respondents

We tried to locate what we may imprecisely term 'opinion leaders' in the context of the conflict — those who directly or indirectly we assumed had some impact on what policies were conducted in the conflict. In other words, we were not concerned with an elite person who held a high position but did not have an articulate stand on the conflict. His reputation was also an important ingredient for selection. Just being a member of an elite was not sufficient for being asked for an interview.

The elite-categories from which we selected were:

active politicians
civil servants in the Ministries of Foreign Affairs
professors and students
editors and journalists
guerrilla leaders (only on the Arab side)

We picked the sample in two ways. From our general knowledge of the conflict we set up in advance a list of persons we thought were influential. In setting up this list, we consulted experts on the conflict in general. In the conflict area, another method was also used. Having obtained an interview, we asked the respondent to name others whom it would be useful to interview, and who would be willing to grant an interviw. This technique, known as chain sampling, helped us to cope with the problem of accessibility. A clear disadvantage with chain sampling is that the respondents will probably choose persons of their own liking. We found it, therefore, important to combine the two methods.[17]

In the second and third rounds of interviewing we also asked area experts to read through previous samples and come up with suggestions for respondents that were not included in the sample, but that they considered important for the interview. This was done to ensure wide coverage of perceptions.

A special effort was also made in this second round to obtain interviews with the same people as in 1970/72, because from 1972 to 1974 a dramatic event of great magnitude had taken place, the October war in 1973. We hoped to find out whether the war had caused change in beliefs. This was linked to considerable problems of accessibility. A shift of regimes as in Egypt, for example, had led to the removal of many people who were interviewed in the first round.[18]

42

We were interested in obtaining interviews with 'influential persons'. The result is demonstrated in the sample obtained, and we leave it to the reader to judge. The respondents range from presidents and guerrilla leaders to students. The sample would have looked different if we had a free choice of whom to interview. In general, however, we were quite amazed at the willingness of high officials to give interviews.

Related to the question of representativeness is to what extent the respondents only speak for themselves or express views representative of larger groups. Previous research supports the idea that activists of the type we have are likely to express beliefs that are common to larger groups of people, since they are more in conformity with the ideas of given reference groups.[19] Given that we have interviewed what we could term 'opinion leaders', this assumption should be even more valid. It is reasonable to expect that the overlap between self-attitudes and those of the reference group is high.

When we interview a political activist, we are not interested in this respondent's idiosyncratic beliefs about the conflict, but in those beliefs that will also be shared by other political activists. What he says to his wife about the conflict may be more personal than what he says to an outsider, but not necessarily more relevant to the beliefs that are constraining his and others' political actions.

What we get in the interview are neither private confessions nor official statements. It is somewhere in between. We believe it to have a close linkage to the type of beliefs considered relevant by decision-makers. We expect that beliefs we have measured overlap to a considerable extent with beliefs important in influence-exerting situations.

Thus we expect the interviewee to report both what he thinks his reference group would expect him to say and his personal beliefs.

Problems of Coding Open Questions

A lot of effort has gone into the interviewing — both as concerns the preparation of questions and the actual field work.

Probably an equal amount of work has gone into the problems of coding. When open-ended interviewing techniques are used, the coding process becomes essential for the results of the study.[20]

The differences between open and closed questions are not crucial from the point of view of quantification. The issue is when one imposes a structure or a classification on the answer. In closed questions the respondent is forced to choose between already fixed alternatives; in open questions the structure is imposed afterwards through the coding scheme.[21]

From a research economy point of view it is of course a lot more time-consuming to impose the structure on answers after they have been given. But for the type of problem we have been dealing with, and the type of data we have been looking at, we think it has been essential for the study to have open questions.

According to Holsti, coding is the process:
'Whereby raw data are systematically transformed and aggregated into units which permit precise description of relevant content characteristics. The rules by which this transformation is accomplished serve as the operational link between the investigator's data and his theory and hypotheses'.[22]

The theory and problem at hand should be our guide in constructing the categories and the rules for classification. The categories are operational concepts of the independent variables that are the different dimensions in the operational code belief system.

As a first step in the coding process we simply wanted to answer the question: Who says what?

Linking it to our anlytical framework, it became important to use this structuring of the content to say something later on about consistency. With this general purpose in mind, a standard and important issue became the size of the categories to be coded. Again the research issue had to be considered when making judgements on the gains and costs associated with many categories as opposed to few.

Applying very broad categories does not enable us at a later stage to disaggregate data, but reliability represents less of a problem. Ultimately it rests upon judgement by the researcher as to where the optimal strategy is. We did settle for rather broad categories.

A main purpose of the study is to make a comparative analysis. The same questions have been asked of all the respondents on both sides in the conflict. It was necessary for us to come up with the same categories for the Arab and Israeli samples. The code-book as it now stands consists of standard categories which will allow for comparisons across sides in the conflict. The coders were asked to code across the protocols, that is to say, a coder would code only one question of a respondent at a time, so as to avoid any 'echo effect'.[23]

Again this is an issue that was left to the researcher's judgement, and again his judgement must be based on or related to his research issue, or otherwise he may make some very wrong decisions. As a recording unit we used a single assertion about some subject.[24]

As context unit we chose the answer to one question. In this way we simply recorded or coded the appearance of a theme, not the *frequency* of the appearance. In asking the question *who* says *what* we are interested in identifying the *patterns* of themes, not the frequency with which they appear. Our theoretical concern is with consistency not intensity.

It suffices to identify simply the appearance of themes. The interesting research question is what themes different respondents mention, in order to assess how the respondent may link beliefs. For the purpose of illustration we may say that we have a set of coding values for each separate question, and that coding rules applied to one question should not be applied to another. We cannot use the coding rules of one question and code the answer to another question. Also if two or more themes appear in the same answer that could be coded in the same category this should be coded only once. In this first stage of coding we were simply interested in charting the patterns of what the respondents were saying. When coding attribution, however, we did also record frequencies of assertions within the same answer. Here our theoretical concern was different, leading up to different coding rules — where our unit of enumeration is not whole answers but each single assertion. However, it turned out that it did not make much difference in the main tendencies in the results, when different systems of enumeration were used.

Reliability did not appear to be a major problem. This can be explained by the type of data we ask for — note-taking is not a serious problem, because the data are rather general in their form, and furthermore the data have been coded in rather crude categories. If we had introduced finer discriminations in the coding of the data, there would probably have been a loss in reliability. But the high reliability also increases the confidence in the quality of the interviewers and the type of questions asked.

Since we did not find any big differences between the samples of 1974 and 1976, we see this as supportive of the claim for reliability. This was the case with most of the questions (see tables in chapter on stability). Both note-taking and interviewer-effect do not seem to have interfered with our results. On questions where we did find big *variations* we examined these more closely. This could be due to change, but also to problems of validity and reliability, or that one or both samples did not mirror the universe of responses very well on those particular questions. So we proceeded systematically to find out what the most plausible explanation would be. Especially on one question we did have some serious problems on the Arab side. It was the following: 'Are there any differences concerning goals and strategies on your side of the conflict?' This question serves as an illustration of how we proceeded in the analysis of these types of questions to assess the quality of the data.

We asked ourselves why the Israelis were much more stable over time on this question than the Arabs. First, we checked reliability.

Our tests indicated that the intercoder-reliability was relatively high (Pi = .75) (ref. formula for reliability test presented later). We even recorded the answers to this question on the Arab side in 1974 and 1976 and came up with results almost identical to those we already had.

Our results on other questions indicate that the *interviewer-effect* is not of great importance.

The next possibility was that of *low response validity*.

To check this we re-analyzed the answers in detail to see whether the question had been properly understood. The re-analyzing of the answers given confirmed a proper understanding of the question. We may point out that a few respondents perceived the question in 'two steps': Are there any differences in your own *country?* versus Are there any differences among the *Arab states?*

But this had already been taken into account when we coded the answers.

We concluded that the discrepancy in results did not seem to be a result of low response validity.

We had now, as far as possible, ruled out any possible 'technical factors' as an explanation for change on this question.

What was left, was a more qualitative evaluation.

Both Arabs and Israelis do see that among the opponents in the conflict there are different policy preferences, and there are both moderate and extreme groups in the opponent's camp. Israelis by and large do see more differences than is the case with Arabs. This of course may reflect objective conditions in the sense that there are more actors and groupings on the Arab side in the conflict.

But then the Israelis should see fewer differences than the Arabs on their own side, but the opposite is the case. So the 'objective' conditions in this sense do not explain the variance.

Another possible explanation could be that Arabs looked upon unity of the Arab world as very important normatively. As a matter of fact it is stated as a goal in the Koran that all Muslims should be united, in other words, it is a religious duty of any Muslim to work for unity. Therefore when asked about differences on the Arab side, this could be considered quite a sensitive issue and then instrumentality increases (see previous discussion on linkage between instrumentality and sensitivity). This also refers to response validity but not in the sense of misunderstanding the question, but deliberately misleading the interviewer.

But why should the Arabs express more unity in 1976 than in 1974? There was more unity in 1974 (after the October war) than in 1976. The normative aspect of the issue obviously does not give the whole explanation. On the other hand, we do not have sufficient data to explore the issue further.

So far, we have considered reliability, response validity, and the 'objective' conditions of change, none of which offers a plausible explanation of the results. We are then left with the possibility that one or both samples do not accurately mirror the variance in the universe. This seems plausible, because we ask about beliefs and attitudes on a subject on which there is probably a great deal of uncertainty as to what answer they should give. There is no ready-made answer, and there is confusion as to what answer they should give. If this is the explanation, the data are equally valid for our analysis, since what is important to us, is that some people see differences and some do not, and we test whether this is consistent with other beliefs of the respondents. It is of less importance to us that the strength between these groups varies between the two samples.

On the use of statistical tests

In this study there is no reliance on formal statistical tests. In part this is due to the nature of the study, which is more an attempt to generate rather than test hypotheses. This reflects the current level of paradigm development in the field. In part formal statistical tests are not reported for methodological reasons. These include the non-random nature of the sampling procedures and the relatively low sample size available for exploring specific questions.

CHAPTER IV

Stability of Beliefs: A Psychodynamic Perspective

Attribution

From theories on attribution, it is hypothesized that when parties to a conflict observe the opponent, the opponent's behavior is seen to be a manifestation of the internal properties of the opponent (abilities, traits, and motives), but the observer will explain his own behavior as a response to the situation (environmental pressures and constraints). This phenomenon, which is called the 'fundamental attribution error', is enhanced when the observer dislikes the actor he is observing and when the actions he is observing are seen to affect himself.

Problems of coding

At first glance, it might look relatively simple to divide statements on causality along internal/external (or dispositional/situational) lines, but looking further into the problem, it becomes apparent that it is not all that simple.

Statements that at first glance may seem to be clearly dispositional in content, for example, may, on closer examination of the context in which the statements appear, prove to be situational. The form of the statement may be misleading, and the context should also be evaluated. Whenever respondents made causal statements about themselves or the opponent, the coder was asked to distinguish between two types of statements:

I explanations that assume only those dispositions that are shared by all men or typical of most men (situational)
II explanations that assume or state something unique or distinguishing about the actor's dispositions (dispositional).

An explanation is only dispositional when the attributor assumes it is something *particular, unique.* Dispositional attribution is also called *person attribute,* which may be a better term, since it is more readily understandable. Does the respondent explain a cause of some event as resulting from some traits of the person (persons) performing the act, or does he refer to reactive behavior caused by stimulus in the situation? When referring to *person attribute* we may say that the respondent in his information-processing behaves as a 'trait psychologist', and when referring to situational variables as a 'reinforcement psychologist'.

Some causal statements interpret behavior as *reactive*. This is the stimulus-response model: the behavior is seen as caused by the situation. Other causal statements will regard behavior as caused by unique traits of the actor. If the behavior is seen as caused by the situation, the behavior is something outside the control of the actor — he does not have any choice. If the behavior, on the other hand, is seen as caused by the person performing the act, it implies that the person has a free choice to act in more than one way; therefore he can do something about his behavior. He is able to control it.

One recurring coding problem is the reference to Zionism. If we look only at the form of the statements, it would be coded as situational. Zionism could be considered a *social force* and would therefore be situational. But the context in which it appears has to be considered. If Zionism is used to describe the state of Israel as being something unique, deviant and odd, or a 'trait' particular to the people of that nation as opposed to the people of all other nations, it should be coded as dispositional. Very often it was used to explain why the people of Israel behave differently from all other peoples. The explanation implies that if Israel had not been based on an alien ideology, called Zionism, the behavior of that state would have been different (normal). Then the explanation is dispositional. The *content* as well as the *form* of the explanations must be examined.

In the first stage of coding we selected a random sample of the protocols, then went through the whole protocol in order to identify those questions that seemed to be most effective in eliciting causal statements. The first problem was to identify causal statements: either explicitly or implicitly the answer to the question 'Why'? 'The enemy behaves like this, because . . .' Open-ended questions will frequently elicit causal statements, but we do have questions that are better in this respect than others.

Image of self and image of the opponent

The first question we selected was:
What do you think are the basic good and bad aspects of your side in the conflict?

49

This question proved useful in eliciting causal statements, because most of the respondents answered the question by explaining *why* they thought they were good, and why they thought they were bad. We are good because we want to live in peace, for example. Or we are good because we have a strong faith and high moral standards, or we are good because we do not discriminate against other people. Or we are bad because there is too much rivalry within our camp, or we are too pessimistic.

On both sides it was claimed that the behavior of our side is good because our intentions are good. 'We fight for a just cause, for peace, for a just solution.' 'We are moderate, our mentality is peaceful, we cherish human life and we do not hate the enemy. There is a strong feeling of justice, we have some inner qualities that are highly praiseworthy; we are great human beings because we try to be human in our dealings with the opponent. We do not have evil wishes, intentions like the enemy does; our purposes are basically good.' So, in sum, there is the idea that we have some human qualities (traits) that are highly admirable, which cause good behavior. The other line of causal analysis refers to intentions.

It can be difficult to determine whether concrete policies (behavior) are dispositional or situational. Again, the context must be taken into account. Sometimes attributions are situational by explaining good results obtained by rational policies, but sometimes the statements are dispositional in that they ascribe rational and efficient policies to inner qualities of the actor. For example: we have a sense of moderation, we are not fanatic; we diagnose the situation in a down to earth way, our thinking is concrete and not abstract (ideological). Some of the respondents coded as balanced or mixed would refuse to speak about 'good' and 'bad' aspects; their causal analyses were typically situational. For them, the causes of the policies of both sides were circumstantial, a part of processes that no one could really be blamed for.

Turning to explanations of one's own bad behavior, policies were criticized as either too lenient or too aggressive. On the Arab side, some policies or groups were characterized as too extreme, and on the Israeli side the Palestinian issue was brought forward. Policies were criticized for not being optimal to their own interests. There was also the criticism that policies could be more efficiently implemented. On both sides the lack of image-building was referred to. Respondents claimed that their own points of view were not explained well enough, or that there was a lack of unity, or that policies were not well enough adjusted to the situation. It was felt that policies do not take into account that the conflict can be solved, or what the true interests of the superpowers are. Bad policies were seen as caused by the opponents' bad behavior (reactive). On the Arab side, dissension within their own camp was mentioned as well as extremism and underdevelopment. The propensity for emotionalism was also referred to.

Table 4.1 Image of self
Q: What do you think are the basic good and bad aspects of your
  side in the conflict? (n = 80)

	Attributions		
	Situational	Dispositional	Both
Israeli	15 %	21 %	64 % (n = 33)
Arab	32 %	23 %	45 % (n = 47)

The Israeli results do not support *the Jones and Nisbett hypothesis* (see Table 4. 1). Israelis make more dispositional than situational attributions. Arab respondents, on the other hand, are more inclined to attribute their own part in the conflict to situational rather than dispositional factors.

The most interesting result is not the frequency distribution of dispositional and situational attributions, where we find contradictory patterns, but the high frequency of respondents making *both* types of attributions. This tells us that there is no systematic bias involved — the majority of respondents are willing to make both dispositional and situational attributions when explaining their own behavior. This result conforms more to the logical schema for attribution processes rather than giving support for erroneous tendencies.

What do you think are the basic good and bad aspects of the other side in the conflict?

When mentioning the good aspects of their opponent in the conflict, Arabs referred to Israel's technological advances, its economic strength, its successful propaganda, and its unity in goals and strategies. As we can see from this, there is a tendency to see the reverse of one's own side in the opponent's camp. A strength for one side is matched by a weakness for the other. We are underdeveloped, the Israelis are developed. We are disunited, the Israelis are united. Underdevelopment causes constraints on optimal policies on our side, while the stage of development in the opponent's camp causes an efficient policy. There was also a hesitancy to express disunity in the respondent's own camp. The tendency was to say that one day we will become united, or that our intentions are to unite. But disunity is implicitly admitted when Arabs mention the unity of the opponent as one of the admirable characteristics of his policies.

There are also respondents that cite contradictory forces in the opponent's camp which may cause changes in policy. The opponent has good aspects because there is internal opposition to his present bad policy in the form of environmental forces and constraints. These types of causal analyses lead to a high expectancy of change: because we see contradictory forces in the opponent's camp, there is the possibility that his policy may change.

Some Arab respondents expressed admiration for traits of the Jewish people, particularly their dedication in the fight for their existence. Sometimes this implies that Arabs are not so dedicated as the other side, but it may also simply be an expression of admiration in that they separate the traits of the Jewish people from the policies generated by the Israeli state, which is hostile, — but that can be reasonably explained by situational or environmental sources or constraints.

Israeli respondents, like Arab respondents, list contradictory forces in the opponent's camp which may trigger change. Egypt was frequently mentioned as an example of these contradictory forces, which may neutralize more hostile tendencies, and which may generate change in hostile policies against the state of Israel. Israelis also referred to traits of Arabs as a people, mentioning hospitality, pride, and self-confidence.

Some respondents would simply not use the label 'good' or 'bad'. When explaining bad behavior of the opponent, Arab respondents mentioned that Israelis have a militaristic attitude, Israelis are militaristic by nature, and Israelis are arrogant. History is cited as inductive support in explaining why Israelis behave differently from other people: these people have complexes from the concentration camps, therefore they deviate from the norm; now they want to take revenge. Racism is another of the opponent's traits cited by Arabs: these people have a tendency to discriminate. For example, it is stated that oriental Jews are not considered equal to European or American Jews. There is also the claim that the opponent tells lies, which can be seen as both situational and dispositional. If the opponent tells lies to support his policies, this was seen as a situational attribution (rational), but more often it was presented as a trait of the enemy (irrational).

Israeli respondents mentioned that Arabs are fanatic, irrational, cannot think logically, lack imagination, have no respect for human life, and have a tendency to hate. Again we see the symmetry in perceptions: admirable traits of their own side (such as rational thinking, a tremendous respect for human life, ability to forgive) are exactly reversed for the opponent. Lack of modernization and lack of democratic institutions in the opponent's camp were also frequently mentioned by Israelis as explanations of bad behavior. Again, we see this symmetry, whereby modernization and democratic institutions explain why our behavior is good, standard or normal, while underdevelopment and lack of democratic institutions explain the bad behavior of the opponent. If the opponent were only as modern and democratic as we, his policies would be rational, and it would be possible to solve the conflict.

It appears, then, that this question is quite useful in eliciting causal statements and will therefore be included in testing attributional tendencies to see whether there is a systematic bias in the attributional process. (Results in Table 4. 2).

Table 4.2. Image of the opponent
Q: What do you think are the basic good and bad aspects of the other side in the conflict? (n = 75).

	Attributions			
	Situational	Dispositional	Both	
Israeli	14 %	41 %	45 %	(n = 29)
Arab	13 %	26 %	61 %	(n = 46)

The results show that there is a higher frequency of dispositional attributions when causes of the opponent's behavior in the conflict are being analyzed. However, as with the previous question, this tendency is weakened by the fact, that most of the respondents have no systematic bias. The majority make both dispositional and situational attributions. So even if we find somewhat stronger support for the hypothesis than we found with the previous question, the main tendency is still to have no systematic bias at all in attributional tendencies.

Results

In explaining the basic good and bad aspects of their own and the other side in the conflict, the respondents came up with causal statements when considering why the parties behave as they do. Our hypothesis predicts that the respondents would make mainly situational attributions when explaining their own behavior, and more dispositional attributions when explaining the behavior of their opponent.

The results (presented in Tables 4.1 and 4.2) do not give strong support for the predicted relationship, (on one question the results were partly counter to what the hypothesis would predict), although the results are in the predicted direction on both questions. Situational attributions are stronger when analyzing one's own behavior, while dispositional attributions are stronger when analyzing the behavior of the opponent, but this tendency is rather weak.

Arab respondents provide somewhat stronger support than Israelis. The Israeli results run counter to our prediction when they were talking about their own side. In making attributions about the opponent in the conflict, however, there is some support in the predicted direction.

The results led us to suspect that the hypotheses are stated in too general a form. The level of generalization tends to hide important variances in the way elites in an international conflict make attributions. Analysis of the data on an impressionistic basis led us to believe that respondents make different kinds of inferences when the observed behavior is considered blameworthy as opposed to praiseworthy.

We may recall that a dispositional attribution places the responsibility for the act with the actor, while a situational attribution leaves the actor free from responsibility. The attribution mechanism will thus enable the observer to take credit when making a dispositional attribution, while avoiding responsibility by 'blaming' situational variables.

Our analysis will go beyond the 'fundamental attribution error' as originally put forward by Jones and Nisbett, in that we claim that *the quality of the act* is important. We expect different types of attributions to be made of different perceived qualities of the act performed.

Jones and Nisbett deal with *evaluatively neutral* situations. In our study the evaluative dimension is very important. We do not deal with neutral 'observers' when it comes to one's own activities or the activities of the opponent. Furthermore, we do not deal with an international situation in general terms, but rather our investigation is related to international conflict with deep emotional involvement. If ego-defensive mechanisms influence the attribution process, we would expect that this could account for variance.

The *evaluation* of the observed activity therefore becomes crucial, and so far we have not taken this into account. We asked the respondents explicitly to mention their own good and bad activity and their opponent's good and bad activity. Consequently, the question provoked responses that are especially well suited for assessing the relative influence of the evaluative content of behavior.

We therefore restate the hypotheses on a lower level of abstraction to see whether we can get any support for the general hypothesis on attributional biases. In emphasizing the importance of the evaluative dimension along with the actor-observer relationship, we may restate the hypotheses in the following form:

1) There is a tendency to make *situational* attributions when observing one's *own bad* behavior.
2) There is a tendency to make *situational* attributions when observing the *opponent's good* behavior.
3) There is a tendency to make *dispositional* attributions when observing the *opponent's bad* behavior.
4) There is a tendency to make *dispositional* attributions when observing one's *own good* behavior.

Table 4.3. Image of self
Q: What are the basic good and bad aspects of your side in the conflict?

	Our side is good			Our side is bad		
	Sit-uational	Disp-ositional		Sit-uational	Disp-ositional	
Israeli	14 %	86 %	(n = 22)	93 %	7 %	(n = 15)
Arab	43 %	57 %	(n = 42)	84 %	16 %	(n = 37)

n = number of respondents

Table 4.4. Image of the opponent
Q: What are the basic good and bad aspects of the other side in the conflict?

	Other side is good			Other side is bad		
	Sit-uational	Disp-ositional		Sit-uational	Disp-ositional	
Israeli	57 %	43 %	(n = 14)	22 %	78 %	(n = 18)
Arab	74 %	26 %	(n = 31)	28 %	72 %	(n = 40)

n = number of respondents

— Sub-hypothesis 1: There is a tendency to make situational attributions when observing one's own bad behavior.

The support is strong in both samples for the postulated tendency. When parties to a conflict explain something considered bad by their own side, they have a tendency to make situational, and not dispositional, attributions. They thereby avoid fixing the blame on themselves: the situation is to blame. The behavior is seen as reactive — caused by situational variables leaving themselves with no choice.

— Sub-hypothesis 2: There is a tendency to make situational attributions when observing the opponent's good behavior.

When the opponent behaves decently, what kind of inferences are drawn? We find some support for our prediction of situational attribution. The support here is stronger on the Arab side than on the Israeli side. When the opponent is decent, he is not given credit. The causal analysis of his behavior concludes that factors in the situation forced him to behave in a decent manner. Again, the behavior is seen as reactive, leaving the actor with no free choice. Since he has no choice, he cannot be given credit.

— Sub-hypothesis 3: There is a tendency to make dispositional attributions when observing the opponent's bad behavior.

Once more, we find support for the hypothesized relationship. The opponent is held responsible for his behavior. He has chosen to behave badly of his own free will, and he is in a position to change this behavior if he wants to. The explanation is then made consistent with an already established devil-image of the opponent. Behavior is no longer seen as reactive, but caused by characteristics of the actor.

— Sub-hypothesis 4: There is a tendency to make dispositional attributions when observing one's own good behavior.

This hypothesis runs somewhat counter to the proposition by Jones and Nisbett on the fundamental attribution error. The proposition may still hold good in its general form, however, even though it appears from our testing that it is not valid given two additional conditions: 1) the observed behavior is not evaluatively neutral; 2) the observer himself is a participant of the activity. Again, our results support our restatement of the original hypothesis. The respondents do not have, as Jones and Nisbett would predict, a bias toward situational attributions. When they observe their own activity evaluated as *good,* the bias is toward dispositional attribution. When something is done that is considered constructive, parties to a conflict want to have credit for it. Their own behavior is no longer caused by the situation but by their internal characteristics. They were in a position to act otherwise, but chose to do something good.

These results demonstrate the flexibility parties to a conflict display in crediting performed behavior. The attribution mechanisms allow for operating with different 'models of responsibility'. Furthermore, the results suggest that the Jones and Nisbett hypothesis may be too general. While we found some support for the hypothesis, there is not a *general* bias toward making dispositional attributions when explaining the behavior of others. Rather, the results show that parties to a conflict have a tendency to mention bad as opposed to good behavior of their opponent. This provides some support for the hypothesis on the general level.

Results

We have found support for our four sub-hypotheses. The respondents are overwhelmingly dispositional when observing their own praiseworthy behavior and their opponent's blameworthy behavior, and overwhelmingly situational when observing their own blameworthy behavior and their opponent's praiseworthy behavior. The results show that the ways respondents make inferences follow more differentiated patterns than would be predicted by the original hypothesis on the fundamental attribution error.

The results also demonstrate the difficulties with triggering attitude change. When observing behavior deviating from the general dichotomy of blameworthy/praiseworthy (their 'expectancy pattern' of behavior), the observer still has mechanisms to explain this behavior without resorting to cognitive change or cognitive reorganization. The way causal inferences are made, gives considerable leeway for avoiding changes in the cognitive system. Attitudes and beliefs about the enemy and themselves can remain the same. Good behavior by the enemy can be explained as forced on him by the situation; hence 'discrepant' information is not allowed to challenge existing negative views of the enemy.

Do you think the other side is threatening you?

We expected the question, 'Do you think that the other side is threatening you?' to elicit causal statements. We expected the respondents not only to answer yes or no, but also to explain why they felt threatened. This was true only to a certain extent. The question was sometimes answered with simply yes or no, or both yes and no, but some respondents did also explain why they felt threatened.

Owing to a relatively high number of yes and no, the answers are only dealt with qualitatively.

The answers to this question emphasized that fear in the conflict is not so much related to what the opponent in the conflict has *done* up to this point as it is to what he *may do* in the future. From this analysis of the conflict there emerges the focus on the intention component that is also very strong in responses about the sources of the conflict. Concrete changes in the situation, concrete events, and the opponent's actions in the past do not seem to be included in causal analyses of why there is a threat. Those who explain why they feel threatened make mostly dispositional attributions. This strong focus on the intentions of the opponent is striking and is common to both Arab and Israeli respondents.

Firm non-probabilistic beliefs seemed to be held about the intentions of the opponent. Common statements were that we feel threatened because the opponent wants to destroy us, exterminate us, liquidate us, finish us, wipe us out. The threat is also conditional on the development of the power configurations between the parties. Instead of making such statements as 'we are threatened because . . .' which could be coded for attribution, some respondents would make 'if . . . then' statements discussing hypothetical future developments. Examples of this type of statement are Israeli respondents saying that if the Arabs became united then the possibility that Israel would be eliminated is very high. Arab respondents would turn this around by saying that if Arabs became united then the conflict would be solved (no threat would exist).

Some respondents simply stated that they do not feel threatened. When answering *why* this is the case, situational attributions were made. It is not that the opponent is so kind that he does not want to threaten us, but his possibilities for doing so are slight. The power component again is present as a strong variable in the causal analysis. The past and the future were referred to by Arab respondents when they see a basic asymmetry developing: Arabs will gradually become stronger, therefore there is no threat. These respondents did not talk about this as a hypothetical scenario but as a given.

Do you think the other side believes you are threatening them?

We also examined the complementary question: 'Do you think that the other side believes you are threatening them?' On this question too, the numbers of yes and no without causal statements were relatively high, and as a consequence the answers are not quantified.

Respondents making causal statements made both situational and dispositional attributions. On the Arab side it was claimed that Israelis felt theratened because of Arab strength. The October war was referred to in this regard. Israelis were justified in feeling themselves threatened because of the superiority of the opponent. These are situational attributions, referring to events or characteristics of the situation rather than of the actor. Dispositional statements included comments to the effect that Israel was a strange element or an artificial fragment in the area. Some Arab respondents also said that Israelis felt threatened because of extreme Arab propaganda. But more frequently reference was made to the propaganda by the Israelis themselves as causing a feeling of threat. These statements can be both situational (propaganda as means to achieve aims) and dispositional (propaganda as reflection of irrational thinking), and each statement must be evaluated in the context in which it appears.

While Arabs were both dispositional and situational in their analysis of the threat to the other side, Israeli respondents made more causal analyses in dispositional terms. For example, there is a feeling of a threat, but this threat is not rational. Or, objectively Arabs should not feel threatened because of their superior position in the conflict, but the existence of myths and make-believe about the character and intentions of Israel makes them feel threatened. The threat was also ascribed to religious and cultural traits of the Arabs. These misperceptions were attributed to factors such as Arab propaganda and fear of democracy.

Some respondents on both sides differentiated between elites and common citizens. Elites instigate irrational fears in the common people. This is also called the 'black top' image, and is a dispositional attribution in that the threat is seen as caused by some particular characteristics of elites, while the common people are 'normal.'

Respondents claiming that the opponent does not feel threatened made mainly causal attributions. Both sides claimed that the generating of fear was used by the opponent as a means to promote policies. Projecting the image of a threat could attract, for example, international goodwill to justify an unjust policy. In this way the threat was not really felt but could be used to promote their own policies. Israelis pointed to the Arabs' use of threats to create Arab unity, mislead international opinion, justify the destruction of Israel, strengthen their side, and so on.

In other words, the belief that the opponent constitutes a threat is propagated by the other party to the conflict solely to promote his own policies. In this way beliefs about a threat were not irrational or dispositional, but determined by situational variables. Beliefs about a threat were used as a convenient means to promote aggressive policies.

It is interesting to note the general tendency to admit that the

59

opponent may feel threatened, but this is his own doing, not ours. This feeling demonstrates how strongly ego-defensive mechanisms operate. While we expected the question to elicit answers with reference to the respondent's own behavior, this was not always true. Quite often the locus of causation was with the opponent, where some genuine characteristics of the opponent as an actor were referred to.

Antecedents of conflict

Our analysis of attribution up to this point has concentrated on how the parties explain what maintains the conflict. We are now moving into the issue of the original roots of the conflict. What caused the conflict in the first place? What respondents see as antecedents of the conflict may not necessarily be the same causes they give to what maintains the conflict today. We deal with this within the same theoretical framework, where the main issue is whether antecedents are seen rooted in dispositional or situational attributions. The data base will be the answers to the first question in the questionnaire: *If you could point out one single factor as the main cause of the conflict in the Middle East, which would you mention?*

In answering the question, respondents attributed causes alternatively to the enemy in the conflict, to themselves, or to both. Some would not put the cause on any one of the parties involved locally, but instead, for example, on the superpowers. Some of the answers did not attribute responsibility to any actor in particular, but to situational forces.

Arab Respondents

Conflict was attributed to both the *establishment* of the state of Israel and to the *behavior* of that state once established. Considerable mention was made of the *intentions* of the Israeli state, of what was perceived as a history of expansion. To prove this point, historical examples were given, the most recent being the occupation of territories in the 1967 June war. Further inductive support for the expansionist tendency of the Israeli state included reference to the lack of willingness to negotiate within the framework of the UN. Looking at the past and the present, Arab respondents focused not so much on the facts of existing Israeli occupation of Arab land, but rather on a theory that this state *by its nature* is bent on expansion. Not only territorial expansion, but economic expansion too was sometimes mentioned: Israel wants cheap labor from the Arabs, domination of all economic activities, and so on. Additional support was found in Zionism, which aimed at getting all Jews to Israel, something

60

inevitably leading to expansion. Some linked Israel to imperialism, and cited the close connection to the USA.

In other words, there was a strong focus on the *intention* component when talking about the main sources of conflict. The intentions of the state of Israel were seen as quite different from those of other states. They have designs for expansion, in which Arabs will consequently suffer. This case of conflict must be seen as something unique, a deviation from the main pattern of behavior. Evaluation of the intentions of Israel were supported not so much by looking at this state's past behavior, but looking at the present, where the perceived lack of willingness to negotiate is attributed to expansionist designs. This was further supported by citing the Zionist ideology, where the stated goal of getting all Jews to Israel is perceived by Arabs as leading to expansion. Furthermore, this policy was linked to Western imperialism, considered a threat to Arab civilization and mentioned as a main cause of the conflict. These respondents regarded the establishment of the state of Israel as an attempt by Western nations to use Israel as a foothold in the Arab world in order to continue their imperialist policies.

The causes of conflict were therefore not seen as conflicts of interest or as rational. Few references were made to situational forces and constraints. Conflict was seen as caused by something irrational, something abnormal, odd and deviant. The perceived intentions of the state of Israel seemed to account for attributed causation as much as Israel's past and present actions, which only serve to give inductive support for the belief on expansion.

The Palestinian refugee problem was also mentioned as a cause of conflict. There is a Palestinian problem because another state was created at the expense of the Palestinians, and these Palestinians need a country of their own. Cultural differences between Arabs and Israelis were also noted, sometimes to underline the artificial character of Israel, and sometimes as a source of misunderstanding between the two peoples. In both cases, we are dealing with dispositional attributions. Situational attributions were present in statements that, for example, conflict was caused by the big powers, especially Great Britain. This policy of great powers and superpowers causing conflict was seen as a rational pursuit of their own interests. Attributing conflict to misunderstandings between the parties, on the other hand, is dispositional, and deviates from a rational pursuit of interests.

The intention of the Arabs to eliminate the state of Israel was seen as the main cause of the conflict. 'The preference of the Arabs is for a world without the state of Israel.' The Arabs refused to recognize the Jews as a distinct independent national entity with legitimate territorial rights. As inductive support for this belief that the Arabs want to eliminate the state of Israel, respondents frequently referred to what the Arabs had *said* in various contexts about the state of Israel — not what they had done.

This strongly dispositional analysis puts the responsibility almost exclusively on one party. Occasionally dispositional attributions were made to their own side. Cultural differences and ways of life were mentioned as causes of conflict. Besides causing misunderstanding, these differences were the bases for irrational policies of the opponent. Because of the present stage of development in Arab civilization, Arabs had to portray Israel as a threat. Feudal and oppressive Arab regimes maintained hatred against Israel to justify their own totalitarian exercises of power. Respondents claimed that an irrational analysis was made by Arabs of the Palestinian problem, and this analysis could be explained by certain special characteristics of Arabs.

These respondents saw the roots of conflict not in environmental constraints, but in unique and abnormal characteristics of Arab civilization preventing Arabs from a rational pursuit of policies. If these deviant ways of thinking were eliminated and Arabs started to make rational calculations on the basis of situational forces and constraints, there would be no conflict, because dealing with someone who would analyze problems rationally would represent no problem for the Israeli state.

There was also a feeling that Arab policies were rooted not only in deviant and odd traits of their civilization, but in gross misunderstandings about Israel and Israeli society. The opponent does not have the correct image of us. If his image of us were correct, his policies would be more rational. Arabs suffered frustration over their own failure; because of this they were aggressive toward Israel. A somewhat comparable attribution to the Arab notion of Zionism was the reference to Islam, which took on meanings of a political ideology to the Israeli respondents. Islam makes it more difficult for Arabs to solve the issues with Israel. It teaches them intolerance. According to Islam, they have to be superior. The very existence of the state of Israel is therefore a blow to Arab pride and culture.

But causes of conflict were also attributed to rational forces such as the national movements of the Jews and the Arabs, which grew out of historical circumstances. The reasoning along these lines stated that the Jews were people who returned to their homeland and re-established their legitimate rights, but that this deprived the native-born population of their legitimate rights.

Finally, another situational attribution was to fix the cause of conflict on the great powers, who exploited local tensions to obtain influence. This was made by both Arabs and Israelis.

The tendency is, of course, for both Arabs and Israelis to see the conflict as caused by the other party to the conflict, but as we have seen, some saw the conflict as caused by both parties, or parties not under their control. We have noted the tendency to analyze the causes of the conflict in both situational and dispositional terms. We will next look further at the strength of these tendencies by quantifying the material, and we will see in this analysis the relative strength of dispositional and situational attributions.

Table 4.5. Arab and Israeli antecedents of conflict
Q: If you could point out one single factor as the main cause of the conflict in the Middle East, which would you mention?

	Situational	Dispositional	
Israeli	62 %	38 %	(n = 65)
Arab	56 %	44 %	(n = 57)

n = total number of attributions made; those making both attributions included.

Results

First we simply counted the frequencies of dispositional and situational attributions without taking into consideration who the 'causal candidates' were. These results are presented in Table 4.5. There is a split between situational and dispositional tendencies, but the overall tendency is to emphasize situational attributions. This result is the opposite of what we found for the attributions on the two previous questions. We find the strongest difference in the Israeli sample.

Why is there a stronger tendency to make dispositional attributions when parties to a conflict explain what *maintains* the conflict as opposed to when they explain the antecedents of the conflict? Objectively speaking, we may say that the roots of a conflict may not be the same as what maintains a conflict. A more plausible explanation is that when looking at history, one can afford to be more *detached* than when observing behavior today. The results indicate a willingness to attribute more to causes stemming from a situation or circumstance the actors cannot control, rather than to resort to explicit blame-fixing. But if the fundamental attribution error disappears with more 'detached' causal inference (because of time), one would not expect the *opposite* tendency to emerge, but simply that the 'erroneous' tendency would be weakened. According to Jones and Nisbett, even a completely detached observer should be subject to the bias. But if ego-defensive mechanisms produce the bias, it still makes sense for the 'erroneous' tendency to be weakened with time. There is a stronger need for self-protection for the actions we perform now than for actions we performed in the distant past. This could give rise to an additional hypothesis: *In cases where ego-defensive mechanisms produce bias, the strength of bias depends on the closeness in time of the observed behavior.*

A more discriminating analysis

We coded the attributions in these categories:

1) Caused by our side
2) Caused by the other side
3) Neutral (caused by everybody or caused by a third party)

In view of previous results we find it important to see whether we are able to find systematic variation in the types of attributions made, depending on the locus of causation.

Drawing on our previous results on attribution, we predict the following: 1) *When respondents explain conflict as caused by their own side, the attributional variable will assume the value situational;* 2) *when they respond that conflict is caused by the other side, the attributional variable will assume the value dispositional.* Note that a respondent can state that the conflict is caused by his own side but still not take any blame. This occurs only in the case of a situational attribution.

Results

Israeli respondents

We can conclude from the results in Table 4.6 that we get strong support for our prediction. The tendency is clearly to make situational attributions if the respondent explains the conflict as caused by his own side, while the reverse is true if he explains the conflict as caused by the opponent.

It is also interesting to note that there is not a predominant tendency for either Israelis or Arabs to see the conflict as caused by the

64

Table 4.6. Israeli antecedents of conflict

Q: If you could point out one single factor as the main cause of the conflict in the Middle East, which would you mention?

	Israel		
Locus of causation	Situational	Dispositional	
Caused by our side	100 %	0 %	(n = 3)
Caused by other side	15 %	85 %	(n = 13)
Neutral	78 %	22 %	(n = 37)

n = 53 is the total number of attributions made. Each respondent can make several attributions, but only one in each category is counted.

other party. Only one-fourth of the Israeli respondents said that the conflict was caused by the opponent. Some even said that the conflict was caused by their own side.

It certainly seems as though one can afford to take a 'cooler' look at the past. The results confirm that ego-defensive mechanisms do not produce so much bias in explaining the more distant past. The main tendency is not to blame anyone for what caused the conflict, but to blame situational forces and constraints. But if there is blame-fixing the results confirm the predicted pattern.

Table 4.7. Arab antecedents of conflict

Q: If you could point out one single factor as the main cause of the conflict in the Middle East, which would you mention?

	Arabs		
Locus of causation	Situational	Dispositional	
Caused by our side	0 %	0 %	(n = 0)
Caused by other side	20 %	80 %	(n = 25)
Neutral	87 %	13 %	(n = 30)

n = 55 is the total number of attributions made; see note under Table 4.6.

Arab Respondents

The results from Arab respondents are presented in Table 4.7, and support the predicted tendency to make dispositional attributions when conflict is explained as caused by the other party. The results for both Arabs and Israelis confirm that the attributions made when explaining the causes of conflict are quite sensitive to the type of blame-fixing we make. In no instances did the respondents in the Arab sample say that the conflict was caused by their own side. (In the Israeli sample we did have some cases.) In these cases, situational attributions were what we predicted. When the conflict is explained as caused by one's own side, environmental influences and constraints are 'blamed'. Thus, saying that the conflict is caused by one's own side is not the same as saying that we are *responsible*. Situational attributions avoid blame. It is therefore not necessarily a more compromising stand in the conflict. (If conflict were seen as caused by one's own side and the attribution was dispositional, it would, of course, be different. But we had no instances of this in either the Arab or Israeli sample.)

As we also found with Israeli respondents, Arab respondents for the most part saw conflict as caused by some third party or everyone involved (coded as neutral). Here, attributions are overwhelmingly situational, as one would have expected. This reflects the weakened need for holding the opponent responsible as time goes by.

Image of change

We now proceed to the respondent's beliefs about means-ends relationships when analyzing the future. Looking at attributional tendencies regarding what could cause change may provide new insight into attributional mechanisms. The data are based on the following question:

Given what you would like to see happen in the Middle East in the near future, what do you think are the most effective ways to achieve these aims?

In this question we wanted to elicit the respondents' theories as to what could cause change, and what would be the best ways to cause change in the direction of expressed desires or preferred state of affairs. According to attribution, elites can see change caused by situational changes or changes in the dispositions of the actors. The present question was a follow-up to a previous question, which was formulated in the following way: *As regards the political situation, what would you like to see happen in the Middle East in the near future?* We will therefore briefly report those answers here to provide the logical sequence in the interviewing procedure.

Examples of Arab responses to this question were that they wanted to see a lasting peace in the area and a just solution of the conflict, or the development of good political relationships of all the countries involved. The Israeli answers were along the same lines, but here there was emphasis on peace as a process, and a sharp distinction drawn between so-called technical peace and real peace. There were some respondents on both sides who said they wanted peace on the condition that their own demands in the conflict were met. On the Arab side, justice and self-determination for the Palestinians were emphasized, as well as Israeli withdrawal from occupied territories. Israeli responses focused on security guarantees and recognition of the state of Israel. Finally, some Israeli and Arab respondents simply stated that they wanted to be stronger in the conflict than the opponent.

When we posed the question about what they would like to see happen in the near future, we expected the answers to be given in a more concrete form than we actually received. By including the near future, we suggested to the respondents that they think of concrete alternatives, but the answers given were mostly in quite general forms. This may demonstrate, or at least indicate, that thinking is not very articulate or advanced on actual resolution of the conflict. What elites typically seemed to discuss, even when asked about the near future, were abstract preferences like total peace, or total absence of conflict.

We then proceeded with the question that will be the subject of attributional analysis: Given what you would like to see happen in the Middle East, what do you think are the most effective ways to achieve these aims? For the views expressed on the most effective ways of achieving their aims in the near future, the level of abstraction was also quite high. There was hardly any articulate thinking about what would initiate processes toward conflict resolution. From the answers, it appears that the dichotomy in attribution is highly relevant. Both types of causal analysis appear. Some respondents emphasized informal processes of the actors (dispositional), while others focused on change in the environment (situational). Some saw change as caused by their own side, others by both sides, or outside powers or the UN, while the majority saw change as caused by modification of the opponent's behavior. For others, resolution of the conflict was a question of more moderation on one or both sides. Once an attitude-change in this direction came about, there would be a resolution of the conflict. This view was presented in dispositional terms, in that moderation was seen as a process internal to the actor. It was a question of becoming less fanatic, less rigid and more rational. In other words, conflict resolution was seen as a process of changing attitudes, and not changing situational influences and constraints.

Other respondents pointed to situational changes. On the Arab side, the magic word was unity. From unity strength was derived, and with strength the opponent would be forced to give in. Strength was seen as a precondition for liberating Palestine. Focus on the power component was also strong on the Israeli side, where military strength was mainly referred to, while economic strength was hardly mentioned. But on the Israeli side the problem was not often perceived as a lack of strength, but as the opponent's misunderstanding of how strong Israel is (dispositional).

Communication and cooperation, as well as negotiations, were expressed as potential sources of change in favorable directions. Change could occur when all countries in the area respected each other's rights. It could occur with the elimination of the influence of the superpowers; conversely, it was also felt that the influence of superpowers could have a constructive role to play. The explanation was that the parties themselves would not be able to progress toward conflict resolution without outside help. Economic and cultural developments were also seen as aiding processes of conflict resolution. For example, it was claimed that education of Arabs would lead to more rational thinking.

Arab respondents saw change as caused by Israeli concessions, such as withdrawal from occupied territories, and solution of the Palestine problem.

In some cases causal analysis was not made at all. Prescriptive statements were given, such as that peace should be based on justice. Or some respondents simply said that peace was a long process, and therefore they could mention nothing that could cause change in the near future.

Table 4.8. Image of change

Q: Given what you would like to see happen in the Middle East in the near future, what do you think are the most effective ways to achieve these aims?

	Situational	Dispositional	
Israeli	77 %	23 %	(n = 39)
Arab	62 %	38 %	(n = 65)

n = 104 is the total number of attributions; see note under Table 4.6.

Table 4.8 presents the distribution of dispositional and situational attributions. The most striking aspect of the results is the emphasis on situational attributions by both Arab and Israeli respondents. In other words, most of the respondents saw changes in desired directions as caused by the manipulation of situational and not dispositional variables. Returning to what caused the conflict, the pattern was the same. We may therefore conclude that for both what the respondents see as original causes of conflict and what could cause it to change, the tendency is to emphasize situational variables.

As with the previous questions, we find it important to proceed with a more discriminating analysis. The dichotomy situational/dispositional is not sufficient. We have to take into account the locus of causation. Do attributional tendencies vary systematically, depending upon the causal candidate of change: the opponent, themselves, or some 'outsiders'? To do this, we coded the causal statements into three categories:

1) Change caused by our side
2) Change caused by the other side
3) Neutral (third party should take initiatives or both parties)

On the basis of previous results, we hypothesize: where change is seen as caused by the opponent, the tendency will be to make dispositional attributions. Where change is seen as caused by themselves, the tendency will be to make situational attributions, and finally, where change is seen as caused by neutral forces, the tendency will be to make situational attributions.

Table 4.9. Image of change
Q: Given what you would like to see happen in the Middle East in the near future, what do you think are the most effective ways to achieve these aims?

	Change Caused by Us			Change Caused by Them			Neutral		
	Sit.	Disp.		Sit.	Disp.		Sit.	Disp.	
Israeli	90%	10%	(n=10)	44%	56%	(n= 9)	85%	15%	(n=20)
Arab	100%	0%	(n=13)	23%	77%	(n=13)	62%	38%	(n=39)

n = 104 is the total number of attributions; see note under Table 4.6.

One interesting aspect of the results is that the majority of respondents on both sides chose a neutral candidate for causing change. This indicates a strong belief in outside help, such as the UN and the superpowers, to promote a solution of the conflict. Arab respondents were somewhat stronger in this regard than were the Israeli.

And again the results support our hypothesis. When change is seen as caused by themselves, the tendency is to make situational attributions, and the tendency is to make dispositional attributions when change is seen as caused by the other side. Stronger support for this latter observation is found in the Israeli data.

These results may give rise to an additional hypothesis, since the postulated bias of Jones and Nisbett may not apply equally in expressions of future predictions or theories on what could cause change. While it is true that a bias is involved whenever any party to the conflict is made the causal candidate of change, the overall tendency is nevertheless to make situational attributions. It is therefore possible for erroneous tendencies in attribution to apply more strongly to post-decision situations than pre-decision stages. When we asked about past behavior, the bias was quite strong. It is possible that a more 'logical' schema applies in the attributional processes concerned with future change, and as a consequence, bias is not found to the same extent. More realism as opposed to, for example, self-esteem may apply. Our new hypothesis derived from these results is: *The attributional bias varies with post-decision and pre-decision stages. In the case of pre-decision, the attributional process wll conform more to a 'logical' schema.*

Change processes are, on the whole, seen as being triggered by changes in environmental forces and constraints. This conforms to the general proposition in social psychology that the easiest way to initiate change is to start off with changes in the environmental intluences and constraints.

Summary

The following questions were used to elicit causal statements:

1) What do you think are the basic good and bad aspects of your side in the conflict?
2) What do you think are the basic good and bad aspects of the other side in the conflict?
3) Do you think the other side is threatening you?
4) Do you think that the other side believes that you are threatening them?
5) If you could point out one single factor as the main cause of the conflict in the Middle East, which would you mention?
6) Given what you would like to see happen in the Middle East in the near future, what do you think are the most effective ways to achieve these aims?

On all questions, the data gave considerable support to our hypothesis.

Attributional tendencies were found to vary systematically with actor and observer as well as with evaluative dimensions of the observed behavior.

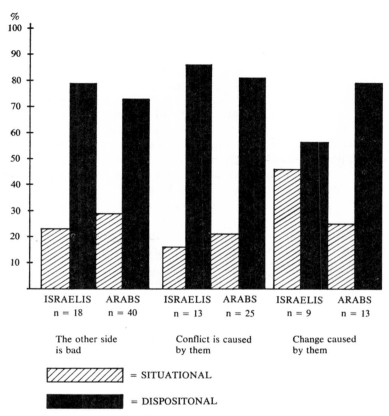

Figure 4.1. Attributional tendencies

The most striking result in Figure 4.1 is the strong dispositional bias in analyzing the behavior of the opponent. The only exception to this is the Israeli result on what the opponent should do to cause change toward a resolution of the conflict, but even here the majority of attributions are dispositional.

Futhermore, we have found that the attributional bias on the whole is weakened in analyses of the distant past (what originally caused the conflict) and the future (what could cause a resolution of the conflict), which has given rise to two additional hypotheses: an attributional bias related to bias as a function of time and bias as a function of pre- or post-decision.

Concluding remarks

In this chapter we have looked at the processes of causal attributions in the Middle East conflict. We have asked how the parties explained causes of their own behavior and the behavior of their opponent. We suggested that the causes could be classified on a dispositional (internal) or situational (stimuli in the environment) basis. We further suggested that even if 'logical' rules of inferences were applied to arrive at causal beliefs, there were still sources of systematic bias. Elite members in the conflict are 'truth' seekers, or open and active information seekers, because knowing the 'truth' would put them in the strongest position to make the right choices. There are, in spite of this, sources of imperfection, one being the bias produced by the attributional process. The results have confirmed our suspicion. But how do we explain the respondents' deviation from logical rules of inferences and the introduction of erroneous tendencies in information-processing? As a starting point we may repeat the four ways mentioned by Bem[1] as explanations of differences between self-perception and interpersonal perception:

a) The private stimuli play a role — even though this varies with the situation — and these private stimuli are, of course, not directly available to the observer.

b) Our experiences of the past that determine the meaning attached to what is perceived (observed) are not available in the same way to the 'stranger'.

c) The protection of self-esteem and defence against threat. This may distort your self-attributions in various ways.

d) Features of the situation are differentially salient to yourself and the observer. There seems to be a difference of focus in attention between the actor and the observer. The actor's attention may be more focused toward situational cues, while to the observer, the actor's behavior is more salient.

As can be seen from this list, Bem leaves open the possibility that bias and distortion can be ascribed to cognitive or informational factors, as well as motivational factors. It is generally acknowledged by attribution theorists that both cognitive and motivational forces can lead to distortion and bias in the attribution processes, and also that these factors can be mutually reinforcing.[2]

Our first result was that the action itself accounted for most of the variance in the type of attributions made. When the actor disliked the observed behavior, the attributional tendencies differed dramatically from the attributional tendencies when the actor approved of the behavior. This relationship points to motivational rather than cognitive factors as an explanation of bias.

Jones and Nisbett emphasize cognitive factors as an explanation of the fundamental attribution error.[3] They point out the rather obvious fact that information on both the effects and the causes vary with actor and observer. Actor and observer may have different information as to the nature of the act, what exactly was done, what effect the action had on the environment, and how the actor himself experienced the act. Furthermore, the observer may not have the same knowledge about environmental influences and constraints on the actor as the actor himself, and the observer is likely to have inferior knowledge about the actor's intention. If Arabs, for example, decide to form a union of Arab countries, they have a different perspective of the nature of this act than the Israelis. The Israelis observing the behavior will have inferior knowledge as to effect of the action, or how the Arabs themselves experience this. Israelis will probably not have the same information on environmental influences and constraints that may have initiated the action, and they must necessarily have inferior knowledge about intentions, since this cannot be measured directly. When explaining the attributional bias by cognitive factors, Jones and Nisbett point both to these informational deficits and the different perspectives of observers and actors.

Our results clearly demonstrate that not cognitive but motivational factors account for most of the variance. This emerges especially when we make a distinction between liked and disliked behavior. Motivational factors are, of course, most likely to produce bias if there is a high degree of involvement in the observed behavior and the affective component is strong. Both these conditions are present for the elites in the Middle East conflict. The motive of maintaining self-esteem is probably strong in producing bias.

If motivational factors are most important in producing the observed bias, this may explain why we did not get the same support for the postulated bias when we asked about the distant past and the future. Motivational factors are strongest in immediate post-decision situations ('pleasure principle').[4] When behavior becomes more distant, the need for protecting self-esteem may not be as great. Looking ahead, at the future or the pre-decision stage, as it were, a 'reality' principle may be stronger than ego-defensive mechanisms. The logical schema for processing causality is given more room. The causal analysis is dictated by the need to operate with an adequate and optimal information based on means-ends relationships. The erroneous tendencies therefore do not apply to the same extent. After the response is given, motivational forces come into play, because there is a need to defend the performed response.

Attributional processes as a means of keeping cognitive balance

The results also provide insight into ways of coping with discrepant information by showing the flexibility an individual has when analyzing the causes of behavior.

In our previous study[5] we explained that discrepant information could be dealt with either by simply ignoring it (selective perceptual process) or by giving added weight to other information (bolstering). The attribution process demonstrates another mechanism for dealing with unexpected behavior and events without changing beliefs. If I have a devil-image of the opponent and the opponent behaves in an indisputably friendly way, I can still maintain my beliefs about the opponent by explaining his friendly behavior as caused by environmental influences and constraints. His disposition to act in an unfriendly way remains the same, but certain characteristics of the situation have forced him to be *temporarily* friendly. In other words, the opponent is not given responsibility (credit) for what he is doing. His behavior is reactive. It also follows from this attribution that the change in behavior will not be seen to be of lasting value, since there is a high expectancy of change in situational variables as opposed to dispositional.[6]

Freedom of choice

Further important implications of the results concern perceived freedom of choice in conflict behavior.[7] We have noted the tendency to attribute the behavior of the opponent to internal dispositions, while seeing one's own choices as governed by environmental influences and constraints.

In choosing a situational explanation the individual assumes that this is something outside the control of the actor (not caused by him) — something for which he cannot be responsible. When choosing a dispositional (internal) explanation, the individual assumes that the responsibility or explanation is with the actor, and that there were two or more options available.

Dispositional attributions imply that actors are faced with *freedom of choice,* while situational attributions imply reaction to stimuli with no real choice involved. Our results therefore tell us that there is a systematic bias involved in perceived freedom of choice. The enemy in the conflict is seen as having alternatives in the conflict, while one's own side pursues policies that are simply reactive to the enemy's policies. In other words, the opponent could have acted otherwise; but one's own behavior, on the other hand, is viewed as having no available options.

Suggestions for further research

Our results on attribution theory suggest the need for differentiating types of situations. The result led us to suspect that attributional tendencies are not the same in a pre-decision stage as a post-decision stage. One should therefore be cautious about generalizing when data are only collected from post-decision situations. We would welcome complementary research on this to see whether our suspicions are confirmed. Previous studies on attribution in international relations fail to make this type of differentiation.[8] In further refining the theory, we also see the need for testing attributional tencencies in typically cooperative situations among nations and groups. This could provide further insight into the theoretical controversy on how to explain the variance predicted by the theory. If the explanation offered by the studies on attribution are correct, attribution in typically cooperative situations should be dramatically different.

One may readily think of situations from our daily experience where attributions will be quite contrary to what attribution theory would predict. In applying the theory to international relations, there is a need to investigate attributional tendencies in different types of situations. Up to this point, those who have applied the theory to international relations have dealt exclusively with conflict. We must leave open the possibility, for example, that attribution works quite differently in processes of de-escalation as opposed to escalation.

In addition, the explanation of the attributional tendencies may be explained in instrumental terms.[9]

It may simply be a 'good' policy for promoting one's interest in the conflict to take credit for behavior considered good while freeing oneself of responsibility for behavior considered bad; it may be also a good policy not to give the opponent credit for his policies that could be considered good while fixing the blame on the oponent for bad outcomes. Thus the attributional tendencies may also be considered highly instrumental in some cases where it promotes one's own position in the conflict.

Who is to blame for this and that? Attribution provides the elites with an instrument to shift blame and take credit that puts their own side in the conflict in a more favorable light.

In bargaining processes, for example, it may be important for getting one's own definition of the problem accepted that one's own analysis of causality is accepted. When the parties in the Arab-Israeli conflict apply different attributions in explaining the causes of their own behavior as opposed to the behavior of the opponent, this could certainly be viewed as a good strategy for fixing blame on the other party to the conflict, and taking credit when this is to one's benefit. Viewing attribution as a verbal strategy in the conflict is intriguing, and demonstrates how it may be helpful for parties to a conflict to convince themselves and others of their rights and the justness of their claims. We imagine that this may be to a party's advantage in many cases, but the reverse may also be true, because operating with these different models of responsibility may produce beliefs that in other situations may be a trap rather than a benefit.

CHAPTER V

Stability of Beliefs: An Intertemporal Perspective

Before discussing consistency, we will analyze the stability of beliefs included in our operational code analysis in an intertemporal perspective. We compare beliefs the respondents had at one point in time (T_1) with beliefs at another point in time (T_2) and thereby assess the stability of these beliefs in the Arab-Israeli conflict.

The tabular data presented are descriptive summaries of the respondents' beliefs, and the frequency distribution of the answers should not be taken as representative of the entire population of relevant elites. The procedure for selecting respondents, as well as the relatively low number of respondents, does not allow for inference generalizations to the universe of relevant elites. The data reported in this chapter therefore are useful primarily for generating rather than testing hypotheses about the stability of beliefs.

Short of a representative sample, interviewing the same individuals over time may produce valuable data for assessing stability. Researchers of international conflict very seldom do interviewing over time, especially with the same respondents. So although our number of respondents reappearing at various points in time is small, we find that these data are valuable enough to justify analysis (list of respondents in appendix).

Before going any further in the analysis, we need to briefly explain questions referring to different dimensions included in the analysis. The dimensions are as follows: 'Image of the Opponent', 'Image of Self', and 'Image of Change'.

Image of the Opponent

The measures of this belief dimension are the following questions in the field interviews:

1) Do you think that the other side is threatening you?
2) What are the goals of the other side in the conflict?

3) Are there any differences concerning the goals and strategies of the other side?
4) What do you think are the basic good and bad aspects of the other side in the conflict?
5) Do you see any elements on the other side working for peace?
6) In what way and how much is the other side dependent on the superpowers?

Image of Self as an Actor

To measure self-image, we posed the following questions in the field interviews:

1) Do you think that the other side is threatening you?
2) What are the goals of your side in the conflict?
3) Are there any differences concerning the goals and strategies on your side?
4) What do you think are the basic good and bad aspects of your side in the conflict?
5) Do you see any elements in your own country working against peace?
6) Do you think that the other side believes that you are threatening them?
7) In what way and how much is your side dependent on the superpowers?

Perception of Change

The measures of this dimension are the following questions in the field interviews:

1) In what way do you think the events in the last years have basically changed the conflict?
2) Now speaking realistically, what would you actually expect will happen in the near future?
3) How long do you think the conflict will last?

Underlying assumptions in the scaling of variance

As in the chapter on attribution, we need to explain the coding procedures used. The independent variables are the operational code beliefs and the dependent variable is the respondent's policy position, which can take on two values: 1) we should negotiate with the enemy now, 2) we should not negotiate with the enemy now. These two values of the dependent variable are seen as the two basic positions toward negotiations at any point in time. The independent variables must capture competing viewpoints within and not only across elites.

Beliefs on which there is consensus cannot predict the different positions in the conflict. Examining the variance in beliefs is therefore central to the study. Our underlying assumption, which we will investigate in the next chapter, is that the variance in the beliefs we have charted and analyzed will account for the differences we find as regards which policies ought to be pursued vis-à-vis the opponent in the conflict.

The study previously referred to aided us in arriving at what we found to be sensible scaling procedures. In this study, we identified three positions, which covered the most interesting tendencies in the conflict for the purpose of evaluating the possibilities for conflict resolution:
1) Advocates of a settlement through negotiations along the lines of the UN Resolution of 1967.
2) Advocates of a Palestinian democratic state including the territory of Israel, having as its preconditions a military solution.
3) Advocates of the status quo. This means being in favor of the present situation in the absence of other options but envisaging a settlement at some unspecified time in the future.

Position 1 is shared by Arabs and Israelis alike, while Position 2 is primarily an Arab position, and Position 3 is held mainly by Israelis. The only goal providing much scope for compatibility, then, is Position 1. These positions we reformulate for the purpose of analysis as two positions (see next chapter).

We should negotiate with the enemy now.
We should not negotiate with the enemy now.

By this we define conflict resolution as a solution along the lines of the UN Resolution 242. The advocates of a Palestinian democratic state on the territory that is now Israel will in our analysis be defined as non-cooperative, because they favor a solution that is far removed from what we have defined as steps toward conflict resolution. Correspondingly, we have defined those supporting maintenance of the boundaries after the June 1967 war as non-cooperative on the Israeli side. This classification may, of course, be criticized; it can be argued for example that the Palestinian guerrillas are standing for the only humane and just solution of the conflict, and that those opposing this solution are the extreme ones. Thus the descriptions 'cooperative' and 'non-cooperative', 'compromising' and 'uncompromising' must be understood in relation to our definition of conflict resolution. Research is not neutral, and our subjectivity is clearly expressed in our scaling of variance. Instead of 'cooperative' and 'non-cooperative' we could have said 'negative' and 'positive', which are perhaps less subjective terms. Still, it does not avoid the problem of subjectivity: what is compromising to one person is not so to another. The underlying logic of scaling must be related to our dependent variable, which is defined as advocating or not advocating compromising with the opponent in the conflict under present conditions.

(For further explanation of this, consult the codebook.)

A good 'test' of the stability of beliefs in the Arab-Israeli conflict would be from the time of our first interviews (1970) to our second round (1974) of interviewing, because there are significant intervening events in this period: the oil embargo and the October war. To assess the extent to which these events affected the basic conflict orientations of our respondents, we will examine the respondents reappearing in samples before and after these events.

In Israel 15 respondents and on the Arab side 12 respondents appeared on our list before and after. Given the small number of cases, the possibility of idiosyncratic results and random variations is present. Furthermore, owing to the fact that we used an unstructured interview schedule in 1970/72 only a few identical questions appear in 1970/72 and 1974.

The results show an overall tendency for stability in the beliefs of Israeli respondents. Events in the years 1970—1974 seem to have had some impact on the belief systems of the Arab respondents. Most worthy of note here is that the Arab respondents in 1970 generally expressed the belief that 'One day we will be stronger than Israel'. This belief was considerably reinforced after the oil embargo and the October war of 1973. The respondents drew different conclusions from perceived changes in the power configuration between the conflicting parties. Some respondents claimed that Israel was no longer expansionist in view of growing Arab strength. Other respondents, however, warned that the Arab world must remain continually on its guard, since Israel would regain its strength for purposes of expansion, and that the Yom Kippur war was merely a temporary setback.

The intervening events, then, may have triggered changes in beliefs. Some Arab respondents see Israel as less expansionist than before: 'Israel is not so strong any more, therefore she is not so expansionist.' For others, the October war was interpreted as a temporary setback for the deterministic expansionist nature of Israel. Other respondents do not seem to make the same linkage between beliefs about *power* and beliefs about *intention* as they did before. The intention component of the opponent is regarded as a constant. Also, the perceived freedom of choice in solutions to the conflict seems to have increased with Arab respondents. More options were seen as solutions of the Palestinian problem.

There was for the Israeli respondents, a noticeable shift toward an uncompromising position in statements dealing with occupied territories.

Both self-image and enemy-image for the Israeli respondents have remained stable. The most stable dimension for Arabs and Israelis is the image of opponent. A noticeable fluctuation can be noted in the Arab self-image. While there was more stability in beliefs for Israeli respondents compared to Arab respondents, the overall tendency for both sides is toward stability.

Image of the opponent, image of self, and image of change

We have discussed the stability of beliefs of respondents who reappeared in samples before and after the October war. Now we will add to our analysis the respondents who were interviewed only once, either before or after the October war. Although we cannot make any direct inferences about stability, we may, by comparing the similarities across all three of the samples for all respondents gain some further insights about the stability of beliefs.

The results from 1974 and 1976 are based on the same questions and the same coding rules. With the first sample, our measures are less exact. Since we used an unstructured interviewing schedule, frequency counts and coding rules had to be somewhat improvised (see appendix on coding). The first sample contains only a few questions similar to questions posed in the second and third samples. It was necessary to sort out questions for which we did have a reasonable data base in all three samples, and therefore the sample of questions is quite accidental, and certainly not the ones we would have chosen if we had had an equally good data base for all.

The dimensions dealt with are: self-image, image of the opponent, image of change. In the first sample, we did have questions about the opponent in the conflict (enemy-image), and there are corresponding questions in the second and the third samples. This is also the case for questions about themselves (self-image), and how they think the conflict will develop in the future (image of change). We will deal with the Israeli and the Arab samples separately, first looking at the Israeli sample of 1972, 1974 and 1976, then at the Arab sample of 1970, 1974 and 1976.

We have two questions with reference to image of the opponent: one question on the perception of the opponent's goals, and the other on the threat posed by the opponent. The results in both the Arab and Israeli samples on these questions show much similarity. There is a high degree of consensus on what the goals of the opponent are (although less in the Israeli sample), and there is a remarkable similarity in these opinions. Equally, the perception of a threat was at al-

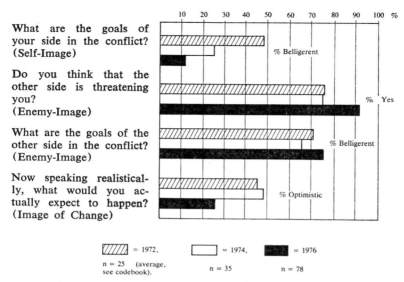

Figure 5.1. Comparison of Israeli responses in 1972, 1974, 1976.

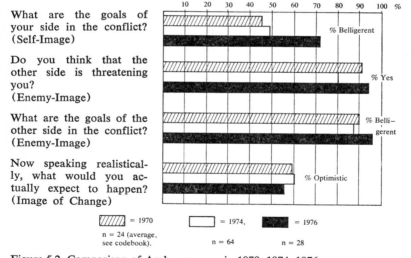

Figure 5.2. Comparison of Arab responses in 1970, 1974, 1976.

most the same level for each sample: the overwhelming majority of respondents in all three samples sees the opponent as threatening.

In the Israeli sample, in response to a question as to their own goals and another as to differences on their own side, we find variations in the perception of their own goals, with the results indicating a pattern of describing one's own goals as less belligerent. The respondents emphasized the accommodative aspects of their sets of goals more strongly after the October war. On the second question, we obtained similar results across samples. The extent to which Israeli respondents saw their side as a unitary or pluralistic actor was similar; the modal category was those who see Israel as a pluralistic actor.

In the Arab sample we have only the question on their own goals, where we find some variation from 1974 to 1976. The most recent sample is more belligerent.

We have only one question referring to what respondents would expect to happen. There is more pessimism on the Israeli side in the 1976 sample. On the Arab side, for all three samples the majority is optimistic.

These results generally support the tendencies we noted when comparing the same individuals over time. Image of the opponent is about the same for each sample, while there are some differences for image of self and image of change.

Comparing samples of 1974 and 1976

Most of the questions are the same in the two samples, which facilitates comparison. On the other hand, we do not have any dramatic intervening events of the type we had when we made the previous comparisons. In assessing the stability of beliefs, the data here are therefore less interesting, and we should hardly expect any dramatic changes in beliefs. The main purpose of the sample in 1976 was to validate the results in 1974. But the interviewing of new elite members in 1976 will help us find out whether the patterns of thinking we found in 1974 apply to wider groups of elites, as well as checking the stability of these patterns. Dissimilar results may be ascribed to loss of reliability, bias in one or both samples, or less stable or more situation-specific beliefs. Similar results suggest reliability and representativeness as well as stability. The comparison will be made on 11 questions posed both in 1974 and 1976.

There is much similarity in the frequency distributions of responses, which suggests stability of the patterns of thinking. We get similar results on five questions for both Arabs and Israelis. (For a complete listing of results, see appendix.) On the whole, Israelis vary less than Arabs. In the Arab samples, we find differences on 6 questions. This may be due to more biased sampling on the Arab side, problems of reliability, more variance in the universe, or that beliefs are more in a stage of fluctuation on the Arab side — a hypothesis supported by previous results. Supporting our previous results is the

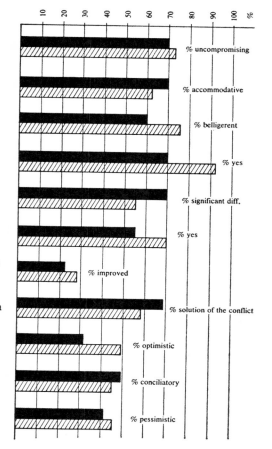

How do you see the solution to the Palestinian problem? — % uncompromising

What are the goals of your side in the conflict? — % accommodative

What are the goals of the other side in the conflict? — % belligerent

Do you think that the other side is threatening you? — % yes

Are there any differences concerning goals and strategies of the other side? — % significant diff.

Do you think that the other side believes that you are threatening them? — % yes

In what way do you think that the events in recent years have basically changed the conflict? — % improved

As regards the political situation what would you like to see happen in ME in the near future? — % solution of the conflict

Now speaking realistically, what would you actually expect to happen? — % optimistic

Given what you would like to see happen, what are the most effective ways to achieve these aims? — % conciliatory

How long do you think this conflict will last? — % pessimistic

= 1974
n = 37
= 1976
n = 78

Figure 5.3. Comparison of Israeli responses in 1974 and 1976.

84

How do you see the solution to the Palestinian problem?

What are the goals of your side in the conflict?

What are the goals of the other side in the conflict?

Do you think that the other side is threatening you?

Are there any differences concerning goals and strategies of the other side?

Do you think that the other side believes that you are threatening them?

In what way do you think that the events in recent years have basically changed the conflict?

As regards the political situation what would you like to see happen in ME in the near future?

Now speaking realistically, what would you actually expect to happen?

Given what you would like to see happen, what are the most effective ways to achieve these aims?

How long do you think this conflict will last?

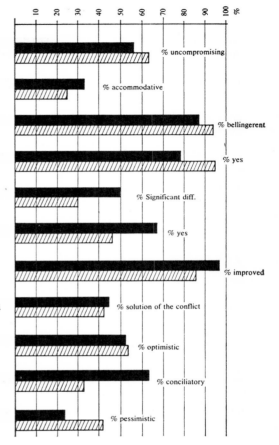

 = 1974
n = 65
= 1976
n = 29

Figure 5.4. Comparison of Arab responses in 1974 and 1976.

85

tendency to less similarity in self-image and image of change than image of the opponent.

Looking at past events on the whole, Arab respondents claimed that they are gradually becoming stronger than the opponent, although more so in 1974 than in 1976. Do Israeli respondents feel the same way? The answer is definitely no. Only a fourth of the Israelis felt that things were moving in their favor, and a fourth of the Israelis really felt that things were getting worse. Israeli respondents had a generally pessimistic attitude in both 1974 and 1976.

There is more pessimism in the Arab sample in 1976 than in 1974. How do we explain this? Perhaps Arabs saw a possible quick solution of the conflict after the October war. This opinion might have been much stronger in 1974 than in 1976.

The impact of the October war may have created strong optimism on the Arab side, but the effect decreased with time. Other questions on optimism/pessimism reinforce the result: a stronger optimism in 1974 than in 1976. This may be a more situation-specific belief then, vulnerable to change by situational changes.

Questions about the future show that the overall tendency has been for the Israeli respondents to be rather pessimistic and Arab respondents to be optimistic. This was somewhat modified in 1976, when Arabs were less optimistic both about past trends and how things will move in the future.

The question dealing with what respondents *expect* to happen in the near future was presented as a follow-up question to: As regards the political situation, what would you *like* to see happen in the Middle East in the near future? Arabs generally, as we have seen, have been optimistic on future developments, but on this question about the near future they are evenly divided between optimism/pessimism.

In the Israeli sample, this question showed a more pessimistic attitude. Those coded as optimistic dropped from 47% in 1974 to 24% in 1976. In the Arab sample the modal category is still optimistic.

We can note a certain pattern on both sides, whereby the overall tendency is to be more pessimistic in 1976 than in 1974. Looking at events in this period, the results make sense, because options for peace decreased and short-term expectations were probably quite sensitive to situational changes. Arabs on the whole tended to be more optimistic as to the final outcome of the conflict (who will win).

Discussion of results

If we examine stability with reference to the operational code beliefs, the most striking result is the stability of the image of the opponent in both Arab and Israeli respondents. No other dimensions have this stability. The questions here refer to the goals of the opponent, the threat of the opponent, how pluralistic is the opponent, and the image of the opponent's image of their own side. The image of self does not have this degree of stability. The questions here refer to their own goals, perception of their own side as being threatening, and pluralism on their own side. It is possible that while the opponent is regarded more or less as a 'constant' in goals and strategies, the respondents may see their own side in the conflict as more changing. The respondents seem to be more confident about the opponent's behavior than about their own. Image of change is also less clear, and at least some beliefs in this dimension seem to be quite situation-specific.

The Israeli respondents show a stronger overall similarity in their beliefs than the Arab respondents, but both groups share the relative similarity of beliefs referring to image of the opponent.

Some beliefs have a high degree of consensus among the elites. But on most of the questions we do find deep cleavages within elites on both sides. The elites in the conflict have different or competing beliefs about what the opponent is like, what their own side is like, and what the processes of change are, or which way the conflict will move.

Competing interpretations are given on both sides. We are therefore able to analyze different patterns within as well as across elites, in the way the elites think about issues. The patterns were visible in the first sample and are confirmed in the second and third. At any point in time there will be many situation-specific beliefs — beliefs that are quite sensitive to change in situations, and situations do change all the time. These situation-specific beliefs are the more peripheral beliefs. What we have dealt with here is the stability of the more basic orientations to the conflict. Given the data base, the results should be regarded as being suggestive. But in the analysis we approach the problem of stability by multiple indicators, where this descriptive analysis constitutes only one of these.

CHAPTER VI

Consistency within Operational Code Components

Consistency

To examine how parties to a conflict arrive at causal beliefs, we dealt in a previous chapter with the role of operational code beliefs in information-processing. Concepts and hypotheses from attribution theory assisted in this analysis. Attribution theory, however, says nothing about how beliefs are linked to each other. We have proposed to study the beliefs as a system, a concept which assumes we are dealing not with a random collection of beliefs, but with linkages, a certain order, and stability. The whole notion of prediction in the operational code is based on the assumption that there are constraints on the way beliefs go together. If this were not the case, prediction would lose much of its meaning. When we investigate consistency in this chapter, we will look at *response-response* consistency, which is a static examination of consistency as opposed to cross-situational consistency, where consistency is looked at over time in different situations. This is the dynamic examination of consistency.

In this study we will take the need for consistency or consistency striving for granted.

Cognitive theory is on safe ground in postulating that there are constraints on the way individuals link and organize and maintain their beliefs, but the extent of constraints or organization, and how these combinations are formed, are subjects open to dispute.

This will not be a test of the theory itself, but we will see to what extent the respondents' beliefs follow hypotheses derived from consistency theory. We will first look at consistency within each separate belief dimension constituting the operational code, which we shall call components of the operational code belief system. On the basis of cognitive theory, we would expect consistency to operate most strongly in these narrow portions of the belief system.

The components are listed below:

Image of Change

In what way do you think the events in the last years have basically changed the conflict?

Now speaking realistically, what would you actually expect will happen in the near future?
How long do you think the conflict will last?

Image of Self
Are there any differences concerning the goals and strategies on your side?
What do you think are the basic good and bad aspects of your side in the conflict?
Do you see any elements in your own country working against peace?
Do you think that the other side belives that you are threatening them?

Image of the Opponent
Are there any differences concerning the goals and strategies of the other side?
What do you think are the basic good and bad aspects of the other side in the conflict?
Do you see any elements on the other side working for peace?

We will look at the response-response consistency in the answers to the questions included in each component. Finding consistency within the components we regard as a precondition for examining consistency within the molar system, which will be investigated in the next chapter.

Image of change

The following are the questions included in our first dimension:

1. In what way do you think that the events in recent years have basically changed the conflict?
2. Now realistically speaking, what would you actually expect will happen in the next few years?
3. How long do you think this conflict will last?

This dimension deals with the respondent's optimism and pessimism about the eventual realization of one's values in the conflict. The questions measure beliefs concerning past trends, the near future or the present, and the long-term future. We hypothesize that the respondent's view of past trends is connected to his analysis of the immediate as well as long-term future predictions. In other words, we expect consistency-seekers who trace favorable or negative developments in the past to extrapolate these trends into their analyses of the near-future and long-term future. In the very long run, it appears that almost everyone is optimistic about ending the conflict. 'Sooner or later there is bound to be an end to it.'

We expect this type of consistency because of our suspicion that the analysis of the movement of the conflict in the immediate future is made consistent with the respondent's views on the past, as well as the more distant future. This type of consistency, while not necessarily conforming to rules of 'logic', conforms to a type of 'psycho-logic' which is common in consistency striving.

We expected some respondents to be influenced by wishful thinking, in that the respondents' preferences, desires, and goals would be tailored to past and future trends.

The questions deal with the expectancy of change and the respondent's diagnoses of these processes. How do the parties in the conflict diagnose forces of change? What are the trends we can see in the conflict? Where are we moving?

We expected the respondents to hold consistent views on this. Those who see favorable trends in the past will, we expect, extrapolate these trends into the future, and those who are pessimistic about the past will also be pessimistic about the future.

When asking Arabs about the past, we focused on dramatic events like the June war 1967 and the October war. Arab respondents claimed that the June war in 1967 had proved to be a good lesson for the Arabs. Their beliefs after this war became more realistic and rational. Their beliefs in the June war 1967 exposed them to a 'reality test' that changed their beliefs to a more 'realistic' model of the conflict. But this war was negative in that the hawks in Israel gained greater influence; while realism was developing in the Arab camp, false conceptions developed in the opponent's camp. This led the opponent into unrealistic policies instead of compromising. This forced Arab leaders to concentrate greater resources on changing the existing situation. The October war came as a result of the unrealistic policy of the opponent. This war was based on a more 'national' Arab approach. It changed the balance of power in the area, offered new possibilities for solution, led to greater unity among the Arabs, proved to Israel that military power could not lead to peace, and changed the attitude of the USA toward the conflict. It is interesting to see how wishful thinking clearly plays a role, in that the event is taken to promote everything considered good in the conflict, while there is hardly any mention of bad effects of the war. This past event is interpreted as having led to a tremendous change in favor of their own side while making everything worse for the enemy. This could be compared to the way Israelis interpreted the June war in 1967, when there was also a clear tendency to interpret the war as promoting all developments considered good, while the bad effects of the war were rarely mentioned. The Israeli victory in the June war 1967 and the relative victory of the Arabs in the October war led the parties into wishful thinking; the diagnoses of the effects of the events were made consistent with the belief that things were really developing to their own advantage.

When viewing the past, we hypothesize that some events are given added importance to make them consistent with one's ideas about which way the conflict is moving. There will be a selection of past events to make predictions for the future consistent with the past.

'Near future' or 'short-term expectations' correspond to the concept 'next few years' on the questionnaire item. The concept 'long-term future' was deliberately left undefined in this question as opposed to the previous question. In coding the answers, we found that some respondents saw the conflict ending in the relatively near future, while others spoke about generations or simply did not conceptualize the time span, but referred to an unspecified interval in an un-forseeable future.

Those respondents not seeing an end to the conflict in the next 20 years are coded as pessimists, while those who envisage a solution within 20 years or so are coded as optimists. Drawing the line between optimists and pessimists at 20 years is, of course, somewhat arbitrary, but in the coding process this did not represent much difficulty because the majority of respondents either did or did not see hope for a solution in the near future. Optimists see favorable trends in the past, and expect improvements in the near future, as well as a final solution of the problem within the next 20 years. The pessimists do not see favorable past trends, do not expect much improvement in the next 20 years, and expect the conflict to continue for some time to come.

Examples of how statements are coded and listed below:

Conciliatory — Arab side
Q 1: The October war changed a lot.
      Now we can go on getting a settlement of our own.
Q 2: Syrian/Israeli disengagement will take place.
      I think we will go to Geneva.
Q 3: If we settle it, it will take 3 years or less.

Non-Conciliatory — Arab side
Q 1: War has come about to prove to the Israelis that they had forfeited that opportunity, perhaps forever.
Q 2: Time is on our side.
Q 3: There is a possibility that the conflict may take generations.

Conciliatory — Israeli side

Q 1: The situation might have changed, but don't know in which direction yet.

Q 2: Possibilities for improvement do exist.

Q 3: I am an optimist.

Non-conciliatory — Israeli side

Q 1: There are no basic changes.

Q 2: For another 5 years they will try again (to destroy us).

Q 3: I just hope I will experience the end of it.

A consistent respondent, according to our definition, would be a respondent who has consistent scoring values on all three questions. In addition, we define as moderately consistent a respondent who has the same scoring value on two of the three questions and mixed or balanced on the third. In other words, if a respondent's answers on all three questions have the same value, he is defined as 'purely consistent'. If a respondent's answers on two questions have the same scoring value but differ only slightly on the third (one movement on the scale), he would be defined as moderately consistent. If, on the other hand, his scoring values differ on all questions, or his scoring value on one question differs fundamentally from his scoring values on the others, he is defined as 'inconsistent'.

Consistent on two questions, but missing data on the third

As already stated, inconsistent respondents will be dropped, because there is no way we can make any predictions from these. But another group will be added. This is the group of respondents for whom we have missing data on only one question within a belief dimension, but for whom we have consistent values on the other two questions included. In cases of this type we may predict the value on the third variable.

Just to take an example: a respondent gives 'pluralistic' answers on two questions on self-image, but has missing data on the third. We predict that he would give a 'pluralistic' or mixed answer to the third question. In both cases he would be counted as consistent (see discussion on operational definition of consistency).

On the other hand, we do not include cases in which we have, for example, a pluralistic answer to one question and a mixed answer to the other, with missing data on the third. These are excluded because this would introduce an additional element of uncertainty, and the result would be less reliable.

We can also offer at least one 'indirect' empirical test that the reliability of this procedure is very high. Our previous tests of consistency have shown that consistency is 60—75% on the average. The probability that a respondent who is consistent on two questions should get the same value or the value mixed is very high indeed. The procedure is of course not 100% reliable, since we cannot test this directly.

We looked at the results when respondents with missing data were not included. The results were very close, but including cases of missing data carries with it the advantage of giving us a bigger number of respondents for further analysis.

We hypothesize that the values represented in the questions will be the same. Or, stated somewhat differently: knowing how a person interprets the past enables us to better predict his beliefs about the future, and the other way around. Also, knowing a person's beliefs about possible short-term improvements enables us to better predict his expectations concerning a final settlement of the conflict.

Table 6.1. Consistency within Image of Change

	Purely Consistent	Moderately Consistent	Inconsistent	
Israeli	11 %	53 %	36 %	(n = 28)
Arab	19 %	36 %	45 %	(n = 53)

Consistent (purely consistent and moderately consistent):
Israeli 64 %,   Arab 55 %
(missing data: 18)

The results presented in Table 6.1 provide some support for the hypothesized relationships. The modal category for both Israeli and Arab elites is on consistency.

Given the fairly weak support for the relationships we had expected, we went back to see if the 'deviant' cases could be an artifact of our coding rules, of if we could find additional patterns of consistency that would be classified as inconsistent according to our measure of consistency. Was it possible that consistency was hidden in our results?

It should also be added that, given the relatively low number of respondents, it is possible that even if there should be such patterns within the deviant cases, they may not emerge in our analysis.

Later on we shall check to see whether it is the same respondents who provide the inconsistencies across the components.

As with the other two operational measures of consistency, Israeli respondents are more consistent than Arabs, whose responses are more complicated to explain. Since we found some differences in the

93

consistency score when looking at different countries, we will deal with each Arab country separately. We will attempt to explain results deviating from the general pattern of consistency deviations which may be tied to the operational measures of consistency.

Eighty percent of the Egyptian respondents are consistent, a result which strengthens previous results on consistency. For Jordan and Lebanon, the modal category turns out to be inconsistent (Jordan 59 %, Lebanon 82 %, but it should be noted that the Jordanian and Lebanese sample is considerably smaller, increasing the possibility that the results may be partly due to random variations).

It appears that Egypt offers the strongest support for the hypothesis, in that 8J % of the respondents are consistent, a stronger showing than even Israeli respondents. In both Jordan and Lebanon, where members of guerrilla organizations or 'identifiers' with these organizations appear in the sample, the modal category is 'inconsistent'. While these respondents hold the same view on the character of the opponent, their views on the future differ strikingly from, let's say those of Egyptian respondents.

Knowing that an Egyptian respondent takes a dim view of the past enables us to predict with confidence that his views on the immediate and long-range future are also dim. The same is true for Israeli respondents, but to a lesser extent.

Table 6.2. Consistency within the Image of Change dimension

	Purely Consistent	Moderately Consistent	Inconsistent	
Israel	11 %	53 %	36 %	(n = 28)
Egypt	24 %	56 %	20 %	(n = 25)
Jordan	18 %	23 %	59 %	(n = 17)
Lebanon	9 %	9 %	82 %	(n = 11)

Consistent (purely consistent and moderately consistent):

Israel	Egypt	Jordan	Lebanon
64 %	80 %	41 %	18 %

(missing data: 18)

We must leave open the real possibility that the linkage between analysis of the past and predictions about the future may not conform to the suggested pattern for many of the respondents. The relationship between analysis of the past and the future may be more complex. It is also possible that optimism about the near future may not be accompanied by optimism about the long-range future. To determine this, we compared the scoring values on the question about the near future with the question about the long-range future (results presented in Table 6.3).

Table 6.3. Consistency within the Image of Change dimension when using only questions 2 and 3

	Purely Consistent	Moderately Consistent	Inconsistent	
Israel	50 %	36 %	14 %	(n = 28)
Egypt	41 %	48 %	11 %	(n = 27)
Jordan	41 %	35 %	24 %	(n = 17)
Lebanon	18 %	36 %	46 %	(n = 11)

Consistent (purely consistent and moderately consistent):

Israel	Egypt	Jordan	Lebanon
86 %	89 %	76 %	54 %

(missing data: 19)

When we isolate these two questions, a considerably higher consistency score is obtained. Of course, a higher score would be expected as a consequence of including only two scoring values as opposed to three, but it is still obvious that the linkage between short-term optimism/ pessimism and long-term optimism/pessimism is quite strong. For the majority of respondents it is therefore true that the question about the past provides the explanation for the relatively weak support for consistency. Knowing that a person views the past optimistically or pessimistically does not enable us to tell very confidently what his future views are; but knowing that a respondent is optimistic about the immediate future does enable us to tell with a high degree of confidence what his long-term views are.

Equally interesting to note is that Lebanese and Jordanian results are contrary to this general pattern, and that support is weaker in Jordan. Many of these respondents obviously do hold negative views of the immediate future but are optimists in the long run. Further analysis into these cases reveals that we are dealing here with patterns that do not conform to our theoretical prediction. These respondents envisage a 'military' solution of the problems, whereby things will be worse before they get better. Since defeating Israel militarily will take time, solutions cannot be envisaged in the near future. These Arab respondents tend to be the same as those who do not feel threatened by the opponent. The majority of these respondents belong to guerrilla organizations or are 'identifiers' with these organizations.

The results demonstrate that linkages made between the past and the future are considerably more complex than we hypothesized. The results furthermore demonstrate that our operational definition of consistency does not capture the pluralism of consistent patterns we find in this respect in the Arab world. We have traced patterns that are certainly consistent, but would be classified as inconsistent by our definition of consistency. These deviant cases show that consistencies on the change dimension are rather complex.

Image of the opponent

The second component of the operational code belief system we will look at is image of the opponent. Here we posed three questions aiming at views referring to the degree to which the respondent saw pluralism:

1. What do you think are the basic good and bad aspects of the other side in the conflict?
2. Do you see any elements on the other side working for peace?
3. Are there any differences conserning goals and strategies on the other side?

On each of the questions, a respondent could have values as follows: significant differences; mixed; no differences. In coding these questions, we counted the respondents in three different categories, which can be thought of as a scaling system where the respondents are expressing views ranging from pluralistic to non-pluralistic. Coding a respondent 'mixed' meant that it was difficult to place him either as pluralistic or non-pluralistic. We expect a respondent expressing a pluralistic view on one question to express pluralistic views on others.

Examples of how statements are coded are given below:

Conciliatory — Arab side

Q 1:   The Israelis are very efficient, they have a high level of intellectual capacity. Their treatment of Arabs within their own country is bad.

Q 2:   I think there are people with clearheadedness who think a future with peace will be more beneficial.

Q 3:   I think there are differences. Within the Labour Party there are great differences.

Non-Conciliatory — Arab side

Enemy-Image:

Q 1: The absence of justice in the Israeli objectives makes it impossible to see any good sides in that conflict.

Q 2: The Israeli people have for long been deluded by their superiority and their dreams of expansion. But, no doubt, the October war dispelled such dreams.

Q 3: Such differences exist, though they are not reckoned with.

Conciliatory — Israeli side

Enemy-Image:

Q 1: In Egypt they realize that the conflict must be solved politically.

Q 2: In Egypt — Economic groups interested in peace. Jordan interested in peace.

Q 3: Some Arab countries less rigid than other countries, some want a political solution, some are hard nuts.

Non-Conciliatory — Israeli side

Q 1: We get the impression that the destruction of the state of Israel is pretty well established in most Arabs' minds.

Q 2: They are sort of fanatic. Human life is not so important to them.

Q 3: No elements working for peace.

We hypothesize that the values of the idea-elements represented in the three sets of questions will take on the same values. There will be a striving toward consistency. A consistent respondent, according to our definition, would be one who has consistent scoring values on all questions. In addition, we define as moderately consistent a respondent who has the same scoring value on two of the questions and a mixed or balanced value on the third (insignificant differences). In other words, if a respondent's answers on all three questions have the same value (significant differences *or* insignificant differences *or* no differences on all three questions), he is defined as 'purely consistent'. If a respondent's answers on two questions have the same scoring value but differ only slightly on the third (one movement on the scale), he would be defined as moderately consistent. If, on the other hand, his scoring values differ on all questions or his scoring value on one question differs fundamentally from his scoring values on the others (if, for example, he sees significant differences on two questions and no differences on the third), he is defined as 'inconsistent'.

Table 6.4. Consistency within the Image of the Opponent dimension

	Purely Consistent	Moderately Consistent	Inconsistent	
Israeli	48 %	26 %	26 %	(n = 23)
Arab	23 %	50 %	27 %	(n = 44)

Consistent (purely consistent and moderately consistent):
Israeli: 74 %,   Arab: 73 %
(missing data: 20)

The results give clear support for our hypothesis that there is consistency on the values of those beliefs represented. (See Table 6.4). The majority of respondents on both sides are consistent on this dimension.

Israel has the biggest share of purely consistent (48 %) and the highest overall score on consistency (74 %). The modal category of Arabs is moderately consistent (50 %). In other words, there is a somewhat stronger consistency pattern among the Israeli respondents, but for both groups the support for the hypothesized consistency pattern is strong (Israel 74 %, Arabs 73 %).

More than one-fourth of the respondents appear to be inconsistent.

Image of self

The questions included in our third operational measure of consistency on image of self, are:

1. What do you think are the basic good and bad aspects of your side in the conflict?
2. Do you see any elements on your own side working against peace?
3. Are there any differences concerning goals and strategies on your side?

The questions deal with the degree to which the respondent is able to make discriminating judgements about his own side. Does he see pluralism — forces pulling in different directions — or does he basically view his own side as unitary? Coding categories and examples of statements falling within the categories are given below.

Conciliatory — Arab side

Q 1: We are convinced that we are fighting for a just cause. But there is a feeling of resignation.

Q 2: I would still think there are a number of people who think of the Arab/Israeli conflict in terms of their basic rights, and have a conviction that Israel will never let us alone.

Q 3: There are differences in strategy. Some say we should have kept on fighting. On the political level some tend to rely on faith in the progress of negotiations.

Non-Conciliatory — Arab side

Q 1: The cause of defending national soil becomes an honour.

Q 2: No elements are working against peace.

Q 3: In general no differences, although the view-points are not identical.

Conciliatory — Israeli side

Q 1: Israel did not accept Palestine as a national entity.

Q 2: The religious rightist people are working against peace.

Q 3: No possible settlement range between them and the Arabs. There are hawks and doves.

Non-Conciliatory — Israeli side

Q 1: The vast majority of the people agree with the view of the government.

Q 2: This is a democratic country, which is something unique in this area.

Q 3: Everyone wants peace, no-one working against peace.

The questions and the operational definitions of consistency are the same as with image of the opponent. To repeat, a respondent is classified as purely consistent if he has the same scoring value on all three questions, moderately consistent if he has the same scoring value on two questions and differs only slightly on the third (one movement on the scale), and a person is inconsistent if scoring values differ on all questions or his scoring value is the same on two questions but differs fundamentally on the third (two movements on the scale). Our hypothesis is that the values of the idea-elements represented in the three sets of questions will take on the same values.

On image of the opponent, we found strong support for our hypothesis on consistency. The results on image of self do not provide equally strong support. Israeli respondents still show a strong support of the postulated relationship, while the modal category for Arabs now is inconsistent. While we cannot say that consistency does not apply to this component, the support of the general proposition of consistency is weaker than was the case with image of the opponent. The Israeli

Table 6.5. Consistency within the Image of Self component

	Purely Consistent	Moderately Consistent	Inconsistent	
Israeli	31 %	46 %	23 %	(n = 26)
Arab	12 %	31 %	57 %	(n = 49)

Consistent (purely and moderately consistent):
Israeli 77 %,   Arab 43 %
(missing data: 12)

respondents also offer weaker support, in that the modal category has changed from consistent to moderately consistent.

It is possible that self-image occupies a qualitatively different position in one's cognitive system than does image of the opponent. Self-image refers to beliefs about the proximal environment subject to direct experience. Image of the opponent, on the other hand, refers to a distant and abstract environment. Image of oneself may be more complex, requiring a more complex model of consistency. The belief patterns may be more pluralistic and more complex, leaving more room for possible hidden consistencies.

As with image of change, we looked for patterns not conforming to the general pattern among those respondents who were inconsistent. We were unable to find such patterns. Inconsistencies were working in all directions. This may again also indicate that we are here simply dealing with more inconsistency, or that beliefs are not as tightly linked and simple in their structure.

Choice propensities

Even though our dependent variable 'choice propensities' has not been introduced earlier, we find it appropriate to include an investigation of consistencies in choice propensities of the respondents in this chapter.

We posed three questions related to choice propensities:

1. If UN Resolution 242 were implemented, who do you think would gain and lose?
2. What parts of the territories occupied during the 1967 war do you consider most vital to keep? (question on Israeli side). To get back? (question on Arab side). If you had to choose, how would you list them?
3. How do you see the solution of the Palestinian problem?

There was a rather even split both within and across the samples on whether these issue are 'compromising' or 'uncompromising', with a small group on both sides holding ambiguous views.

Is there a tendency to maintain a consistent stand on policy issues? Will a respondent who is 'hawkish' on one policy issue be likely to be 'hawkish' on other policy issues? We do expect consistency to operate among statements on these issues, because we assume that most elites see them as related, and therefore, according to cognitive theory, there will be pressure towards consistency. Moderation on one issue should lead to pressure toward moderation on other issues, for example.

A note on what is meant by consistency in this context may be in order. Consistency does not mean that the respondents *across* time will make the *same* policy statements, which is one of the ways in which consistency has been applied; for example, this could mean always the same position on territories. As a matter of fact, we do know that these positions do fluctuate over time. So this is not the type of consistency we deal with here. Some choice propensities may be quite situation-specific, in that we do deal with positions on issues which are quite sensitive to change. The position on the Palestinian issue probably does have a greater cross-situational consistency than the position on territories. But on both issues there have been noticeable shifts across the time period during which we have conducted interviews. Also, this varies with the party to the conflict. An issue with a high cross-situational consistency in Israel may fluctuate considerably on the Arab side and vice-versa. The stability of the operational code beliefs, however, tells us that these beliefs have a high cross-situational consistency as well.

What we examine directly here could be termed *response-response* consistency, which occurs if all three responses are located on the same side of the compromising-uncompromising dimension.

We expect, even if not tested directly, consistency to be dynamic in the sense that even if the respondents make different choices over time, these choices could be classified as either consistently compromising or uncompromising. We do not expect a respondent to be a hawk one day and a dove the next.

The concept of choice propensities is applied to indicate that we are not really dealing with actual choice, but with the policy statements of the respondent before he makes the actual choice. We only want to account for his propensities in compromising or uncompromising choices if intervening variables do not force him to modify his original position.

We still have the three-point scale where the verbal expressions of values are compromising, mixed, or uncompromising. The underlying logic for the scaling should be explained before we proceed, even though we have discussed this before.

There is a pluralism of goals on both sides in the conflict, and these goals change over time. We may look at goals on a continuum ranking from the most extreme to the most moderate. We assume that the most conciliatory goals in both camps overlap. These operant goals could be placed along this continuum.

	Coalition A goal	Coalition B goal	
Extreme goals			
			Extreme goals

Resolution of conflict

Our previous research leads us to the assumption that moderate goals in both camps will lead to conflict resolution (issues would be viewed integratively and common solutions would be found). But also, our previous research makes us able to move toward meaningful simplification on the issue of goals.

With reference to strategic goals, there are roughly speaking two different goals in each coalition. One regards it as realistic to try to reach a compromise with the enemy today — this will be labeled conciliatory. The alternative goal pursued is that compromise with the enemy today is not feasible. This goal will be labeled non-conciliatory.

Below are listed examples of how statements have been coded in answers to the three questions:

Non-Conciliatory — Israeli side

Q 1: UN is completely unable to solve the conflict, anti-Israeli forces have the upper hand.

Q 2: Should stay in Golan. We cannot give the West Bank away.

Q 3: Don't agree to an independent Palestinian state.

Conciliatory — Israeli side

Q 1: 242 a good point of departure. My basic view is that the conflict is a non-zero-sum game.

Q 2: Problem of territories must be agreed to by negotiations. Israel must have sea-passages. Jerusalem a very difficult problem.

Q 3: I am against that Israel imposes a solution for the Palestinians. They have national feelings. I am for a Palestinian state. They should decide themselves.

Non-conciliatory — Arab side

Q 1: The genuine winner will be the Palestinians.

Q 2: Impossible to choose what part of our national soil we want back (we want it all).

Q 3: The Palestinians must have all their national rights back.

Conciliatory — Arab side

Q 1: Neither side will completely gain or lose; there will be pluses and minuses on both sides.

Q 2: You find varying answers on the Arab side as to what territories are most vital to get back. There is generally so much sacrosanctity on the Arab side about Arab soil being occupied.

Q 3: Palestinians in general agree on a partition of Israel. But there will be a fringe of Palestinians not willing to accept this, and they will go on causing trouble.

Table 6.6. Consistency within the Choice Propensities dimension when breaking down the Arab sample

	Israel (n = 29)	Egypt (n = 29)	Jordan (n = 17)	Lebanon (n = 9)
Consistently compromising*	34 %	21 %	6 %	11 %
Mixed	0 %	0 %	0 %	0 %
Consistently uncompromising*	48 %	14 %	59 %	44 %
Inconsistent	17 %	65 %	35 %	44 %

(missing data: 13)

* We use the label 'consistently compromising' and 'consistently uncompromising' because it is of interest for the operational code. 'Consistently compromising' includes 'moderately consistently compromising' and 'purely consistently compromising'. 'Consistently uncompromising' includes 'moderately consistently uncompromising' and 'purely consistently uncompromising'.

Table 6.7. Consistency within the Choice Propensities dimension

	Israel (n = 29)	Egypt (n = 30)	Jordan (n = 17)	Lebanon (n = 9)
Consistent	83 %	33 %	65 %	56 %
Inconsistent	17 %	67 %	35 %	44 %

There is, as shown in Table 6.7, overall support for consistency in statements on policies (60 %). The support is especially strong for the Israeli respondents (83 %). In the Arab sample more complicated patterns emerge. Variation appears in the Arab sample, with Jordan and Lebanon not conforming entirely to the Egyptian sample. We have therefore chosen to break down the Arab sample to control for nationality to find an explanation for results contrary to our expectations. As regards differences between countries, the Jordanian and Lebanese respondents provide some support for the expected relationship, while Egyptian respondents generate results quite contrary to predictions. How is it that the majority of Egyptian respondents and a great deal of Jordanian and Lebanese did not conform to the expected pattern?

There is some support for consistency in the Jordanian sample (65 %) but considerably less consistency in the Egyptian (33 %), while Lebanon is in between (56 %).

Given the low consistency score, we have to be open to the possibility that there are more pluralistic patterns of consistency among the Arab respondents. The operational definition of consistency probably offers no appropriate model of the way consistency operates for many Arab respondents. Consistency is therefore hidden in the results, because the operational definition does not reveal it. We have to recheck our operational definition.

One group favors UN Resolution 242, expresses a dovish position on the Palestinian problem, but expresses hawkish views on territory. This type of 'inconsistency' may be quite 'logical' when we take so-called 'national interests' into account. Some may find it important to have an uncompromising position on territories, but a compromising position on the Palestinian problem. The Palestinians do not touch directly on Egyptian national interests, for example. Therefore a respondent may not experience inconsistency by being compromising on one position and uncompromising on the other. This is, nevertheless, inconsistent with our definition of consistency. (Thirty-five percent of the inconsistent respondents fall into this category).

Another group, which appears to favor UN Resolution 242, is uncompromising on the Palestinian problem and territories. Here we should like to control for the attitude we find in the Arab world toward the UN. It is possible that we have groups who think it both desirable and feasible to establish a Palestinian state and return territories, while at the same time believing in negotiations, because they view the UN as generally favoring the Arab position in the conflict. These respondents are inconsistent according to our definition, but probably do not see themselves as inconsistent. (Thirty percent of inconsistent respondents fall into this category.) If this is the case, it also reveals a lack of consistency in the coding rules for some respondents. Insistence on implementation of the UN resolution is scored as evidencing an accommodative or compromising orientation. While this may be true for Israeli respondents and the majority of Arab respondents, insistence on the UN resolution by some Arab respondents may indicate uncompromising choice propensities as well. When this is the case, it makes no sense to include this question in the operational measure of consistency. The Arab respondents are deviant, because for the majority attitudes toward implementations differ widely.

We find the same tendencies in Jordan and Lebanon, where 67 % of the Jordanian inconsistent respondents and 50 % of the inconsistent respondents in Lebanon fall into one of these two patterns.

Contrary to previous results, we are here able to find certain consistent 'inconsistent' patterns, which show that consistency does operate, but not in the way we expected. We have identified two additional consistency patterns in the Arab sample, which can be explained by looking at *national interests* and *attitudes toward the UN*.

Our original model of belief relationships is invalid for many respondents. In other words, there are different kinds of hawks and different kinds of doves. What we need, then, are two additional operational measures of consistency. Our original operational definition of consistency did not take sufficiently into account the possibility of defining the compromising-uncompromising dimension differently by different participants. Consequently, consistently compromising or uncompromising choice behavior does not mean the same to the various participants. This should be taken into account in assessing response-response consistency.

Table 6.8. Consistency within the Choice Propensities dimension when consistency is measured by two additional operational definitions

	Israel (n = 29)	Egypt (n = 30)	Jordan (n = 17)	Lebanon (n = 9)
Consistent	83 %	77 %	88 %	78 %
Inconsistent	17 %	23 %	12 %	22 %

On the basis of this additional operational definition of consistency, the overall consistency, as shown in Table 6.8, is stronger, as well as the support in each individual country. Now the modal category is consistency for all countries. Support for consistency on the Arab side as a whole is now 80 %. Support for consistency on choice propensities is found on both sides. This consistency makes it a far easier operation to find out the relationship between the independent variables (image of the opponent, image of self, image of change) and the dependent variable (choice propensities).

Concluding remarks

If the same respondents provide most inconsistencies from one set of questions to another, the inconsistent respondents would have probably been more easily dealt with and more readily explained. Unfortunately, this was not the case. An inconsistent respondent on one dimension was just as likely to be consistent as inconsistent on another dimension.

The most consistent beliefs of the respondents are those referring to image of the opponent.

On image of self, image of change, and choice propensities the same amount of consistency is not found. Especially in the Arab world, pluralistic patterns emerge as to how the respondents combine their beliefs within these dimensions. Especially beliefs on image of change appear to have weaker consistency than we thought.

CHAPTER VII

Linkage between Belief Dimensions

Consistency on the macro-level of operational code beliefs

In the previous sections, we considered consistent patterns in belief molecules or micro-units of the operational code belief system. The results were encouraging in that we found consistent beliefs within these units for most respondents.

The following section will examine the linkages between these micro-units in the system. As we move away from the more narrow portions of the belief system to the molar level, we expect weaker support for consistency. Cognitive consistency theory states that the need for consistency applies more strongly to narrow portions of a person's beliefs than to the broader set of beliefs. Therefore there is a greater chance that beliefs will not be linked in the same way in the respondent's cognitive system, and the threshold for inconsistencies will increase as we consider broader parts even if the beliefs are connected.

In looking at consistency on this molar level, we experience a considerable data loss. From an initial sample of 95 respondents we only retain approximately 33 respondents on the average with a range of 26—45. This is explained by the belief inconsistency we have found previously. For a respondent to be included at this stage in the analysis he has to be consistent on two belief dimensions or more.

A respondent previously found to be consistent on image of the opponent, but not on other dimensions, for example, will be excluded.

The quantitative analysis is therefore meant to be suggestive. However, these analyses are carried out because they do provide a pivotal link in the operational code study.

Having examined linkages between the components, we will proceed to see how well the operational code belief system accounts for the variance in choice propensities of the respondents.

Figure 7.1 illustrates what we are examining in this chapter. The arrows indicate where we expect to find linkages between dimensions, and our study seeks to determine the existence and strength of these linkages. Knowing, for example, a respondent's image of his oppo-

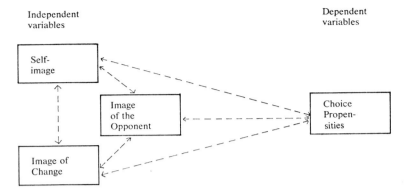

Figure 7.1. Suggested linkages between the dimension examined.

nent, with what success can we determine his self-image or his image of change?

Before defining our operational measures of consistency, we shall briefly describe how our empirical measures are related to the theoretical construct of the operational code.

In the operational code, Philosophical Belief I is listed as three questions: What is the essential nature of political life? Is the political universe essentially one of harmony or conflict? What is the fundamental character of one's political opponents?

In our analysis the first question is translated to: What is the self-image of political life? A comparison of the 'coding' of previous operational code studies seems to make this reasonable.

Relevant questions in the field interviews are:

What are the goals of your side in the conflict? Are there any differences concerning the goals and strategies on your side? What do you think are the basic good and bad aspects of your side in the conflict? Do you see any elements in your own country working against peace? Do you think that the other side believes that you are threatening them? In what way and how much is your side dependent on the superpowers?

In our analysis the question 'What is the fundamental character of one's political opponents?' is translated or limited to: 'What is the fundamental character of one's major opponent?' Pertinent questions in the field interviews are: Do you think that the other side is threatening you? What are the goals of the other side in the conflict? Are there any differences concerning the goals and strategies of the other side? What do you think are the basic good and bad aspects of the other party to the conflict? Do you see any elements on the other

108

side working for peace? In what way and how much is the other side dependent on the superpowers?

Optimism/Pessimism

Philosophical Belief II is concerned with the following questions: What are the prospects for eventual realizations of one's fundamental values and aspirations? Can one be optimistic or must one be pessimistic on this score? And in what respect the one and/or the other? Questions in the field interviews were: In what way do you think the events in recent years have basically changed the conflict? Now speaking realistically, what would you actually expect will happen? How long do you think the conflict will last? All these questions apply to the 'image of change'.

These questions mirror how respondents view past trends, the near future and the long-term future prospects, and the final outcome of the conflict.

While the previous two dimensions (image of opponent and self-image) dealt with what the conflict looks like; this dimension involves calculations concerning which way the conflict is moving.

Image of the opponent/Image of self

We expect that a respondent who holds consistently pluralistic beliefs of the opponent will also hold consistently pluralistic beliefs of his own society, while those holding consistently unitary beliefs of the opponent will also hold consistently unitary beliefs of their own society.

We expect those seeing many differences in policy views within their own society also to see many differences in the policy views in the opponent's camp. And those who see no differences in policy views on their own side should also see no differences in the enemy's policy views. Individuals seeing elements working against peace in their own society would be more inclined to see elements working in favor of peace in the opponent's society, and those perceiving no elements working against peace in their own society will, we expect, see no elements in favor of peace in the opponent's camp. Finally, those who see their own behavior as almost totally justified will see the opponent's behavior as nearly completely unjustified, while those viewing their own behavior as only partly unjustified will see the opponent's behavior as partly justified.

In the previous section we examined the degree to which beliefs were consistently pluralistic or unitary with respect to image of the opponent and image of self. We will now find out the degree of consistency across the two micro-units on the pluralism/unitary dimension. Respondents who provide the inconsistency across the two dimensions result in a considerable data loss, since no comparison could be made except for respondents consistent on both dimensions. Again, we regard the results as suggestive and the examination of linkages as exploratory.

Table 7.1. Consistency between Image of the Opponent and Self-Image (n = 31)

		Image of the Opponent		
		Pluralistic	Unitary	
Self-Image	Pluralistic	100 %	0 %	(n = 16)
	Unitary	33 %	67 %	(n = 15)

Results on linkages between Image of the Opponent and Image of Self

The results presented in Table 7.1 suggest cognitive linkages between these two dimensions (given the correctness of our assumption that having consistent values across the two dimensions indicates such a linkage). If a respondent expresses consistently pluralistic beliefs about the opponent, there is a good chance that he expresses consistently pluralistic beliefs about his own side. Conversely, if a respondent expresses consistently unitary beliefs about the opponent, there is a good chance that he expresses consistently unitary beliefs about his own side. Some respondents have a pluralistic view of the opponent and a unitary view of their own society. In the previous chapter we noted the tendency to see exactly the opposite in the opponent to what they saw in themselves. Weakness on their own side was matched by perceptions of strength on the other side, and vice versa. On the pluralism component of image of the opponent, this is definitely not the general pattern: we do not get reverse scoring values on image of the opponent and image of self. But it does not 'logically' follow that scoring values will be the same for the two dimensions. It is therefore interesting to note that the majority of respondents see both their own side and the opponent as either pluralistic or unitary. In some cases, we have respondents who see the opponent as consistently pluralistic while viewing their own side as consistently unitary.

Image of the opponent/Image of change

We expect respondents who hold consistently pluralistic beliefs about the opponent also to hold consistently optimistic views about change processes. They are likely to see favorable trends in the past and to express optimism toward developments in the near and long-term future. On the other hand, we expect respondents holding consistently unitary beliefs about the opponent to see unfavorable trends in the past and to be pessimistic regarding developments in the near future as well as the long-term future.

Table 7.2. Consistency between Image of the Opponent and Image of Change (n = 35)

		Image of the Opponent		
		Pluralistic	Unitary	
Image of Change	Optimistic	67 %	33 %	(n = 27)
	Pessimistic	63 %	37 %	(n = 8)

Results on the relationship between Image of the Opponent and Perception of Change

The results as shown in Table 7.2 do not support our expected relationships. When a respondent is an optimist, he is more likely to have a pluralistic image of the opponent than a unitary one, but at the same time it appears that a pessimist is also more likely to have a pluralistic view of the opponent, which is contrary to our expectations. The previous consistency results on image of change suggested that we omit the analysis of the past and look only at consistency for future expectations.

Again, the results are not as expected. Knowing that an individual in the conflict has a pluralistic or a unitary image of the opponent does not enable us to say with any confidence that he is pessimistic or optimistic about future developments. Image of change has been noted as a central belief-dimension in the operational code belief system. In view of this, we will now look at possible linkages between image of change and image of self.

Image of self/Image of change

We expect respondents holding consistently pluralistic views of their own society to express consistently optimistic views about change processes.

Table 7.3. Consistency between Self-Image and Image of Change (n = 27)

		Self-Image		
		Pluralistic	Unitary	
Image of Change	Optimistic	29 %	71 %	(n = 17)
	Pessimistic	50 %	50 %	(n = 10)

The results on linkages between self-image and image of change in Table 7.3 are clearly contrary to our expectations. As a matter of fact, it seems that if a respondent has an optimistic view of change, a better chance exists that he has a unitary view of his own side in the conflict. For the pessimists, there is an even split between a pluralistic and unitary view of their own side, which suggests no systematic bias in either direction.

In view of these results, we will make a further analysis of this dimension to determine whether patterns are 'hidden'. We will here, as previously, see if there are any differences between Arab and Israeli respondents.

It appeared that knowing that an Israeli is an optimist or pessimist in relation to the conflict does not enable one to say anything about his image of self. On the Arab side it appears that optimism and a unitary image of self go together, contrary to our expectation. We can form no opinion about the Arab pessimist, since none of the respondents was consistently pessimistic. These results led to a recheck of the coding rules to see whether they could have been more discriminatory on the Arab side. We found this not to be the case.

These results reveal that a better prediction of whether a person is an optimist or pessimist in the conflict is made by knowing which side he belongs to than by knowing any of his other operational code beliefs.

There is an overall tendency for Israelis to be pessimists and a tendency for Arabs to be optimists. But the results also serve to demonstrate the higher degree of conformity found in the Arab world with regard to processes of change. This conformity is expressed by the commonly held view that the conflict is moving toward the Arabs' advantage. There is more variation in thinking on the Israeli side, but the modal category is the reverse of the Arab side: Israelis are overwhelmingly pessimists. This explains why the results tend to neutralize each other.

These results obtained do not indicate that this dimension is of no value in the operational code. It is of limited value in accounting for variance within elites, but may be valuable in accounting for the overall variance across elites in the conflict.

The operational code and choice propensities

The present study is based on the expectation that a systematic relationship exists between operational code beliefs and choice propensities of the respondents. This expectation is based on the general notion of consistency-striving, which claims that respondents will seek consistency between beliefs and behavior. When we know a respondent's beliefs, we should be able to say what policies he would support or recommend in the conflict. In this section we will see how closely these expectations match our results.

In asking what policies the respondents would recommend, we referred to a set of interrelated issues linked to a negotiated settlement of the conflict. We expected the respondents to express a response-response consistency with regard to these sets of issues, and the results did match our expectations in this regard. The results have been presented in a previous section and show a high degree of consistency. Moderation on one issue will in most cases be matched by moderation on other issues, while hawkishness on one issue will in most cases mean hawkishness on other issue. It should, however, be added that the compromising-uncompromising dimension did not take on the same meaning for all participants, necessitating a readjustment to our operational measures of consistency to account for different definitions of compromising-uncompromising.

The high consistency score enables us to deal with all policy issues 'collectively'. In this way it is unnecessary to view individually the relationship between operational code beliefs and each policy. Additionally, since we have no respondents giving consistently 'mixed' scoring values on policies, we may assign only two values to the dependent variable, 'compromising' and 'uncompromising'. These correspond to the two basic policy orientations we noted previously: those wanting negotiations at some unspecified time in the future and those recommending negotiations presently. It also appears that only a few respondents came up with scoring values consistently mixed on beliefs. Leaving out these respondents, we can limit ourselves to dealing only with the two *substantive* scoring values on beliefs — compromising and uncompromising orientation.

Previously we have spelled out these positions as:

1) Our policies vis-à-vis our enemy should be to take steps to compromise now (enter negotiations with the intent of reaching a settlement), or:

2) Our policies vis-à-vis our enemy should be not to compromise now (not enter negotiations with the intent of reaching a settlement presently).

We see this as the two basic policy positions at any point in time, from which most other policy positions can be derived. The time dimension is here very important where *now* or *presently* have to be underlined because in principle everybody looks to a compromise at some point in time. The dividing line is between those who see it as a feasible policy to compromise with the enemy on the basis of what the situation looks like today and those who do not see this as a feasible policy.

It is important to distinguish between beliefs and policies. Our independent variables deal with the respondent's beliefs about himself, his opponent and his beliefs about change. The dependent variable refers to policies that our respondents will choose, recommend, or identify with.

Theoretically, there exist 256 combinations of belief dimensions included in the study, but empirically the number is narrowed down to very few of these possible combinations. This is, of course, a precondition for the whole approach. Empirically, the respondents link beliefs in ways that limit the universe of possible patterns. The direction of linkage is constrained by rules of consistency.

Relationship between Image of the Opponent and Choice Propensities

We expect that respondents with a pluralistic view of the opponent will recommend or support compromising (dovish) policies, while respondents who have a unitary view of the opponent will recommend or support uncompromising (hawkish) policies.

Table 7.4. Relationship between Image of the Opponent and Choice Propensities (n = 45)

		Image of the Opponent		
		Pluralistic	Unitary	
Choice Propensities	Compromising	95 %	5 %	(n = 19)
	Uncompromising	54 %	46 %	(n = 26)

The results as shown in Table 7.4 are encouraging. Knowing that a respondent has a pluralistic view of his opponent in the conflict enables us to say with some degree of likelihood that the policies he supports or recommends will be compromising. Knowing that a person has a unitary view of the opponent enables us to say that he is more likely to recommend uncompromising policies in the conflict. The difference in sensitivity of the unitary and pluralistic image of the opponent to the policies recommended by the respondents emerges as an interesting aspect of the results.

Respondents holding a unitary image of the opponent are easier to make predictions about than are respondents with a pluralistic image of the opponent. This suggests that those having a unitary (dogmatic) image of the opponent will consistently stick to 'hawkish' policy positions with little flexibility. Those having a pluralistic view of the opponent (less dogmatic) have considerably more leeway for their actions. This explains why the behavior of this group is harder to predict, or makes it possible to predict that this group will not display the same cross-situational consistency. In some instances these may be hawkish, in other dovish. To test this, we need data for the policies recommended by these respondents over time, or rather interviews taken over time. We are currently only in the position of posing this as a suggestion for further hypothesis-testing. There is, of course, also the possibility that for some respondents a pluralistic image of the opponent can be consistent with support for uncompromising policies depending on the situation.

Relationship between Self-Image and Choice Propensities

We expect respondents with a pluralistic view of their own side in the conflict to support compromising policies, while we expect respondents expressing a unitary view of their own side to support uncompromising policies in the conflict.

Table 7.5. Relationship between Self-Image and Choice Propensities (n = 36)

		Self-Image		
		Pluralistic	Unitary	
Choice Propensities	Compromising	75 %	25 %	(n = 12)
	Uncompromising	33 %	67 %	(n = 24)

Again we find support for the expected pattern. Table 7.5 shows that if a respondent has a pluralistic view of his own side, this enables us to say with some likelihood that he is compromising. Knowing that a respondent has a unitary (dogmatic) view of his own side enables us to say with some likelihood, that he will recommend uncompromising policies in the conflict. These results correspond to what we found for image of the opponent. But, the difference in sensitivity to the dependent variable between unitary and pluralistic is not supported.

It is not easier to say which policies are supported by holders of a unitary (dogmatic) view of their own society as opposed to those holding a pluralistic view.

But knowing a respondent's image of self does not enable one with equal confidence to say which policies this respondent will recommend, even if the results are similar on the two dimensions. The overall consistency will also have to be taken into account. There is a far better chance that beliefs on image of the opponent will be consistent than is the case with image of self. Therefore, image of the opponent is more valuable in predicting which policies a respondent will recommend, because there is no way to determine which policies an inconsistent respondent will recommend.

Image of Change and Choice Propensities

We now turn to the third dimension in our operational code model, the image of change. We expect the optimist to recommend compromising policies, while we expect the pessimist to recommend uncompromising policies.

Table 7.6. Relationship between Image of Change and Choice Propensities (n = 38)

		Image of Change		
		Optimistic	Pessimistic	
Choice Propensities	Compromising	94 %	6 %	(n = 16)
	Uncompromising	64 %	36 %	(n = 22)

Table 7.6 shows that if a respondent is an optimist, this enables us to say that he is likely to recommend compromising policies. When a respondent is a pessimist this enables us to say that he will most likely recommend uncompromising policies in the conflict.

Discussion of results

The results show that *image of the opponent has the highest predictive power,* but we did find support for the expected relationships with the other two belief dimensions.

Knowing that a person has a consistently unitarian view of his own or his opponent's side in the conflict enables one to predict with confidence that he will advocate uncompromising (hawkish) policies. But knowing that a person has a pluralistic view of the enemy or his own side gives less reason to predict that he will be compromising (dovish). He is likely to be uncompromising (hawkish), and the modal category is compromising. Furthermore, if a person is consistently pessimistic, he will probably be uncompromising, but

116

the proposition that a person who is consistently optimistic will be a compromiser is more doubtful.

Our ability to predict when pairing dimensions in the code turned out according to our expectations. One can make the strongest predictions by combining self-image and image of the opponent, and the weakest by combining self-image and perception of change, while the pairing of image of the opponent and image of change falls in between.

Table 7.7. presents a summary of the results. Percentages in each square represent the amount of consistent values of different pairs or combinations. Linkages between the dimensions are strongest between image of the opponent and self-image (84 %) and weakest between self-image and image of change (38 %).

Table 7.7. Relationship between different dimensions of the operational code

	EI	SI	O/P	PP
EI	—	—	—	—
SI	84 %	—	—	—
O/P	60 %	38 %	—	—
PP	67 %	70 %	60 %	—

EI = Enemy-Image
SI = Self-Image
O/P = Optimism/Pessimism
PP = Policy Position

Combining belief dimensions in the Operational Code

So far we have looked only at the degree to which separate belief dimensions account for variances in policies supported by the respondents. In this section we attempt to explain more of the variance by combining belief dimensions.

Image of the Opponent and Image of Change Combined

The first two independent dimensions we combine are image of the opponent and image of change. Here, we expect a respondent having a pluralistic view of the opponent and an optimistic view of change processes to recommend compromising policies. A respondent having a unitary view of the opponent and a pessimistic view of change processes should recommend uncompromising policies.

117

Table 7.8. Combined effect of Image of the Opponent and of Change on Choice Propensities (n = 27)

		Image of the Opponent/Image of Change			
		Pluralistic Optimistic	Pluralistic Pessimistic	Unitary Optimistic	Unitary Pessimistic
Choice Propensities	Compro-mising	82 %	9 %	9 %	0 % (n = 11)
	Uncompro-mising	31 %	19 %	31 %	19 % (n = 16)

The hypothesis is supported in Table 7.8 by results that a respondent with a unitary view and a pessimistic outlook will recommend uncompromising policies.

When a respondent is both pluralistic and optimistic, we can say with some confidence that he is more likely to support compromising policies. The number of consistent patterns is also high with this combination. When image of self and image of change were combined, the modal category was on inconsistency, but here the modal category is consistency, increasing the overall value of the combination in accounting for variance.

Combining Image of the Opponent and Self-Image

We expect a respondent with pluralistic views of the opponent and his own side to recommend compromising policies, while we expect a respondent with unitary views of the opponent and his own side to recommend uncompromising policies.

Table 7.9 supports tendencies we have found throughout. It appears that there is a greater likelihood that a person who is pluralistic in his views of the opponent and his own side will recommend compromising policies. It also shows that a respondent who has a unitary view of the opponent and his own side is likely to recommend uncompromising policies.

Most of the respondents (and a greater number than on the previous combination) are consistent, increasing the value of the potential for accounting for variance. It suggests, as we have noted earlier, that a fairly strong linkage exists between these two belief dimensions.

Table 7.9. Combined effect of Image of the Opponent and Self-Image on Choice Propensities (n = 26)

		Image of the Opponent/Self-Image			
		Pluralistic Pluralistic	Pluralistic Unitary	Unitary Pluralistic	Unitary Unitary
Choice Propensities	Compromising	73 %	18 %	0 %	9 % (n = 11)
	Uncompromising	31 %	20 %	0 %	49 % (n = 15)

Finally, Figure 7.2 suggest linkages and predictability of the belief dimensions of our code. The broader the lines, the stronger the relationship, while broken lines indicate a very weak relationship or no relationship. We may sum up by saying that of the belief dimensions in our code, a strong relationship between EI and SI and these in combination will best predict policy positions of the respondents. The image of change dimension, which has no strong relationship to the

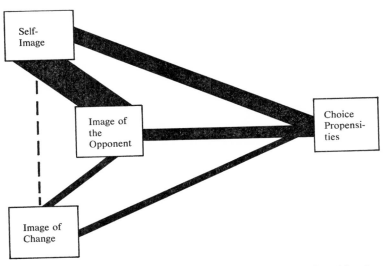

Figure 7.2. Indication of the strength of the relationship between the dimensions

other dimensions, has the best predictive value in combination with image of the opponent.

Self-image and image of change combined produce poor predictions. The image of change dimension in our model is therefore not a very useful belief dimension in accounting for variances in policy positions within elites on each side.

CHAPTER VIII

Implications for Conflict Resolution

In this last chapter we will examine how much we can say about the problem of conflict resolution on the basis of the results. What does this cognitive perspective tell us about the problem of resolving the conflict? What has the cognitive approach identified as the essential issues and what are the key problems for conflict resolution? What we can say about this will be tempered by some of the limits of the operational code approach. What are the weakness and possible sources of error of this approach to the study of conflict? The study will not resolve if variables other than cognitive are important because we have not looked at these other variables. But we will try to demonstrate that the cognitive approach can give us new and fruitful ideas on how to look at the problem, and that the operational code is a useful framework to use in the study of conflict.

The interpretations offered thus far in the analysis have pertained to the data collection and the theoretical formulation within which the data have meaning. They have therefore been guided by standard norms of scientific practice that relate to limitation in the sample, number of cases, etc.

At this point, however, I wish to place my investigation in a broader frame of reference and discuss the implications of my results for what is the major underlying interest that guided this study, conflict resolution in the Middle East.

In the introduction to the study we suggested such questions as: why do some recommend concilatory moves while others do not? Is this in part because of systematic differences in beliefs? What are the beliefs that together form the whole which defines the actors' interpretation, diagnosis, and prescription vis-à-vis the conflict situation? More specifically, what characterizes the beliefs and thinking of those favorable to conciliatory moves and those who are not?

Before starting the discussion a few words on conflict resolution may be in order. A solution to the conflict in the Middle East can obviously take many forms. Implementation of a 'solution' would not necessarily mean that the conflict would be solved in the sense of its being entirely eliminated. On the contrary, a considerable amount of conflict is likely to continue. As is common in international conflict, resolution on one level may intensify conflict on another, and resolution of one issue may exacerbate conflict over other issues. Indeed, the issues themselves may change entirely, with original issues replaced or eclipsed by new problems, with the original cause of the conflict differing from that which sustains it.

A distinction is often made between 'conflict management' and 'conflict resolution'. With conflict management some steps have been taken toward conflict resolution. But once there is conflict management some elements of conflict resolution are also achieved. It is difficult to imagine a conflict resolution not having its roots in a process of conflict management in some sort of agreed accommodation of differences. Conflict resolution is here regarded as a process in which the system is not static but rather as one in which the interaction of states moves along a scale from open extreme violence to positive peace.

The more specific issue to be dealt with is how conflicting parties tend to respond to initiatives for a settlement of the conflict. We have asked throughout our research efforts what would bring about successful steps toward resolution of the conflict. The conclusions from our previous study were that the possibilities for such a process were greatest when the relative strength between the parties is balanced, and when the situation of status quo or no negotiation is experienced by both parties as costly in political and military terms. A gradual process of binding commitments to the status quo situation was seen as seriously jeopardizing moves toward peace.[1]

The conflict interaction is characterized by a great degree of uncertainty. There are few 'reality checks' that allow one to draw undisputed conclusions on the effect of a given policy.

Moves toward war as well as toward peace were linked to considerable uncertainty. In other words, it was concluded that certain characteristics of the situation were important for an amicable settlement; but, in addition to this, the interpretation or the meaning ascribed to the situation was important.[2]

In this study we have dissected the problem, in that we have not dealt with all the various characteristics of a situation required for a 'settlement', but have focused exclusively on the necessary cognitive preconditions.

What impact do conflicting beliefs have on the way in which information is processed? How do we ascribe *meaning* to what takes place, and what implications does this have for resolution of the conflict? The study is based on the assumption that there are certain cognitive constraints and biases that impede a settlement and that these are important.

122

It should, however, be underlined that we recognize policies to be quite sensitive to situational variables, and that the specific choice in any given situation will be a dynamic interaction between beliefs and characteristics of the situation.

Beliefs and action are interactive. *Beliefs determine action, while, on the other hand, action determines beliefs.* Action is the testing ground for beliefs and may cause beliefs to be modified, changed, or given up altogether. But then the newly formed beliefs again become determinants of consequent action.[3]

The overall interaction pattern over time in the Arab-Israeli conflict can be described as a mixture of accommodative and belligerent behavior, but there is also behavior that could be characterized as 'neutral' or 'balanced'.

Which policies will ultimately lead to conflict resolution can also be argued — and a party to a conflict will not usually view its own actions as belligerent.

A 'tough' or 'soft' line could in principle be accommodative if it has the effect of promoting a compromise. A 'soft' policy may also promote belligerency. If one side believes for example, that the other side is now soft, 'down on its knees', for example, this might raise the expectation of gains and consequently make a compromise more difficult. Accommodative behavior by one side can, therefore, promote belligerent behavior by the other, while it is also possible that belligerent behavior by one coalition can promote accommodative behavior by the other.

When we analyzed our first interview data from the Arab world, we concluded that there seems to be a very even power relationship between the adherents of a military solution and the adherents of a political solution.[4] We then drew the conclusion that if the adherents of a military solution in the Arab world (of which the guerrilla was the primary exponent) should be defeated, it would be far easier to reach a negotiated settlement along the lines of the UN resolution. But we made the fallacy of omitting the interaction process with the adversary in the conflict. The defeat of the guerrillas in Jordan did not increase the possibilities of a political solution. The day-to-day troubles with the status quo went sharply down in Israel, which had the effect of strengthening the position of groups in Israel wanting to hold on to the occupied areas — not a settlement along the lines of the UN resolution.

Variation in the behavior of one side is likely to lead to variation in the behavior of the other side. The literature on negotiations of international conflicts gave us some leads in the previous study as to characteristics of the situations that are the most favorable for initiating negotiations with the aim of a compromise of outstanding issues. The conclusion here was based on a cost/benefit analysis (subjectively expected utilities).[5] How much will it cost to keep the conflict going rather than to negotiate? If both parties perceive the other party as roughly equal in military capabilities, we concluded that the possibilities for negotiations are then best. Response is not only determined by who has the greatest leverage in the decision-making process — moderates or extremists. Extremists will also make their cost/benefit calculations and may come out with a response that can be classified as accommodative. 'Hawks' in the conflict are not insensitive to 'reality'.

Given the fact that over the years the parties to the conflict responded to each other in both a refractory and conciliatory way, the crucial question becomes: When does a party to the conflict respond in a conciliatory way and when does it not? The interpretive patterns that can be derived from the parties' respective beliefs may account for some of this variation.

We have demonstrated in our study how these beliefs determine information-processing and vary critically with *policies advocated* in the conflict.

The study has sought to identify constraints on cognitive functioning which may result in policies that are not optimal in relation to how the contending parties want relations between themselves to develop. We have sought to identify errors or biases elites make in the selection and treatment of data that may have repercussions on resolution of the conflict. We will now discuss how these errors or biases may be counterproductive.

The rigidity of established paradigms in information-processing about the Opponent in the conflict

Psychological research on international conflict has been quite concerned with the psychological processes leading to the devil-image of the opponent and how the establishment of this paradigm is highly resistant to change, taking on the character of self-fulfilling prophecies.

Parties to a conflict have rigid beliefs. Events that coincide with already established beliefs are easily understood and interpreted. Events that will break with already established beliefs can be coped with in different ways without changing beliefs, as demonstrated in our study.

Conflict resolution presupposes processes of change, and a critical issue is what may trigger change. Our results point to how the rules and psychological processing of information may inhibit these processes. Human beings as information processors generally tend to be conservative, and we may say that this is a rational way of dealing with information. But in situations of intense international conflict, it may be irrational.

The present research has produced more specific answers regarding how this general rigidity works in situations of international conflict.

In our previous study we did point to ways of avoiding change in already established beliefs by simply ignoring (selective perceptual process) or giving added weight to other information (bolstering) whenever discrepant information occurred.[6]

In this study we are able to further support this claim in that it gives added insight into ways of coping with discrepant information by showing the flexibility of an individual when analyzing the causes of behavior (attribution). The descriptive analysis also revealed that some beliefs are far more resistant to change than others. Not all beliefs we charted were equally rigid. The most resistant beliefs are at the same time the beliefs most critical to conflict resolution (image of the opponent). This we shall return to later in this chapter.

Attribution theory especially provided new insight into how we can avoid changing beliefs. The dichotomy in the attribution process allows one to deal with unexpected behavior and events without changing beliefs.

Instances of this may be when the opponent initiates moderate policies. If the enemy behaves in an expected way, the behavior is quite likely attributed to him. If, on the other hand, the enemy behaves in a manner not expected, the behavior will be attributed to environmental forces and constraints In this way, it is not necessary to change beliefs about the enemy. If I have a devil-image of the opponent and the opponent behaves in an *indisputably* friendly way, I can still maintain my beliefs about the opponent by explaining his friendly behavior as caused by environmental influences and constraints. His disposition to act in an unfriendly way remains the same — certain characteristics of the situation have forced him to *temporarily* behave in a friendly way. In other words, the opponent is not given responsibility (credit) for what he is doing. His behavior is seen as reactive. Selective perceptual processes will not sufficiently explain this process. The information is received, but the explanation of how it can be ignored lies in the cognitive process itself. This general rigidity may make the parties insensitive to the possibilities to change. Their information-processing is not optimal, in that there is a bias involved that works against the identification of change processes that may facilitate resolution of the conflict if properly reacted to.

The attribution of causality is one of the mechanisms that tends to sustain an already established belief system about the conflict. There will then (looking at behavior as reactive to situational constraints) be a strong tendency to ignore the possibility of change.

This in turn may be a self-fulfilling prophecy: since we ignore the possibility that change has taken place with the opponent, moderate policies run the risk of not being followed up with similar initiatives that could initiate processes toward resolution.

The unexpected behavior of the opponent is not interpreted as a change in his goodwill, nor a change in his aggressiveness, nor taken as a sign of possible moderation. Rather, it will be explained as *reactive*. The opponent is nice to us now, but this is because he has to be; he is forced to do this and does not really want to.

If the parties to a conflict are subject to this type of biased information-processing, there is no subjective need to offer moderate policies to reciprocate the opponent's conciliatory moves. The conciliatory moves of the opponent may of course, nevertheless, produce international or domestic pressure to reciprocate, which in turn may constrain decision-makers in moderate directions.

Our conservatism against changing beliefs is quite rational in many situations. It would not be wise — or rational — to change beliefs about the enemy every time we observed behavior that did not conform to these beliefs. After all, the already established beliefs are based on past experiences.[7] But a mechanism that functions optimally in many situations could also be a hindrance toward conflict resolution, and we suggest on the basis of our study that due to systematic biases in information-processing the opponent will not be given credit when initiating moderate policies.

An observed moderate change in the Opponent's behavior will be seen as temporary

It also follows from the previous point that moderate change in the opponent's behavior will not be seen as lasting, since attributing change to situational variables (as opposed to dispositional) means that change will be considered highly temporary. The extent to which the opponent's behavior is seen as caused by his stable disposition leads to a low expectancy of change. Inner qualities are stable and permanent, as opposed to situational variables; as a consequence, when seeing the behavior of the opponent as caused by his disposition, the observer cannot possibly expect sudden changes. But alternatively when behavior is explained by constraints in the situation, expectancy of change will be high. If a moderate policy by the opponent is seen as related to certain situational characteristics only, it gives little incentive for changing one's own policies, since the opponent is soon expected to fall back on previous policies rooted in his stable disposition.

In instances like this, information-processing may be erroneous, leading to sub-optimal policies. It works against the kind of convergent steps necessary to solve international conflicts of this type. Conciliatory moves of the opponent are not greeted in a manner that 'objective' characteristics of the situation should dictate.

The Opponent has many alternative options available in his policies while we have none

The results also indicate a tendency to think that the opponent has many options available, while one's own party in a conflict is simply seen as reacting to the opponent's moves. The elite participants in our sample erroneously think that only the opponent's policies determine conflict resolution processes.

In analyzing what causes conflict it is easy to forget that it is an interactive process in which the opponent's policies are quite sensitive to one's own moves. As we stated earlier, we made the mistake early in our analysis of ignoring the interactive process between parties when estimating outcomes. Elite members make the same mistake — there is almost an exclusive tendency to focus only on the moves of the opponent in the conflict, implying that outcomes will be determined by his moves.

As we noted earlier, in choosing a situational explanation the elites assume that this is something outside the control of the actor (not caused by them) — something they cannot be responsible for one way or the other. When choosing a dispositional (internal) explanation, the elites assume that the responsibility or explanation is with the actor. In other words, there were *two* or *more options* available in the situation.

Making dispositional attributions implies that actors are faced with freedom of choice, while situational attributions imply only reaction to stimuli with no real choice involved. Our results therefore, tell us that there is a systematic bias involved in *perceived freedom of choice*. The enemy in the conflict is seen as having many available alternatives, while one's own side is pursuing policies that are simply reactive to the enemy's policies. In other words, the opponent could have acted otherwise.

It is logical to assume that both parties do have freedom of choice — alternative policies to pursue. In their information-processing, however, members of the elites mistakenly think that the opponent has more freedom of choice than they have themselves. This can readily be identified in our sample and is prevalent on both sides.

This view inhibits processes toward conflict resolution, in that it prevents the type of integrative thinking that enables one to see more common options and alternatives in the situation, from which both parties may gain.

'Over-psychologizing' the problem

Another important implication of the erroneous tendencies we have noted is that one tends to 'over-psychologize' the cause of conflict. For example, it is noticeable how discussion about the opponent in the conflict is focused on his intentions, or what Kelman calls his dreams and not his operational program.[8] There is sometimes almost an exclusive focus on what the opponent has said in the conflict, not what he has actually done. This tendency leads to a systematic underestimation of the extent to which the opponent's behavior is determined by environmental forces and constraints.

The problem is seen as a question of changing the opponent's attitudes and beliefs, while the conflict of interests over land, frontiers, and statehood are left in the background.

This erroneous tendency leads the elites in our sample to over-emphasize the psychological aspect of the problem, while de-emphasizing the need for concessions on concrete interests. It may be good tactics to focus on dispositions even if they are slower to change, because one does not wish to have any changes in the actual situation (status quo). But even if one is in favor of maintaining the status quo, this psychologizing may be counter-productive to the status quo in that it fails to focus the debate on resolution of issues in the environment (conflict of interest) that may initiate change that in turn may change beliefs and attitudes.

Changes in situational variables are more likely to trigger change than are efforts at convincing the opponent that he should change his abstract preferences.

Finally we feel the need for issuing a warning as to the generalizing of the biases we have pointed at. We are just saying that these *may be* present in certain situations.

Attribution theory has been helpful in accounting for the overall biases and tendencies in information-processing. On the other hand, attribution theory does not seem to account for the variations within elites that we regard as important for the resolution of a conflict. All elite members in our sample seem to display roughly the same tendencies in making attributions both within as well as across samples. Our efforts to divide the respondents into groups in order to search for systematic differences within the sample resulted in clearly negative results.

Attribution theory does not seem able to account for the intra-elite variances, and cannot tell us how elite members linked beliefs. In this respect, cognitive consistency theory was helpful. The application of the theory was useful in our search for answers to questions of centrality and relevance, as well as explaining linkages in the system.

We examined such questions as:

Where do we find the emphasis on cooperative thinking and where do we find the emphasis on non-cooperative thinking?

Do those elites who empasize non-cooperative thinking in one area consistently tend to think non-cooperatively in other areas?

How does this affect policies advocated in the conflict by these elites?

To some extent, all participants in a conflict are victims of the psychological processes leading toward black/white thinking, but there are variations that we find critical to the problem of conflict resolution.

In accounting for the striking differences in the way elites in the conflict vary in policy positions and processing of information, it is not enough to look at where they stand in the conflict (what you believe depends on where you stand) or to attributional processes. Even though this to a considerable degree can account for variances in the dependent variable, it is also necessary to consider differences in operational code beliefs.

Our results tell us that some operational code beliefs typically tend to be shared by a large proportion of the elite in a given country. Examples of such beliefs are judgments on the intentions of the opponent in the conflict.

Examples of such beliefs are on the Israeli side:

'The Arabs want to eliminate us'

and on the Arab side:

'The state of Israel wants expansion'

But beneath these beliefs, considerable disagreement emerges as to what the opponent is like and what can cause him to change.

The Innovator and the Traditionalist

Much of this study has focused on screening those operational code beliefs that are most critical or most sensitive to the policy preferences advocated by the respondents — thereby also locating the beliefs most critical and relevant to the problem of conflict resolution.

We have found basically two different belief-patterns or types in the conflict. For illustrative purpose we shall call these the 'Innovator' and the 'Traditionalist'. We suspected that the compromiser is more of an innovator, while those opposed to conciliatory moves are more traditionalist in not believing (or wanting to believe) that a new relationship is feasible. The traditionalist may be more competitive and see conflict in a zero-sum perspective. The innovator, less competitive and more inclined to see the conflict in a non-zero-sum perspective, has the ability to imagine and initiate change. Neither is insensitive to objective characteristics of the situation, and many times both will agree simply because the characteristics of the situation more or less determine the choice. But rather different styles are revealed when the situation is more ambiguous and linked to a higher degree of uncertainty as, for example, in making major conciliatory moves. Here, the traditionalist does not want to take risks for peace. The innovator and the traditionalist analyze the situation differently, and have different theories on what will lead to peace. The innovator sees more freedom of choice for the opponent but also to some degree for himself. The innovator is more sensitive to possibilities for change, while the traditionalist either expects no change or expects it too slowly to warrant a change in policies. The labels 'traditionalist' and 'innovator' here suggest how elite members think differently on issues and adhere to different theories of peace, but we cannot expect elites to correspond to these 'pure types'.

To review:

We hypothesized that linkages would be formed in the patterns as illustrated in Figure 8.1.

We expected a respondent with a pluralistic view of the opponent also to take a pluralistic view of his own side in the conflict, as well as an optimistic view of possibilities for a solution of the conflict.

We furthermore expected a respondent with these belief linkages to have an inclination toward advocating conciliatory moves in the conflict. On the other hand, we expected a respondent with a unitary view of the opponent also to have a unitary view of his own society, as well as being pessimistic about a final solution of the conflict.

Furthermore, we expected a respondent with these types of linkages to be inclined toward advocating non-conciliatory moves in the conflict.

The need for a typology of operational codes is argued on the basis of the necessity for making the research cumulative, as well as for research economy. Unless one is able to arrive at meaningful typologies, comparisons and cumulative research on operational codes become very difficult. Moving toward meaningful typologies would also imply a simpler structuring of belief as something that would make the operational code more easily applicable from the point of view of research economy.

In developing typologies, it becomes crucial to identify the nuclear and discriminatory components in the belief system, in order to have a few manageable categories along which a typology can be defined. Also, selection of the components of an operational code for typology development should be made with references to the uses to which a typology is to be put. We think that these types can tell us something meaningful about the problem of conflict resolution.

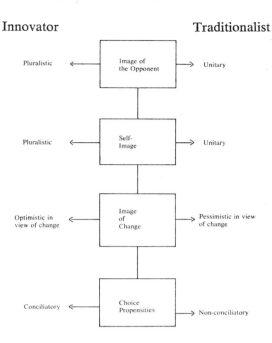

Figure 8.1. Hypothesized linkages of beliefs in conflict.

In arriving at these conclusions we investigated the problem by looking at multiple indicators. We looked at the stability of beliefs by examining attributional tendencies. Another indicator was the descriptive analysis of belief stability by looking at beliefs expressed at different points in time (cross-situational consistency). Finally we assessed consistency between different operational code beliefs statically. When investigating this, we first examined the degree of consistency between sets of questions intended to measure the components before proceeding to look at linkages between the components. We investigated the problem through multiple independent indicators in order to see whether the results on one indicator tended to support the results on another indicator.

Some did see both the enemy and their own society as unitary, while others saw pluralism in the opponent's camp as well as in their own. Some emphasized that what is good for them is good for the opponent, while others maintained that what is good for the opponent is bad for them. Some saw consensus within their own society, while others emphasized conflicting forces. Some viewed the opponent as a unitary bloc, while others found reconciliatory tendencies. The 'innovator' thus can see that even though the enemy is hostile, there are still some friendly or peaceful forces at work. The 'traditionalist', on the other hand, does not list good aspects of the opponent, and does not mention trends and groups in the opponent's camp that may be peaceful.

Furthermore, traditionalists do not see contending strategies in the opponent's camp, some of which may be friendly to their interest in the conflict. The mixed or balanced respondents are ambivalent concerning these issues: they do not deny that there may be some trends and groups deviating from the totally unitary image of the opponent, but they are unwilling to attribute to these opposing trends and groups any important role in the conflict. We find a corresponding pattern of thinking for the self-image dimension.

Most elite members we have interviewed — and this may sound obvious — display a mixture of cooperative and non-cooperative thinking, while the extent to which cooperative and non-cooperative thinking dominates elite members differs. The linkages we hypothesized did not turn out quite as we expected. In Figure 8.2 we illustrate how we found the relationship to work.

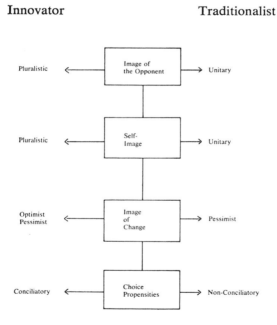

Figure 8.2. Modal types constructed on the basis of empirical results

Knowing that a respondent is either pluralistic or unitary in his view of his own side in the conflict or the opponent does not enable us to say very much about his having an optimistic or pessimistic view on change. Having a pluralistic view on one's own side and the opponent does not imply that one is likely to be an optimist as to the final solution of the conflict. The elite member in Israel is just as likely to be a pessimist.

Arabs tend to be far more optimistic when it comes to the final outcome of the conflict. They see the conflict as lasting longer but at the same time adhere to non-probabilistic beliefs that the conflict will develop in their favor. There does not seem to be a strong linkage between the image of the opponent and 'on whose side is time'. It is therefore not possible to predict one belief from the other. A strong belief in time being on their side would, we hypothesized, lead to conflictual policy positions, but this belief seems to give more leeway for different policy positions. Also with this belief, we do not seem to get the u-curve distribution that we got within each national elite on image of the opponent and image of self.

This also demonstrates that respondents scoring 'highly conflictual' on some dimension in the belief system may not score conflictual on others.

We found considerable variations in the degree to which the components included in this analysis of the operational code were stable, consistent, linked to other components in the system, and the degree to which variance in the dependent variable (policy preferences) is accounted for.

We are all the time speaking about questions of degree. We found Image of the Opponent to be clearly the most stable, consistent and discriminatory of the components.[9] A certain stability, consistency, and discriminatory value are also found in the other components — especially in Image of Self. But Image of Self and Image of Change would probably require a more elaborate construction of categories to increase their value. The results suggest that it is necessary to come up with considerably more differentiated categories.

Having located the pluralism/unitary dimension as the most promising, we proceeded to look at the covariation of these beliefs, and the dependent variable (choice propensities). The results were highly encouraging in that a unitary image of the opponent seemed to correlate strongly with a non-conciliatory stand in the conflict as well as a pluralist view with a conciliatory stand.

In other words, knowing that a respondent has a unitary or pluralistic view of the opponent enables us with considerable confidence to say what policies he will advocate in the conflict. The covariation here is strong. If at the same time we know his self-image, it increases our ability to say what his policy preference may be, whereas knowing his image of change does not help much.

Cognitive consistency theory tells us that when we get these results on image of the opponent it means that these beliefs are frequently used as organizing concepts. This explains why they tend to be both simple, stable and consistent. Parties to the conflict do need theories on what the opponent is like and how he is likely to respond. We are typically dealing with situations of uncertainty. The uncertainty is solved by forming these firm, non-probabalistic beliefs about the opponent. Disagreement in the conflict tends to focus on what the opponent is like. This disagreement tends to be polarized, and the contending parties develop firm convictions. This explains why by relatively few questions we were able to trace both the structure and the content of beliefs about the opponent.

Moving toward peace as well as toward war involves a considerable amount of uncertainty. To solve this uncertainty, theories are needed as to how the opponent will respond to conciliatory as well as non-conciliatory moves. Out results suggest that firmly established beliefs on the image of the opponent have a considerable impact on solving these uncertainties. These beliefs are, of course, seldom put to any reality test, but will form the explicit or implicit assumptions on which the disagreement rests.

Our basic argument on the basis of these results is that the ability to see the opponent as pluralistic with forces pulling in different directions may be critical to the problem of conflict resolution. Being able to see conflictual as well as moderating forces in the opponent's camp sensitized one to the possibility that one's own policies may interact with these tendencies, and that policies of one's own side may be influential in bringing about change.

Those sensitive to this fact are also more on guard for changes in the opponent's camp that may open up possibilities for greater options for peace. To some degree, we think that everyone in a conflict is a victim of the fallacy of not detecting shifts in the opponent's camp that may significantly alter the situation in the direction of peace or war. Respondents having a pluralistic view, however, are more sensitive to possible changes.

In other words, some elites remain quite insensitive to moderate changes in the opponent's camp — changes that could initiate a cumulative process toward peace, given reciprocity. It should be added that one may also have an overly optimistic view on which conciliatory moves could lead to change in the opponent's camp. Conciliatory moves may backfire.

Our basic argument is that elite members differ substantially in their ability to differentiate the image of the opponent. Elites with a differentiated view are more adaptable to changing situational characteristics as well as more favorable toward conciliatory moves as a whole, because their information-processing is not subject to the same degree of bias as those with a unitary view.

For example, it may be quite difficult to signal moderation in a very clear and unambiguous way, given domestic considerations. It is therefore important for policy-makers to be differentiated enough in their theories about the opponent in order to detect significant shifts in the opponent's policies. In this respect, there is substantial variation within elites.

In other words, our study has led us to believe that variations in the policy recommendations of elites in the conflict can be traced to fundamental differences about the meaning ascribed to the conflict — their definition of the situation, where beliefs as to the pluralism of the opponent are critical.

Sometimes the logic of the situation will determine the response. There tends to be consensus on what should be done. A situation of all-out war generally leads to almost complete consensus (there is cooperation between innovators and traditionalists). If one strategy is perceived as a success (instant), it is also likely to give this strategy great prevalence over alternative strategies. The Six-day war created great cohesion in Israel, while disagreement characterized the losing Arab side. Correspondingly, we found disagreement in Israel after the October war, while a great amount of agreement existed in the Arab camp.

Failure of one strategy reinforces alternative strategies. It leads to a re-evaluation of the cost/benefit analysis. But taking steps toward resolution of a conflict is likely to involve a high level of uncertainty. In cases like this we expect the variances in intra-elite belief patterns demonstrated to account for what policies would be recommended to a high degree.

Strategies for countering biases in information-processing and political choice

How can one counter the biases that may lead to sub-optimal policies?

It is not enough to make the party concerned aware of biases in information-processing. Even though elite members would be made aware that these biases exist, it might have no implications for behavior. Letting a decision-maker in the conflict understand how these biases operate certainly does not guarantee that this decision-maker will change his methods of processing information or the way he makes choices. It is certainly not sufficient merely to make elite members aware of the problem. This is what in psychology is called the irreversibility phenomenon.

A strategy suggested by some social psychologists is the use of so-called intergroup techniques, whereby elite members from both sides in the conflict are brought together to generally learn to understand the perspective of the other party.[10]

Research to date, however, generally seems to confirm that persuasion and communication alone seem insufficient to change people's beliefs, and the implications for behavior are even more doubtful.

Recently social psychologists have pointed to the need for focusing on which changes in the situation could bring about change in beliefs. It is possible that we start at the wrong end of the spectrum by trying to change beliefs before the situation is changed. This goes back to our previous point that there is too heavy a focus on attitudes and beliefs in the conflict — over-psychologizing as it were — while there is not enough attention given to situational changes that may produce these changes.

Of course it is not one thing or the other — improvement in communication and understanding may be one of the possible paths.

We have seen, for example, that even though parties to a conflict may admit that the opponent is threatened by them, there is a strong tendency to fix the blame not on themselves, but on the opponent's own behavior. An increased understanding of the genuine fears of the opponent may *possibly* lead to the advocacy of more moderate policies in the conflict, even though this is not at all certain. Getting a party in the conflict to say and understand that a threat is caused by him does not necessarily change his policies, or one may even argue that it is not even likely.

Discussing the implications of a cognitive analysis of this type may tend to ignore the conflict of interests which is obviously present. It is important to keep in mind that the psychological processes are only one aspect and, in part, a reflection of a conflict of interest that may be much more difficult and complicated than conflict arising from these psychological mechanisms. Any approach to conflict resolution, therefore, must take the real conflict of interest into account. One must not deal with the psychological conflict as independent of the realities that these psychological dispositions represent.

While we do not suggest explicit strategies to counter the erroneous tendencies in information-processing, we feel it is an important step in research on conflict resolution to identify the critical areas. We have tried to point out what may be psychological stumbling blocks to peace. We have issued a warning on the basis of our results that researchers and analysts of conflict as well as direct participants tend to draw erroneous conclusions from events that may inhibit processes of conflict resolution. A word should also be added as to what could trigger change. This should certainly not be based on an evaluation of the various patterns of thinking in the conflict. So-called 'representative samples' may be quite misleading, because the initiating of change may come from minor groups — even quite idiosyncratic beliefs of individual leaders.

Appendix A

List of respondents

Sample 1970—72

EGYPT

President Gamal Abdel Nasser
Vice-President Hussein El Shafei
Muhamed Sayd Ahmed (Editor) (Al Ahram)
Loutfi El Kholy (Editor) (Al Taliaa)
Hassan Fouad (Editor) (Al Ahram)
Moussa Sabry (Chief editor) (Al Akhbar)
Anis Mansour (Editor) (Al Akhbar)
Professor Muhamed Anis (Cairo University)
Ahmed Shukeiri (Editor) (Al Moussawar)
Kamel Zouheiri (Director) (Press Syndicate Rossad Yossef)
Tarek Foda (Journalist) (Al Akhbar)
Kamel Bakr (Director) (Leader of the Press Centre)
Minu Besieso (Journalist) (Al Ahram)
Khairy Aziz (Editor) (Al Taliaa)
Dr. Ahmed Kamal (The Popular Front)
Abou Nidal (El Fatah)
Ahmed al Shukeiry (Former leader of PLO)
Rolv Moltu (Director)* (UNICEF)
Mohamed Sameh Anwar (Secretary of State) (Ministry of Foreign Affairs)
Ahmed Esmat Abdel-Meguid (Government Spokesman) (Ministry of Foreign Affairs)
Ahmed Sabry Kamal (Ministry of Foreign Affairs)
Adel Taher (Minister of Tourism)
Said Mustafa Salim (Student) (Cairo University)
Yussef Abbass (Student) (Cairo University)
Knut Mørkved (First Secretary)* (The Norwegian Embassy)
Svein Tobiassen (Student)* (Norwegian student at Cairo University)
Abou Soheil (El Fatah)
Mohammed Raid (The Popular Front)
Joseph Abou-Firas (The Popular Front)
Yussef el Sebaiy (Editor) (Secretary General of Afro-Asian Organization)

JORDAN

Rev. Raouf Najjar (Director)* (UNRWA)
George Khoury (Norwegian Consul)
Joseph Thompson* (World Lutheran Federation)
Rouhi El Khatib (Mayor of Jerusalem, partly also during the Israeli occupation)
Ahmad Tuqan (Ministry of Foreign Affairs)
Rafet O. Ramzi (Ministry of Foreign Affairs, student)
Ahmad Al Azhary (El Fatah)
Dr. George Habbash (Leader of the Popular Front)

Dr. Motmoud Hijazi (El Fatah)
Professor Sir Nasir (Head of Sociology at University of Amman)
Professor Mohamed Sakr (Economics, University of Amman)
Professor Atallah Doany (Architecture, University of Amman)

SYRIA

Mahmoud El Youssef (Director) (Norwegian Consul General)
Robert Mulky (Lawyer) (Palestine Arab)
Mr. Dalati (Head, Political Department of the Ministry of Foreign Affairs)

LEBANON

Professor Hassan Saab
Ghassan Twenie (Editor) (Jour, An Nahar)
Reni Aggiouri (Editor) (L'Orient)
Professor Joseph Malone (AUB)
Raymond Eddé (President du Bloc National)
Edmond Rabbath (Lawyer) (Expert on Aqaba)
Gebran Majdalany (Former Chairman of Baath in Lebanon)
Dr. Fayez Sayegh (Director) (PLO Research Centre)
Sir John Renni (Dep. Commissioner General) (UNRWA)*
Antoine Boutros (Director) (Institute for Palestine Studies)
Tunberg (First Secretary)* (The Swedish Embassy)
Professor Naffat Nase (AUB)
Professor Barakat (AUB)
Professor Elie Salem (AUB)
Professor Zurayk (AUB)
Samir Coshe (The guerrilla group DFCG)
Professor Ibrahim Ibrahim (AUB)
Ljøstad* (Area Manager SAS)

ISRAEL

Israel Herz (Member of the Executive Committee of Histadrut)
Dr. Michael Shuster
Yossi Goel (Professor) (Hebrew University)
Oresio Vester (Director)* (American Colony, Jerusalem)
Yaakov Bialik (Student) (Hebrew University)
Shimon Halevi (Student) (Hebrew University)
Richard Oestermann (Director of Information, Hebrew University)
Yehezkel Dror (Professor) (Hebrew University)
Ted Lourie (Editor) (Jerusalem Post)
Michael Brecher (Professor) (Truman Center of Peace Research)*
Mordechai Nahumi (Journalist) (Al-Hamishamar)
David Lazar (Professor) (Hebrew University)
Louis Guttman (Professor) (Hebrew University)
Gabriel Bron (Journalist)
Kochavi Shemesh (one of the 'Black Panther' leaders)
Bjørn Dvorsky (Member of the Histadrut international secretariat)
Dan Pattir (Journalist) (Davar)
Moshe Zak (Editor) (Maariv)
Dov Bar-Nir (Journalist) (Haaretz)
Simha Flapan (Editor) (New Outlook)
Daniel Dishon (Researcher, Editor) (Shiloah Institute for Middle East Studies,
    Middle East Record)

Dan Shiftan (Researcher) (Shiloah Institute for Middle East Studies)
Mordechai Gazit (Director General) (Foreign Ministry)
Yehoshafat Harkabi (Professor) (Hebrew University)
Erwin Frenkel (Editor) (Jerusalem Post)
Lt.Col. Menachem Zohar (Military spokesman)
Shmuel Tamir (Member of the Knesset, Free Center)
Dov Zakin (Member of the Knesset, Mapam)
Gad Ranon (Jerusalem Foreign Press)
Moshe Sasson (Assistant Director General, Foreign Ministry)
Tuqan (Candidate for the municipal elections in Hebron) (Palestinian)*
Ohan (Businessman) (Palestinian)*
Fouad Aref (Businessman) (Palestinian)*
Anonymous student (Palestinian)*
Tawfiq Salman (Director of Tourism) (Palestinian)*
Akiva Eger (Director) (Institute Afro-Asiatique)
Eliezer Livneh (Author, Journalist)
Israel Stockmann (Researcher) (Shiloah Institute for Middle East Studies)
Matityahu Peled (Professor, previous general) (Tel-Aviv University)
David Werner Melchior (Party secretariat of Mapai)
Jan Jølle (First Secretary)* (Norwegian Embassy, Tel-Aviv)

Sample 1974

EGYPT

Ahmed Khaled Abdo, doctor
Ali Amin, editor in chief, Al Ahram
Magda Amin, student, American University, Cairo
Ahmed Anis, government spokesman
Ahmed Attia, professor, Institute of Strategic Studies, Al Ahram
Mohammed Ayesh, student, American University, Cairo
Abdel Halim Badawy, minister
Tahseen Basheer, spokesman of the Foreign ministry
Amin Hosny Bonnah, student, American University, Cairo
Abdelwahab M. Elmessiri, Institute of Strategic Studies, Al Ahram
Mohammed El Farra, associate director, The Arab League
Ezz el Din Foda, professor, Cairo University
High-ranking Officer, anonymous
Ali Hamdi El Gammal, editor, Al Ahram
Boutros Ghali, professor, Cairo University
Ali el-Din Hillal, professor, Institute of Strategic Studies, Al Ahram
Aida El Kashef, student, American University, Cairo
Nora Koshef, student, American University, Cairo
Akram Nabulsi, student, American University, Cairo (Palestinian)
Saphinaz Naguib, professor, Cairo University
Sadek Radwan, professor, American University, Cairo
Wahid Rafaat, professor, earlier member of government
Ramzy E. Ramzy, student, American University, Cairo
Abdel al-Raouf el-Reedi, spokesman of the Arab League
Foud Riad, professor, Cairo University
Mohammed Riad, Under-secretary of Foreign Affairs, Foreign Ministry

* Interviews which were dropped in the final preparation of data.

Adly El Sharif, Red Cross liaison officer
Mofid Shihab, professor, Cairo University
Hamed Sultan, professor, consultant to the Foreign Ministry
El Sayed Yassin, professor, National Center of Sociological and Criminological
Research

JORDAN

Munzer Anabtawi, professor, Jordan University
Kamal Bisharat, farmer
John Benar, correspondent, Financial Time/Associated Press
Fuad Farradj, engineer, Jordan Office for Geological and Engineering Services
Sami Habayeb, lawyer
Ahmed el Khalil, senator
George M. Khoury, businessman/Norwegian council
Taher el Masri, minister of the occupied areas
Naseef Kashif Murad, student, American University, Cairo
Raouf Najjar, Catholic priest
Sari Nasir, professor, Jordan University
Mokbel Shukri, economist
Naher Shukri, economist
Joseph Thompson, doctor, World Lutheran Federation*

LEBANON

Riad Ashkor, researcher, Institute for Palestine Studies
Hakkam Darwaza, researcher, Institute for Palestine Studies
Solikan Frezili, editor in chief, Beirut Daily
Mohammed Hamdan, professor, American University of Beirut
Mohammed Ibrahim, professor, American University of Beirut
Mohammed Ghalib Kaysi, student, American University of Beirut
Nafhat N. Nasr, professor, American University of Beirut
Edmond Rabbath, professor
Anis Sayegh, director, PLO's research center
Moufid Shahim, spokesman (PFLP)
Bassam Abu Sharif, spokesman (PFLP)

ISRAEL

David Altman, president, National Union of Israeli Students
Daniel Amit, professor, Hebrew University, Jerusalem
Abi Atias, Ministry of Housing
Yehuda Avenel, journalist, Jerusalem Foreign Press
Michael Brecher, professor, Truman Institute, Jerusalem*
Abraham Cohen, engineer
Jacob Cohen, Head of Arab Department, Histadruth
Daniel Dishon, professor, Shiloah Institute, Tel-Aviv
Yehezkel Dror, professor, Hebrew University, Jerusalem
David Farchi, director general, Minister of Information
Simhan Flapan, editor in chief, New Outlook
Erwin Frenkel, editor, Jerusalem Post
Joseph Ginat, the office of the Prime Minister, Arab Affairs
Hanna Greenberg, Foreign Ministry, Department of Information
Louis Guttman, professor, Hebrew University, Jerusalem

Alouph Hareven, director, Foreign Ministry, Department of Information
Michael Harish, member of parliament
Yehoshafat Harkabi, professor, Hebrew University, Jerusalem
Israel Herz, member of the executive committee of Histadruth
Chaim Herzog, ambassador to the UN
Benjamin Jaffe, director, international department, World Zionist Organization
Eliezer Livneh, author
Nevil Lamdon, Foreign Ministry
Jacob Majus, director, Middle East Peace Institute, Tel-Aviv
Nawaf Massalha, director, Arab Department of Histadruth
Eli Marx, associate director, Afro-Asian Institute, Tel-Aviv
Meron Medzini, director, Government Press Office
David Werner Melchior, Party secretariat of Mapai
Boaz Moav, member of parliament
Mordechai Nahumi, journalist, Al Hamishmar
Dan Pattir, journalist, Maariv
Richard Oestermann, director of Information, Hebrew University, Jerusalem
Ari Rath, journalist, Jerusalem Post
Anan Safadi, journalist, Jerusalem Post
Benjamin Sella, international department in Histadruth
Gabriel Sheffer, researcher, Hebrew University, Jerusalem
Mohammed Abu Shilbayeh, journalist, author, (Palestinian)*
Israel Stockmann, researcher, Truman Institute, Jerusalem
Yael Vered, director, Foreign Ministry
Gideon Weigert, journalist
Noam Yaffe, student, Hebrew University, Jerusalem
Hanan Ben Yehuda, Vice President, National Union of Israeli Student
Muky Zor, Kibbutz En Gev

Sample 1976

JORDAN

Mohammed A. Aamiry, Former Minister of Foreign Affairs
Wassfi Anibtawe, Professor, Former Minister
Jamil Barakat, Secretary General, Amman Chamber of Commerce
N.Y. Bulos, Engineer
Hamad El Farhan, Businessman, Former Under-Secretary for Ministry of Economics
Emile Ghory, Political author, Former Minister
John Halaby, Correspondent for Associated Press
Sheikh Saeh, Abdul Hamid, Former Minister for Religious Matters
Dawoud Husseini, Doctor, Former Minister
Salah Inibtawe, Medical Doctor
Nizar Jerdaneh, President of the Pharmaceutical Union of Jordan
Ahmed El Khalil, Senator/lawyer
George M. Khoury, Businessman, Norwegian Honorary Consul
Adnan Abu Odeh, Senator.

EGYPT

Mohammed Sayed Ahmed, Editorial writer, Al Ahram
Mohammed El Ashmawy, Attaché, Foreign Ministry

Safwat Baraka, Minister Plenipotentiary
Boutros Ghali, Professor, Cairo University
El Said Kamal, Director of the PLO office in Cairo
Khaled El Komy, Second secretary, Department of Palestinian Affairs, Foreign Ministry
Gamal Mansour, Under-Secretary of State, Foreign Ministry
Fouad Abdel Moubdi, Ambassador, Director of Department of Arab Affairs, Foreign Ministry
Amre M. Moussa, Counsellor, Foreign Ministry
Fayza Aboul Naga, Attaché, Foreign Ministry
Mahmoud Aboul Nasr, Minister Plenipotentiary
Prominent officer, Anonymous
Ibrahim Sabri, Ambassador, Director of Diplomatic Institute
Abdel Monem Said, Institute of Strategic Studies, Al Ahram
Abbas Helmy Sidki, Ambassador, Director of Department of Palestinian Affairs, Foreign Ministry

ISRAEL

Prof. Reuven Yaron, Faculty of law, Hebrew University.
Prof. Emanuel Guttmann, Hebrew University.
Mr. Amazia Baram, researcher, Truman Institute.
Mr. Mordechai Nissan, researcher, Truman Institute.
Mr. Benjamin Jaffe, Director of Jewish Agency, External Department
Prof. Yeshayahu Leibowitch, Hebrew University.
Dr. Jack J. Cohen, director. B'nai Brith Hillel Foundation at the Hebrew University.
Mr. Richard Oestermann. Chief of Dept. of Information and Public Affairs, Hebrew University.
Dr. Zeev Sternhall, Hebrew University, Dept. of Sociology.
Dr. Dan Horowitz, Hebrew University, Dept. of Sociology.
Dr. Meir Pa'il, Member of Knesset, Jerusalem.
Dr. Peretz Tishby, assistant director of Jewish National and University Library, Hebrew University.
Mr. Shlomo Argov, adviser to Director General of Foreign Ministry, Jerusalem
Mr. Samuel Katz, author, Tel-Aviv.
Dr. Dan Ronen, Assistant Minister of Education and Culture, Jerusalem.
Dr. Yoram Beck, head of French-speaking countries, Jewish Agency, External Department, Jerusalem.
Mr. Ari Rath, editor and managing director of 'Jerusalem Post', Jerusalem.
Miss Tirza Gur-Arie, head of English-speaking countries, Jewish Agency, External Department, Jerusalem.
General Uzi Narkis, Director, Jewish Agency, Aliya Department, Jerusalem.
Prof. S. N. Eisenstadt, Van Leer Foundation, Jerusalem.
Mr. Yehoshua Justman, editor of 'Ma'ariv', Jerusalem.
Mr. Abba Eban, MK, Knesset, Jerusalem.
Mrs. Doris Lankin, legal adviser to 'Jerusalem Post', Jerusalem.
Mr. Moshe Yegar, Director of Information, Foreign Ministry, Jerusalem.
Mrs. Rivka Hadary, Director of Liaison Office for American Professors for Peace in the Middle-East, Jerusalem.
Mrs. Yocheved Sussmann, head of Scandinavian Information Dept., Jewish Agency, Jerusalem.
Dr. Raphaella Bilskey, adviser to Prime Minister, Van Leer Foundation, Jerusalem.
Prof. E. O. Schild, Dean, School of Education, Haifa University.

Prof. Knei-Paz, Department of Sociology, Hebrew University, Jerusalem.
Mr. Aharon Yariv, MK, Knesset, Jerusalem, (former chief of Intelligence).
Mrs. Nuzhat Katsab, MK, Knesset, Jerusalem.
Mr. Itzhak Moday, MK, (president, Israel-America, Chamber of Commerce and Industry).
Mr. Zev Chefets, Director of Information Services, Liberal Party, Tel-Aviv.
Mr. Anan Safadi, journalist, 'Jerusalem Post', Jerusalem.
Mr. Eliahu Lankin, M. J. Advocate, former member of Knesset, Jerusalem.
Mrs. Hanna Palti, Ministry of Foreign Affairs, Jerusalem.
Mr. Yehezkel Flomin, MK, Tel-Aviv.
Dr. Leon Dycian, MK, Advocate, Tel-Aviv.
Mrs. Yossi Sarid, MK, Knesset, Jerusalem.
Mr. Raphael Horowitz, spokesman of 'La'am' party, Moshav Ben-Noon.
Mr. Dan Leon, author, Jewish Agency, Jerusalem.
Mr. Avraham Katz, MK, Knesset, Jerusalem.
Mrs. Shulamit Aloni, MK, Knesset, Jerusalem.
Mrs. Esther Herlitz, MK, Knesset, Jerusalem.
Prof. Moshe Arens, MK, Knesset, Jerusalem.
Mr. Raphael Gvir, Ministry of Foreign Affairs, Jerusalem.
Mr. Walter Eytan, Director of Israeli Broadcasting, (former director general of Foreign Ministry).
Mr. Kalman Yaron, Director of the Martin Buber centre for adult education, Hebrew University, Jeusalem.
Mrs. Malka Keynan, historian, Van Leer Foundation, Jerusalem.
Mr. Erwin Frenkel, editor, 'Jerusalem Post', Jerusalem.
Mr. Izhak Bar-On, Brig. General, Director General, Tel-Aviv University.
Mrs. Rachel Enbar, editor, 'La'mathil', Jerusalem.
Mr. Moshe Rivlin, Director General, Jewish Agency, Jerusalem.
Mr. Ehud Olmert, MK, Advocate, Knesset, Jerusalem.
Mr. Israel Yesha'yahu, Knesset-president, Knesset, Jerusalem.
Dr. Shlomo Schafir, foreign correspondent, 'Davar', Tel-Aviv.
Mr. Gideon Samet, editor, 'Ha'aretz', Tel-Aviv.
Mr. Shmuel Segal, Director of Mevasseret Zion, Jerusalem.
Mr. Benjamin Abileah, Spokesman and assistant director of the press division, Ministry of Foreign Affairs, Jerusalem
Mr. Dan Pattir, adviser to Prime Minister, Prime Minister's Office, Jerusalem.
Mr. Eytan Gilboa, lecturer in international relations.
Mr. Haim Gouri.
Mr. Yoshua Tan-Pai Haaretz, editor.
Mr. Michael Mizan, lawyer, Welfare Dept.
Mr. Amnon Sella, doctor, international studies.
Mr. Yehiel Limor, journalist.
Mr. Zvi Schiffrin, univ. professor.
Mrs. Eli Eyal, TV-journalist.
Mr. Ellis Joffe, univ. professor.
Mr. Bar-Yaacov Nissim, univ. professor.
Mr. Ben-Ami Shillony, Hebrew University.
Mr. Joshua Bitzur, journalist.
Mr. Zev Klein, univ. professor.
Mr. Aharon Leva, Davar.
Mr. Shlomo Ginossar, Davar.
Mrs. Tuvia Mendelson, Davar.
Mr. David Lazar, univ. professor.

List of respondents interviewed in both 1970 and 1974 Arab side

Egypt: Moussa Sabry

Jordan: Raouf Najjar
              Sir Nasir
              Mohamed Sakr

Lebanon: Edmond Rabbath
              Naffat Nasr
              Ibrahim

List of respondents interviewed in both 1972 and 1974 Israeli side

Israel: Israel Herz
              Richard Oestermann
              Yehezkel Dror
              Michael Brecher
              Mordechai Nahumi
              Louis Guttmann
              Dan Pattir
              Simhan Flapan
              Daniel Dishon
              Yehoshafat Harkabi
              Erwin Frenkel
              Eliezer Livneh
              David Werner Melchior

Purposive sample 1970 — 1972

	Active Politicians		Civil Servants		Editors/ Journalists		Professors/ Researchers		Students		Guerrilla Leaders		Others		Total	
	No.	%	No.	%	No.	%	No.	%	No.	%	No.	%	No.	%	No.	%
Egypt	5	18.5	1	3.7	12	44.4	1	3.7	2	7.4	6	22.2	0	—	27	30.3
Jordan	1	10.0	1	10.0	0	—	3	30.0	1	10.0	3	30.0	1	10.0	10	11.2
Syria	0	—	1	33.3	0	—	0	—	0	—	0	—	2	66.7	3	3.4
Lebanon	2	13.3	0	—	2	13.3	9	60.0	0	—	1	6.7	1	6.7	15	16.9
Israel	5	14.7	2	5.9	10	29.4	12	35.3	2	5.9	0	—	3	8.8	34	38.2
Total	13	14.6	5	5.6	24	27.0	25	28.1	5	5.6	10	11.2	7	7.9	89	100.0

Note: Palestinian respondents, including guerrilla leaders, are attributed to the country in which they happened to be interviewed.

145

Purposive sample 1974

	Active Politicians		Civil Servants		Editors/ Journalists		Professors/ Researchers		Students		Guerrilla Leaders		Others		Total	
	No.	%	No.	%	No.	%	No.	%	No.	%	No.	%	No.	%	No.	%
Egypt	4	13.3	2	6.7	2	6.7	12	40.0	7	23.3	0	—	3	10.0	30	31.6
Jordan	2	15.4	1	7.7	1	7.7	2	15.4	1	7.7	0	—	6	46.2	13	13.7
Lebanon	0	—	0	—	1	9.1	7	63.6	1	9.1	2	18.2	0	—	11	11.6
Israel	3	7.3	9	22.0	8	19.5	11	26.8	2	4.9	0	—	8	19.5	41	43.1
Total	9	9.5	12	12.6	12	12.6	32	33.7	11	11.6	2	2.1	17	17.9	95	100.0

Note: Palestinian respondents, including guerrilla leaders, are attributed to the country in which they happened to be interviewed.

Purposive sample 1976

	Active Politicians		Civil Servants		Editors/ Journalists		Professors/ Researchers		Students		Guerrilla Leaders		Others		Total	
	No.	%	No.	%	No.	%	No.	%	No.	%	No.	%	No.	%	No.	%
Egypt	3	20.0	7	46.7	1	6.7	2	13.3	0	—	1	6.7	1	6.7	15	14.2
Jordan	2	14.3	1	7.1	1	7.1	1	7.1	0	—	0	—	9	64.3	14	13.2
Israel	19	24.7	13	16.9	14	18.2	21	27.3	0	—	0	—	10	13.0	77	72.6
Total	24	22.6	21	19.8	16	15.1	24	22.6	0	—	1	1.0	20	18.9	106	100.0

Note: Palestinian respondents, including guerrilla leaders, are attributed to the country in which they happened to be interviewed.

Appendix B

Questions posed in 1970/72:

ARAB SIDE

Questions about the adversary

Why does not Israel want direct negotiations with the Palestinian Arabs?

What part of the territories occupied during the 1967 war do you consider most important for Israel to keep?

Why do you think Israel stresses the importance of being recognized as a state?

Is it more important for Israel to be recognized than to keep the territories occupied in 1967?

If there had been a co-ordinated diplomatic action right after the 1967 war, how do you consider the chances would then have been to force the Israelis to withdraw from the occupied territories?

Do you see any faction in Israeli politics able to satisfy Arab expectations and demands?

Questions about local actors on the Arab side

What do you consider to be Egypt's main goal — to force Israel from the areas occupied in the 1967 war or to fight for the legitimate rights of the Palestinian Arabs?

Do you think the Egyptian government under certain circumstances could have been willing to cede to Israel the old part of Jerusalem, the Golan Heights and the Gaza Strip?

How great do you consider is the influence of the Egyptian government?

Is it not true that Jordan and Israel almost came to terms some weeks after the war and that such an agreement between the two has been very close on other occasions as well?

What are the attitudes of Jordan and Lebanon?

Why does not Syria want to take part in the negotiations?

Do you think Syria would have to accept a solution already accepted by Egypt, Jordan and Israel?

In your opinion, what trends are there to be found in the military development since the war of 1967 and how do you judge the future military development?

How did the changing patterns of cooperation influence Arab politics after 1967?

How do you rate the balance of power between those who advocate a military solution and those who would prefer a peaceful solution?

In the escalation of the 1967 war we could identify some uncontrolled elements.

Can you also *after* the 1967 war identify similar uncontrolled elements?

Internal disagreement has been reduced in Israel due to the Arab-Israeli conflict. Why has this not been the case in the Arab world?

To what extent do you think public opinion plays a role?

What are the goals of the guerrilla movements, and do they actually look upon these goals as realistic?

What difference of opinion do you find in the guerrilla movement, and what significance does this difference imply?

Do the Marxist-oriented and revolutionary regimes commit themselves more to the guerrillas? If so, what is the reason for this?

Questions about third parties

How is it that the UN was able to contribute strongly to a diplomatic solution in 1957, but unable to do so later in the present conflict?

What are the differences of opinion held by USA and the Soviet Union as to negotiations?

What changes are to be found in the commitment of the Great Powers after the 1967 war, and to what extent have these changes influenced their objectives when working on a conflict solution?

How do you think a European detente could influence the situation in the Middle East?

What goals does France pursue in her Middle-East policy and to what extent is this policy appreciated?

Is Egypt more dependent on the Soviet Union than Israel on the USA?

Questions on negotiation set-ups and gains

Who would gain from direct negotiations between Israel and the Arab governments and between Israel and the Palestinian Arabs?

Who would gain from a negotiated agreement through UN?

Why do the Arabs refuse to negotiate directly with Israel? Who will gain or lose from the system of negotiations propagated by the UN and the Great Powers?

The future

How do you think the conflict will develop?

ISRAELI SIDE

Questions about the adversary

How would you explain the differences in opinions in the Arab world concerning the state of Israel?

How do you evaluate the Arab strategy?

How would you explain the differences in opinions between Sadat, the guerrillas and the Arabs on West Bank?

Which question do you feel is the most difficult one in the conflict with the Arab world?

What do you think would happen to the Jews if the Arabs gained a military victory over Israel?

Egypt

If Egypt agreed to a peace treaty with Israel, do you think Egypt would give up the idea of fighting against Israel?

Why do you think Egypt wants peace?

How do you estimate the influence of Egypt?

Jordan

What do you think are the objectives of the Jordanian government?

What is the opinion of King Hussein of a Palestinian state on the West Bank?

Syria

How would you describe the desires and demands of Syria and Lebanon?

Guerrillas

What are the chances that the guerrillas will once again represent an important factor in the conflict?

Do you think the guerrillas will grow in a more revolutionary direction?

Israel

What are the differences in opinion as to Israeli demands on the Arabs?

Do you see any faction in the Arab world that is able to satisfy Israeli expectations and demands?

Do you expect that Israel will always remain the stronger military party?

Do you think the state of Israel will always preserve its Jewish character?

If you should rank the occupied territories according to their strategic, economic and religious importance, what ranking would you suggest?

How would you shortly describe the difference between maximalists and minimalists in the Israeli society?

What are the differences of opinion within the Israeli government?

In what fields can Israel compromise with the Arab world?

To what extent does public opinion play a role?

Questions about third parties

How do you think the position of the United States has been influenced by the increased Russian engagement?

Do you think the United States will always support the state of Israel?

How do you think a European détente could influence the situation in the Middle East?

Do you find any differences between the Russian and American attitudes toward the questions of borders?

Is Israel more dependent on the USA than Egypt on the Soviet Union?

In which ways do you feel that powers outside the conflict area have influence on the development of the conflict?

How would you describe differences in attitudes in the EEC?

Questions on negotiation set-ups and gains

Who would gain from direct negotiation between Israel and the Arab governments and between Israel and Palestine Arabs?

Who would gain from negotiated agreement through UN?

Did the demand for direct negotiations come as a wish to be the superior in the negotiations?

Who will gain or lose from the system of negotiations being prepared today?

How do you think the conflict will develop in the future for Israel — for the Arabs?

Questions posed in 1974:

I *Causes of conflict*

    a) If you should point out one single factor as the main cause of the Middle East conflict, which would you mention?

II *Strategies*

    a) If UN resolution 242 were implemented, who do you think would gain and lose?

    b) What parts of the territories occupied during the 1967 war do you consider most vital (question on Israeli side) to keep? (question on on Arab side) to get back? (If you had to choose, how would you list them?)

    c) What parts of the territories do you consider most vital for the other side to get back (Israeli side)/ to keep? (Arab side) (If you had to choose, how would you list them?)

    d) How do you see the solution of the Palestinian problem?

III *Self-image*

    a) What are the goals of your side in the conflict?

    b) Are there any differences concerning the goals and strategies on your side?

    c) What do you think are the basic good and bad aspects of your side in the conflict?

    d) Do you see any elements in your own country working against peace?

    e) Do you think that the other side is threatening you?

IV *Third parties*

    a) In what way and how much is your side dependent on the superpowers?

    — militarily?

    — morally?

    — politically?

    — economically?

    b) In what way do you think the superpowers and UN can influence a peace solution?

    c) In what way and how much is the other side dependent on the superpowers?

V *Enemy-image*

    a) What are the goals of the other side in this conflict?

    b) Are there any differences concering the goals and strategies of the other side?

    c) What do you think are the basic good and bad aspects of the other side in the conflict?

d) Do you see any elements on the other side working for peace?
e) Do you think that the other side believes that you are threatening them?

VI *Change*

a) In what way do you think the events in the last years have basically changed the conflict?
b) In what way have the following events influenced the conflict?
   1) The civil war in Jordan?
   2) The activities of the guerrillas abroad?
   3) The Oil Embargo?
c) What were the basic causes of the October war, and how has the war influenced the conflict?

VII *Future*

a) As regards the political situation, what would you like to see happen in the near future?
b) Now speaking realistically, what would you actually expect will happen?
— concerning the new generation?
— concerning the military situation?
— concerning international public opinion?
c) Given what you would like to see happen in the Middle East in the near future, what do you think are the most effective ways to achieve these aims?
d) How long do you think this conflict will last?

Question posed in 1976

1. Do you expect another war in the coming years?
2. Are you in favour of a Palestinian state on the West Bank and the Gaza Strip?
3. What are the goals of your side in the conflict?
4. Are there any differences concerning the goals and strategies on your side?
5. Do you think that the other side is threatening you?
6. What are the goals of the opponent in this conflict?
7. Are there any differences concerning the goals and strategies of the other side?
8. Do you think that the other side believes that you are threatening them?
9. In what way do you think the events in the last years have basically changed the conflict?
10. Do you think the Sinai Agreement
    a) has been favorable to both sides? □
    b) has been favorable only to your side? □
    c) has been favorable only to the opponent? □
    d) has had no effect? □
11. In what way do you think the increased international recognition of the PLO has influenced the conflict?
12. In what way has the civil war in Lebanon influenced the conflict?
13. How do you see the solution of the Palestinian problem?
14. As regards the political situation, what would you like to see happen in the Middle East in the near future?
15. Now speaking realistically, what do you actually expect will happen?
16. Given what you like to see happen in the Middle East in the near future, what do you think are the most effective ways to achieve these aims?

17. Question in Israel: Frequently Arab leaders say that your side wants to expand. Why do you think they say that?
    Question on Arab side: Frequently Israeli leaders say that you want to eliminate them. Why do you think they say that?
18. How long do you think this conflict will last?

Appendix C

CODING MANUAL FOR ATTRIBUTION

General introduction

In the first stage of coding we selected a random sample of the protocols; then we went through the whole protocols in order to identify those questions on which there seemed to be the best data for coding attribution.

The first problem was to identify so-called *causal statements*. They are either explicitly or implicitly an answer to the question *why*. The enemy behaves like this, because ... Open-ended questions may yield data on attribution on all issues, but we do have questions that are more related to attributional statements than others.

In the coding process we shall always have a basic dichotomy in mind: Does the causal statement (explanation of an event) make reference to *dispositional or situational* variables or both? Dispositional attribution is also called *person attribute,* which may be a better term, since it would be more readily understood. In other words, does the respondent, when he expresses a cause for some event, explain this as caused by *some traits of the person* (persons) performing the act, or does the respondent refer to *some kind of reactive behavior* caused by stimulus in the situation? When referring to *person attribute* we may say that the respondent in his information-processing behaves as a 'trait psychologist', and when referring to situational variables as a 'reinforcement psychologist'.

Another rule of thumb should be:
Is the causal statement:
. . ., 'because of the situation'
or
. . ., 'because of the actor' (himself).

And please note, we did not only want to identify the causal processing when the respondent observes the behavior of others. We are equally interested in *how* the respondent makes causal statements about his own behavior. Therefore causal statements on both one's own and the enemy's behavior should be coded.

Coding problem number one is, of couse, to identify dispositional as opposed to situational attributions. The dichotomy is not as simple as it may sound. The same causal statements can be interpreted as both. A guidance here must also be the context within which it is said. The form of the statement may be misleading, and the context should also be evaluated. In difficult cases it should be helpful to have this in mind:

(i) Explanations that assume only those dispositions that are shared by all men or are typical of most men. (Code as situational.)

155

(ii) Explanations that assume or state something unique or distinguishing about the actor's dispositions. (Code as dispositional.)

It should also help to see whether the explanation seems to imply a Stimulus-Response model (situational) rather than a theory about something unique about the actor in question (dispositional). Some causal statements interpret behavior to be *reactive*; this is the Stimulus-Response model.

The observer refers to stimulus in the environment as an explanation for the observed behavior. Nation A did this because of Nation B — for example. We did this because we had to (observing one's own behavior — self-perception).

The coding problem will not be solved by using a forced choice format (listing of content) unless this is based on context. But bear in mind that the dispositional is linked to *uniqueness* while the situational is *general*.

'Narrow' (dispositional) versus 'broad' (situational) may sometimes be helpful to think of.

A matter is only dispositional when the attributor assumes that it is something *particular, unique*. The attributor may be referring to a trait, but still it would be coded as situational if the attributor assumes this trait to be shared by everybody, including himself.

It may also be helpful to think of behavior seen as 'rational' (situational) or behavior seen as 'irrational' (dispositional).

What kind of attributions you make is also linked to perceived freedom of choice. What you think you can do about it.

Making a situational attribution is the same as saying that it was something you thought you had no control over. Dispositional attribution implies freedom of choice.

The fact that we are talking about a very familiar situation should make it easier to evaluate the context and thereby facilitate the solving of the coding problems. One quite special problem that we should like to discuss with you is the coding of *Zionism*. As a general statement we could say that it could be both dispositional and situational, and that it has to be considered within the context in which it appears. If Zionism is considered a *social force*, we would code it as situational. On the other hand, if Zionism is used to describe the state of Israel as being something unique, a 'trait' particular to the people of that nation as opposed to the people of all other nations, it should be coded as dispositional. If it is used, so to speak, to explain that the people of Israel behave differently from all other peoples because of *Zionism*, it is dispositional.

If you have read this introduction carefully, you can proceed to code the first question — code only one question at a time, since this will increase reliability. Before you start on each question, study also the examples we have listed below each question. Only the questions listed should be coded.

We have one coding-sheet for each respondent.

As can be seen, we code both the presence of an attribution and the number of attributions within each category — if they make more than one attribution.

What do you think are the basic good and bad aspects of your side in the conflict?

Good:
( ) Dispositional .... number ( )
( ) Situational   .... number ( )
Bad:
( ) Dispositional .... number ( )
( ) Situational   .... number ( )

What do you think are the basic good and bad aspects of the other side in the conflict?

Good:
(   )   Dispositional   ....   number   (   )
(   )   Situational   ....   number   (   )
Bad:
(   )   Dispositional   ....   number   (   )
(   )   Situational   ....   number   (   )

Examples of coding:

Good/bad o t h e r side
Good — situational

Arabs   'They have a strong army'
'They are more developed than us'

Arabs   'New movement in Israel wants to stop expansion, I am thinking about the leftist movement.'

Israeli   'Sadat has good intentions.'
'Good point in coming closer to the US.'

Good — dispositional

Arabs   'They are very efficient and hardworking.'
'They have a fantastic cohesion, they are very united.'
'Their patriotism.'

Israeli   'Arabs more realistic.'
'They are very hospitable'.
'Strong sense of their own weakness'.

Bad — situational

Israeli   'They give refuge to Arab guerrilla organizations.'
'They will not respect UN resolution 242.'

Arabs   'Terrorism against Palestinians.'
'No respect for UN resolutions.'
'They take advantage from their sufferings during WW II — they have public opinion on their side.'

Bad — dispositional

Arabs   'The superior race thinking.'
'They are aggressive.'
'Israel is a threat to every Arab nation.'

Israeli   'Somehow they want to kill us.'
'They are irrational.'

Good/bad your side:
Good — situational

Arabs   'Our government better now than before 73-war.'
'We have never occupied any country.'
'We have the oil.'

Israeli   'Arab workers in Israel have achieved high standard of living.'
'The labor movement is leading.'
'We can apply western science.'

Good — dispositional

Arabs   'We are hospitable and tolerant.'
'We are fighting for a just cause.'
'Our attitude has become more open and flexible.'

Israeli	'Our society built on equality.'
	'We are basically very optimistic.'
	'We have natural unity, high morale and strong beliefs.'

Bad — situational

Arabs	'Our influence on the outside world not very good.'
	'There is much disagreement among Arab states.'
	'We still belong to the underdeveloped world.'
Israeli	'Some faults as a democratic system.'
	'Our historical complexes.'
	'Didn't recognize the Palestinian entity.'

Bad — dispositional

Arabs	'We are very emotional.'
	'We are too naive, this make us frustrated.'
Israeli	'We have become more chauvinistic.'
	'Bad manners, impatient.'
	'Self-assurance, think we can achieve everything.'

One coding sheet for each respondent. We also here code both presence of an attribution and frequency.

If you should point out one single factor as the main cause of the Middle Ease conflict, which would you mention?

( ) We are to blame .... ( ) Situational .... number ( )
( ) Dispositional .. number ( )

( ) They are to blame .... ( ) Situational .... number ( )
( ) Dispositional .. number ( )

( ) Third parties are to blame .. ( ) Situational .... number ( )
( ) Dispositional .. number ( )

( ) Neutral (we can all be blamed) ( ) Situational .... number ( )
( ) Dispositional .. number ( )

Besides coding the causal statement as situational or dispositional, it is necessary to make a further classification of the statements. We also code the statements along a blame-fixing dimension.

Examples of codings:

'They are to blame' — situational attribution

Arabs	'The essence of the conflict lies in the plan worked out by the World Zionist movement at the conference of Basle in 1897 to set up a Jewish state on the land of Palestine.'
	'Occupation of Palestine by the Israelis.'
Israeli	'Growth of the Arab world, economically, strategically and their pressure elements.'
	'Arab refusal to accept Jews as a national entity.'

'They are to blame' — dispositional

Arabs	'Israeli imperialism — Zionism.'
	'The Israeli fanaticism.'
Israeli	'Arab pride — their beliefs, their culture.'
	'That the Arabs are determined to destroy Israeli.'
	'Arab suspicion.'

158

Israeli
> *We are to blame — situational*
> 'The existence of a Jewish state.'
> 'Jewish return after 100 years.'

Israeli
> *We are to blame — dispositional*
> 'We are committed to Zionism.'

Third parties / Neutral — Situational

Israeli 'Two nations claim the same territory.'
'Big power conflict. SU interested in tension.'
'Clash between two nationalistic movements.'

Arabs 'The opposition between the North and the South in the world.'
'The creation of the State of Israel in Palestine in 1948.'

Third parties / Neutral — Dispositional

Arabs 'Western imperialist design.'
'Lack of assimilation in the area.'
'Lack of understanding for the Arabs.'

Israeli 'Two cultures fighting each other.'

One coding-sheet for each respondent. Here too we coded both presence of an attribution and frequency.

Besides coding along the situational/dispositional dimension we also classified along what we might call a 'responsibility dimension.'

Given what you would like to see happen in the Middle East in the near future, what do you think are the most effective ways to achieve these aims?

Up to *us* .... ( ) Situational .... number ( )
( ) Dispositional ...... number ( )

Up to *them* .... ( ) Situational .... number ( )
( ) Dispositional ...... number ( )

Up to *third parties* ...... ( ) Situational .... number ( )
( ) Dispositional ...... number ( )

Neutral .... ( ) Situational .... number ( )
( ) Dispositional ...... number ( )

Examples of coding
Up to them — situational

Arabs 'Israelis must withdraw from areas occupied in 1967.'
'Depends on Israeli approval of UN res. 242.'

Israeli 'New leadership in Arab world.'

Up to them — dispositional

Arabs 'Process of re-thinking in Israel.'
'Dezionization of Palestine.'

Israeli 'Arab attitudes should be re-educated.'
'Arabs must start teaching love — not hatred.'

Up to us — situational

Arabs 'Guerrilla actions.'
'Opening the canal.'

	'Egypt more open economically.'
Israeli	'A strong Israel in every sense.'
	'That Israel return the occupied territories.'

Up to us — dispositional

Arabs	'Arab solidarity.'
Israeli	'Recognition that creation of Israel created the Palestinian problem.'
	'Re-education of basic Israeli perceptions.'

Neutral / Third Parties — situational

Arabs	'That we don't get any further interventions by big powers.'
	'Every party give in and come together and talk.'
Israeli	'Use political and military tools on both sides to push the process in the right direction.'
	'Successful continuation of Geneva talks.'

Neutral / Third parties — dispositional

Arabs	'Trying to co-exist peacefully.'
	'Understanding and goodwill.'
Israeli	'General readiness to negotiate.'

Coding Manual for Consistency

This booklet provides you with instructions on how to code the protocols from the interviews. Before starting to code you may find it useful to read some articles and papers on the general approach to the study.

For example:

Alexander L. George: The Operational Code: A Neglected Approach to the Study of Political Leaders and Decision-Making. *International Studies Quarterly* (June 1969), 190—222.

Ole R. Holsti: The Operational Code Approach to the Study of Political Leaders: John Foster Dulles' Philosophical and Instrumental Beliefs. *Canadian Journal of Political Science* (March 1970), 123—157.

Daniel Heradstveit: *The Operational Code as an Approach to the Study of Foreign Policy Decision-making.* NUPI-notat No. 119, Oslo 1976.

Instructions for the list code.

You are asked to code the answers on a three point scale. You will not be asked to make any further discrimination between the answers than this. For each question the booklet provides you with a number of concrete examples of how to place the answers along this evaluative scale. However, before proceeding to the concrete examples, it is also important that you have some notion of what this cognitive scale means. If you look at how we have verbalized the scale, you will gain a better idea of this. For example, we quite frequently use terms like compromising $(+1)$, mixed (0), uncompromising (1). It may also be helpful to think of the various operational code beliefs ranging from one extreme to the other. For example, there may be either conflict or harmony in politics, the future may be predictable or unpredictable.

We have come up with three basically different goals pursued in the conflict area. The actors in the area should be classified according to their attitude toward these three goals. Empirically, of course, the situation is far more complex. The pluralism and the complexity of a conflict of this character is enormous. For analytical purposes, however, we have to move toward simplification. In spite of pluralism in goals pursued, we find that these three different goals cover most of the interesting tendencies in the conflict for the purposes of evaluating the possibilities for conflict resolution. Those seeking these goals are:

1. Adherents of reaching a settlement through negotiations along the lines of the UN Resolution of 1967.
2. Adherents of a Palestinian democratic state, including the territory that is now Israel, having as its preconditions a military solution.
3. Adherents of the status quo. This means being in favor of the present situation in the absence of other options, but envisaging a settlement at **some unspecified time in the future.**

Goals 1 and 2 are mainly shared by people in the Arab world, while goals 1 and 3 are mainly shared by people in Israel. It follows from this that it is only goal 1 that is shared by both conflict parties, and thus the only goal about which there is scope for compatibility.

In coding we shall define beliefs along the dimension of positive-negative toward a negotiated settlement. When positive the actor is characterized as conciliatory, when negative he is called non-conciliatory.

In the interviews there will hardly be any respondent who is purely conciliatory or non-conciliatory. There will be a mixture of both conciliatory and non-conciliatory thinking. But some respondents will emphasize conciliatory thinking more than others. It is this variation in thinking that we are interested in revealing through the coding of the answers.

To get a better idea of how the answers should be coded, it is important that you study the examples listed below.

To avoid any 'echo' effect in the coding process, that is, the coding of an answer being influenced by knowing the respondent's answer to other questions, you should take five protocols at a time and code each single question across all protocols before starting on the next question.

(The category 'don't know' has been dropped in the analysis. It appeared in a very low frequency.)

In the category 'mixed' all statements that are ambiguous in content should be coded, but do study the statement *very* carefully before coding in this category. Many statements appearing at first glance as ambiguous, can often by a more careful examination be scaled as belonging to one of the other two categories.

If UN Resolution 242 were implemented, who do you think will gain and lose?

FAVORABLE
Arab categories: THE ARABS WILL GAIN
— the Arabs will get back the occupied areas
— the resolution puts an end to Israel's expansionist strategy
— the resolution opens the way for a peaceful solution of the conflict
— the resolution will enable the countries in the area to use their resources for social and economic development and thus be advantageous for everybody

Israeli categories: THE RESOLUTION WILL GIVE TERRITORIES TO THE ARABS AND SECURITY TO ISRAEL
— both will gain
— the conflict is not zero-sum
— it is too vague, but contains some elements of cleverness

6 — The Arab-Israeli Conflict

MIXED

Arab categories:
— the resolution will not lead to a final solution of the conflict
— the Arabs will only control 25 % of Palestine if the resolution is implemented

Israeli categories:
— thePalestinians will remain refugees forever if the resolution is carried through
— we will gain provided that the Israeli interpretation is respected, then it might lead to peace

UNFAVORABLE

Arab categories:
ISRAEL WILL GAIN
— the resolution is a favorable barter for Israel; by returning territories that have never belonged to them, the Israelis will achieve peace
— the resolution guarantees secure borders for Israel

THE PALESTINIANS WILL LOSE
— the established regimes will gain — the Palestinians will lose the rights to their homeland
— the resolution will not solve the Palestinian problem

Israeli categories:
THE RESOLUTION IS OF NO INTEREST
— it will not lead to peace
— it only gives vague promises to Israel and those are not worth anything
— it presupposes involvement by the superpowers and that is no good

Don't know:
Depends on the interpretation

What parts of the territories occupied during the 1967-war do you consider most vital for you to keep (Israeli side)/to get back (Arab side)?

UNCOMPROMISING

Arab categories:
ALL OF THEM
— every inch of the occupied territories is important for us to get back
— all of the occupied territories, of course; would you give away parts of your own country?

Israeli categories:
— all of the territories are important to keep
— most of the territories are important to keep

MIXED

Arab categories:
ALL OF THEM AND IT IS POSSIBLE TO RANK THEM IN IMPORTANCE
— Sinai, Golan and the West Bank
— Jerusalem, West Bank, Golan and Sinai
— Egypt; Sinai; Syria; Golan; to Arabs: Jerusalem; to Palestinians: their homeland

Israeli categories:
SOME OF THEM, BUT IT IS NOT POSSIBLE TO RANK THEM IN IMPORTANCE
— if they mention anyone of the following, code as mixed:

162

Golan, Sinai, West Bank, Jerusalem, Gaza-Strip, Sharm-el-Sheikh
— they mention only: Golan, Sharm-el-Sheikh, Jerusalem
— views differ

COMPROMISING

Arab categories: SOME OF THE TERRITORIES, BUT IT IS NOT POSSIBLE TO RANK THEM IN IMPORTANCE
— Jerusalem
— West Bank
— Golan
— Sinai
— Gaza
— Suez Canal
— Golan, Jerusalem
— Sinai, Golan, Jerusalem
— Sinai, Sharm-el-Sheikh, Golan, Jerusalem, Gaza Strip, West Bank

Israeli categories: NONE OF THE TERRITORIES IS IMPORTANT TO KEEP

What parts of the territories do you consider most vital for the other side to get back (Israeli side)/to keep (Arab side)?

UNCOMPROMISING

Arab categories: NONE OF THE TERRITORIES IS VITAL FOR ISRAEL TO KEEP
— several answers fall within this category, but the answers are generally not commented on further

Israeli categories: — we have to keep the territories for strategic reasons
— if we felt secure, we would need no territories
— no territories should be given back before the Arabs show peaceful intentions
— historic and religious rights say we should keep the West Bank
— we should keep all the territories

MIXED

Arab categories:

Israeli categories: — territories can be given back if compensated by security guarantees
— we must keep Jerusalem
— we should keep the Golan
— we should keep some of the territories

COMPROMISING

Arab categories: SOME OF THE TERRITORIES ARE IMPORTANT FOR THE ISRAELIS TO KEEP, BUT IT IS NOT POSSIBLE TO RANK THEM IN IMPORTANCE
— Golan heights
— West Bank
— Jerusalem

— Sinai
— Gaza

SOME OF THE TERRITORIES ARE IMPORTANT FOR
THE ISRAELIS TO KEEP, AND IT IS POSSIBLE TO
RANK THEM IN IMPORTANCE
— Golan heights
— Golan heights, Tiran Straits, Gulf of Akaba
— Golan heights, Jerusalem, Sharm-el-Sheikh
— Golan heights, Mitla Pass

Israeli categories: — the territories should be given back (some of them) because of the idea of a Jewish state
— the territories should be given back (some of them) because it is not fair to take them from the Arabs
— we should give the territories back except some minor parts
— all the territories should be given back

How do you see the solution of the Palestinian problem?

UNCOMPROMISING
Arab categories: BY RESTORING THE LEGITIMATE RIGHTS OF THE PALESTINIAN PEOPLE
— self-determination for the Palestinians
— Palestinians should be allowed to return to their homes in the areas now controlled by Israelis
— a democratic secular state should be established (Palestinian democratic state consisting of the Palestine Mandate area where Jews and Palestinians live together)

CONTINUED BATTLE AGAINST ISRAEL.
END OF ZIONISM

Israeli categories: THERE IS NO SOLUTION — DO NOT BELIEVE IN A SOLUTION
— the problem is not important to me
THE OPPONENT MUST FIND THE SOLUTION
THE PALESTINIANS THEMSELVES MUST FIND THE SOLUTION
— there should be more unity among the Palestinians
— Jordan/Palestinian state
— I don't know what the problem is
— Palestinians not a nation
— part of solution Israel-Jordan

MIXED
Arab categories: THE PALESTINIANS MUST DECIDE
— a plebiscite among the Palestinians should be held in order to determine the establishment of a Palestinian state

Israeli categories:

COMPROMISING
Arab categories: — those Palestinians not wishing to return should be compensated by Israel

— a separate Palestinian state should be established consisting of the West Bank/Gaza/Jerusalem

IMPLEMENTATION OF UN RESOLUTIONS
— implementing all the UN resolutions from 1947 to 1974
— implementing UN resolution 242

CHANGE IN MENTALITY
— Israel must recognize the PLO
— better communication between Israel and Arabs/Palestinians
— negotiations between Israel and PLO

Israeli categories: OUR SIDE SHOULD CONTRIBUTE MORE TO THE SOLUTION
— we should change our mentality

BOTH SIDES COULD DO MORE TO FIND A SOLUTION
— better communication
— change of mentality

CONCRETE PROPOSALS
— some kind of entity is necessary

What are your goals in the conflict?

BELLIGERENT

Arab categories: RESTORATION OF THE NATIONAL RIGHTS OF THE PALESTINIAN PEOPLE
— establish a Palestinian state outside Israel on parts of the old Palestine

REVOLUTION IN THE ARAB WORLD
LIBERATION OF THE WHOLE OF PALESTINE
— establish a secular state where rights and duties are not determined by religious affiliation

STOP ISRAELI EXPANSIONISM
— crush Zionism

GET RID OF WESTERN IMPERIALISM

Israeli categories: STRENGTHEN THE JEWISH PEOPLE (ZIONISM)
— it is very important to get all Jews to Israel

WE WANT TO STOP ENEMY ATTACKS
— we have to be strong enough to withstand the enemy
— we should go back to our culture

MIXED

Arab categories: REGAIN OCCUPIED TERRITORIES
— our goal is to liberate all the occupied territories

— it is necessary to regain the occupied territories to bring
about peace
— because of Israeli expansionism our main goal has
become to regain the occupied territories
— to achieve Arab Unity

Israeli categories: WE WANT RECOGNITION
— all we want is to be recognized by the Arabs

WE WANT SECURITY
WE WANT TO STOP ENEMY ATTACKS
— we have to be strong enough to withstand the enemy
— we have to be strong economically

ACCOMMODATIVE

Arab categories: RESTORATION OF PEACE IN THE MIDDLE EAST
— our goal is peaceful relations with all the countries in the
area, even Israel
— we want a peaceful settlement of the conflict

IMPLEMENTATION OF THE UN RESOLUTIONS
— implementation of the UN resolutions is the best way to
create peace

CONVINCE ISRAEL ABOUT PEACEFUL
COEXISTENCE
— our goal is to convince Israel that it is best for her to
live in peace with her neighbours
— we have to force Israel to live in peace with her neighbours .

CONVINCE ISRAEL THAT SHE WILL NOT WIN

MILITARILY
CULTURAL INDEPENDENCE
— our goal is cultural independence based on a strong
economic basis

ECONOMIC DEVELOPMENT
— our goal is economic development, social development
and social reforms

Israeli categories: WE ARE WILLING TO WITHDRAW IF THE ARABS
LEAVE US IN PEACE
OUR GOAL IS PEACE
— our goal is to establish social justice inside Israel
— our goal is survival
— to be recognized as part of the Middle East
— the majority of Israelis want peace

*Are there any differences concerning the goals and strategies of your side in the
conflict?*

NO DIFFERENCES

Arab categories: — there are no differences concerning the goals and strategies of Egypt/Jordan/Lebanon
— there are no differences concerning the goals and strat-

egies of the Arab side
— these are national goals
— our goals are also approved by all our Arab friends

Israeli categories: — there are no differences concerning the goals and strategies of Israel
— there is one basic issue for all of us

NEUTRAL (INSIGNIFICANT DIFFERENCES)
Arab categories: — small groups in Egypt/Jordan/Lebanon disagree, but these have very little influence
— there are some minor groups in the Arab world that disagree, but they have no/little influence
— differences concerning tactics only
— the majority agrees on the present goals

Israeli categories: — minor groups in Israel disagree, but they have little or no influence
— only differences on the surface — basic agreement on security
— basic agreement — despite some differences

SIGNIFICANT DIFFERENCES
Arab categories: — disagreement about the use of political or military strategy in Egypt/Jordan/Lebanon
— disagreement in Egypt/Jordan/Lebanon about accepting Israel as a sovereign state
— major differences between reactionary Arab states (Jordan, Egypt, Saudi-Arabia) who want status quo, and the Palestinians who want revolution and liberation
— the Arab states want to get back what they lost in the June war, the Palestinians want a secular state

Israeli categories: — no differences concerning religious, secular, nationalistic aim, but differences of *means*
— differences in ideology
— everybody has his own definition of peace

What do you think are the basic good and bad aspects of your side in the conflict?

WE ARE GOOD
Arab categories: WE ARE DOING THE RIGHT THING
— we are fighting for a just cause
— we are fighting for our rights
— all we want is to live in peace/get back our land
— we are fighting in order to bring about a peaceful solution/negotiated solution/just solution
— we have peaceful intentions
— we are fighting to achieve the legitimate rights of the Palestinians

WE ARE GETTING MORE AND MORE REALISTIC
— we understand that we have to solve our own problems

— we have started to concentrate on internal economic and social development
— we are less concerned with ideology
— we have proved to be good soldiers
— we have shown that we can use our resources effectively
— we have learnt to explain our cause to the world

WE ARE GETTING UNITED
— unity has enabled us to carry out the oil embargo

THERE IS NO DISCRIMINATION

WE DO NOT PLAN ON ELIMINATING THE ENEMY

Israeli categories:
— we have a strong faith and a high morale
— there is a strong solidarity
— Israeli mentality is peaceful
— we cherish human life
— we do not hate the enemy like the Arabs
— we recognize the rights of all people
— we have an enormous strength
— history has made the Jews a strong people
— we do not want to die without meaning
— we keep to reality
— suffering gives achievement
— Israel works for peace
— we are willing to experiment
— Israel carries on a reasonable humanistic policy
— Israel is democratic, which is unique in this part of the world

MIXED (BOTH GOOD AND BAD)
Arab categories:

(If the respondent starts out by mentioning bad sides first, this often indicates a more balanced attitude)

Israeli categories:
— it is not possible to generalize
— you cannot speak about good and bad aspects
— we are what we are because of the historical process
— not good or bad
— some of our policies are good — some are bad

WE ARE BAD
Arab categories:

BAD STRATEGY
— we are not able to explain our point of view to the world
— we have bad propaganda
— Arab leaders use extreme expressions

LACK OF UNITY
— rivalry between Arab countries
— different use of goals and strategies

DO NOT ACT WITH SUFFICIENT REALISM
— have not realized that the superpowers want to promote their own interests
— extreme actions (guerrilla actions abroad)

168

MINOR GROUPS WANT TO ELIMINATE ISRAEL
— extremism

Israeli categories:
— we are intolerant
— we are impatient
— we are too self-confident
— we are chauvinistic
— we have bad manners
— we are too pessimistic
— we have a strong emotional shift
— we interpret information in an extreme way
— we have too much fear of the enemy
— we have not managed to demonstrate Arab aggressiveness clearly enough to the world
— our relationship with the Palestinians can be criticized
— Israel should have recognized the Palestinians as a national unity
— we looked at the conflict as not solvable
— we have some fanatics
— there is poverty in Israel
— we have isolated ourselves in relation to the Arabs

Do you see any elements in your own country working against peace?

NO ELEMENTS WORKING AGAINST PEACE
Arab categories:
— there are groups with special views and meanings about a peaceful solution, but this does not mean they are against peace
— if peace means that the occupied areas will be given back to Egypt, there is nobody against peace
— there is nobody in the Arab world working against peace, but there are different views on how to solve the conflict
— it might look as if some groups are working against peace, but they are working for justice

Israeli categories:
— everyone wants peace

NEUTRAL (INSIGNIFICANT ELEMENTS WORKING AGAINST PEACE)
Arab categories:
— minor groups are working against peace, but they have no significance
— a few extreme groups are working against peace
— some religious fanatics are working against peace
— some communists are working against peace
— some minorities are working against peace

Israeli categories:
— those who work against peace have no influence on Israeli policy
— a small fraction. Some of the tactics of Likud

SIGNIFICANT ELEMENTS WORKING AGAINST PEACE
Arab categories:
— all the students are against peace
— those who support UN resolution 242 are against peace

— the Palestinian resistance movement is working against peace
— the reactionary Arab regimes are working against peace

Israeli categories: — some conservative and religious groups make compromise more difficult
— there are people who refer to themselves as 'Land of Israel movement'

Do you think that the other side is threatening you?
YES
Arab categories: ISRAEL IS THREATENING US
— Israel's policies are Zionism or of a Zionist character
— Israel is expansionistic
— Israel has expansionist goals
— they want to establish greater Israel from the Euphrates to the Nile
— Israel is constantly threatening us by military means

ISRAEL IS THREATENING US BECAUSE OF POTENTIAL ECONOMIC DOMINANCE
— Israel is planning to become a local superpower
— Israel is a technologically advanced society with the support of the US and may be able to dominate the area economically

ISRAEL ABSORBS THE ENERGY AND RESOURCES OF THE ARAB WORLD
— the conflict with Israel prevents economic and social development

Israeli categories: — the Arabs want to destroy us
— the Arabs want to exterminate us
— the Arabs want to liquidate us
— the Arabs want to finish us
— the Arabs want to wipe us out
— we should not trust peace feelers
— the Arabs *may* try to exterminate us, but I am an optimist
— if all Arabs united, Israel may possibly cease to exist

MIXED (BOTH YES AND NO)
Arab categories: THE THREAT IS REDUCED AFTER THE OCTOBER WAR
Israeli categories: — we hope that the streams of moderation will influence the leadership

SOME WILL ELIMINATE US, SOME NOT
— Egypt wants peace, others not
— they want to see Israel disappear but have realistic considerations as well

NO
Arab categories: ISRAEL IS NOT THREATENING US
— we don't feel threatened after the October war because

170

of the Israeli defeat
— our victory in the October war shows that we have become as strong as/stronger than the Israelis

WE ARE GETTING STRONGER
— Israel is threatening us, but that is rapidly changing with the strengthening of the liberation movement
— Israel is very pleased with the present situation

Israeli categories: THE ENEMY WANTS TO ELIMINATE US BUT THEY ARE NOT STRONG ENOUGH
— they want to, but the possibilities are slight
— the danger of wiping out Israel is now far less
— they would like to, but realize now that it is not possible, do not have the capabilities
— in the past they wanted to, but not now
— not at the moment

In what way and how much is your side dependent on the superpowers?

DEPENDENT ON BOTH SUPERPOWERS
Arab categories: — we need the support of both superpowers
— militarily we are dependent on the SU, politically on the USA
— to establish peace we need the support of both superpowers
— like most developing countries we depend on support from the superpowers
— we are dependent on the superpowers because they have a monopoly of modern arms
— we try to stay equally dependent on both superpowers in order to maximize the support they can give us

Israeli categories: — we are dependent on the relationship between the superpowers (to reach a settlement)
— directly on USA, indirectly on the SU

DEPENDENT ON THE USA
Arab categories: — politically we are solely dependent on the USA, because USA is the only power that can push Israel back
— we are dependent on the USA militarily
— we are dependent on the USA economically
— USA is the only superpower that can supply us with foreign currencies needed for social and economic development
— Jordan is the country most dependent on the USA

Israeli categories: — we are dependent on the shipments of armaments from
— we are politically dependent on the USA
— the withdrawal from Sinai in 1956 and the last part of the October war proves that we are both militarily and politically dependent on the USA
the USA

WE ARE ECONOMICALLY DEPENDENT ON THE USA

— we are getting more strongly dependent on the USA

THE SU MAKES US DEPENDENT ON THE USA
— for arms we are dependent (USA does not have to be
mentioned explicitly)

DEPENDENT ON THE SOVIET UNION
Arab categories:
— we are dependent on the SU in the military field
— since 1955 we have been very dependent on the SU
— Syria is the country most dependent on the SU
    — both militarily and economically

Israeli categories:

NOT DEPENDENT ON ANY OF THE SUPERPOWERS
Arab categories:
— we cooperate with all the countries that want peace and
friendship
— we depend on the superpowers both militarily and economically, but this does not mean that we are satellites
of the superpowers — politically we are totally independent
— the dependency is mutual — the superpowers are also
dependent on the Arabs because of their oil monopoly
— other nations are becoming more and more dependent
on us
— all countries in the world are dependent on the superpowers

Israeli categories: WE CAN ONLY TRUST OURSELVES, THEREFORE
WE SHOULD FIGHT FOR INDEPENDENCE

WE WILL BECOME LESS DEPENDENT ON THE USA
BECAUSE OF OUR MILITARY PRODUCTION

WE ARE NOT DEPENDENT ON THE USA
— it is of vital interest to defend Israeli existence indepen-
dently of the USA
— not more than Norway
— it is a two-way relationship

*In what way do you think that the UN and the superpowers can influence a
peace solution?*

FAVORABLE
Arab categories: THE SUPERPOWERS CAN INFLUENCE A PEACE
SOLUTION
— the superpowers have influence to secure an implementation of UN resolution 242
— the policy of détente between the superpowers will enable
them to take initiatives for peace
— the superpowers are able to enforce a peaceful solution
in the Middle East
— as a result of the Arab victory in the October war and
the Oil Embargo the superpowers have already started
to cooperate in order to bring about a peaceful solution
— if the superpower cooperation is carried out within the
framework of the UN they can influence a peace solution

172

— the superpowers — especially the USA — can force Israel to accept UN resolution 242

THE UN CAN PLAY A CONSTRUCTIVE ROLE
— the UN can only influence a peace solution if the superpowers cooperate within the Security Council

Israeli categories:
— in principle the superpowers can, but they have not managed so far
— the superpowers can if they agree
— superpowers can influence but within certain limits
— we are mere puppets of the superpowers

MIXED
Arab categories:
Israeli categories:
— superpowers can influence, but peace basically has to be worked out here

UNFAVORABLE
Arab categories:

THE SUPERPOWERS CANNOT INFLUENCE A PEACE SOLUTION
— the superpowers have no interest to influence a peace solution
— the Soviet Union is interested in a high level of conflict in order to maximize political influence
— the USA is unable to act unbiased because US Middle East policy is determined by the Jewish population in the US

THE UN CANNOT PLAY A CONSTRUCTIVE ROLE
— the UN has not the power to influence a peace solution
— the UN is unable to make guarantees for a peace solution
— the UN becomes tied hand and foot if the superpowers disagree

Israeli categories:
— one power works for peace, the other not
— if they agree the superpowers can, but I don't believe it

In what way and how much is the other side dependent on the superpowers?

DEPENDENT ON BOTH SUPERPOWERS
Arab categories:
— that the Jews are allowed to emigrate from the SU shows that the superpowers work together with Israel

Israeli categories:
— underdevelopment in the Arab world makes the Arabs dependent on the superpowers
— because they are backward and underdeveloped the Arabs are dependent on the superpowers
— get the maximum out of both superpowers

DEPENDENT ON THE USA
Arab categories:
— Israel cannot survive without economic or military help from the USA
— Israel is totally dependent on the USA both militarily, economically, morally and politically
— Israel is a springboard for US imperialism

— it is not friendship, but an alliance — Israel and USA both need each other
— Israel is the 51st state in the USA
— Israel is dependent on the USA from the loaf of bread to the Phantom fighter
— the October war proved Israel's total dependence on the USA

Israeli categories:

DEPENDENT ON THE SOVIET UNION
Arab categories: — the immigration of Soviet Jews has made Israel dependent on the SU
— SU provides a lot of indirect support to Israel by refusing weapons to Egypt
— SU supported Israel by maintaining status quo
— there must be some understanding between the SU and Israel since Jews are allowed to emigrate
— the SU supported the foundation of the state of Israel

Israeli categories:

SOME ARAB STATES ARE NOT SOVEREIGN STATES

BECAUSE OF THEIR DEPENDENCY ON THE SU
— it is not only a question of dependency, it goes further than that

THE ARABS ARE DEPENDENT ON THE SU FOR WEAPONS
— without the weapons from the SU the Arabs will not be able to do anything

NOT DEPENDENT ON ANY SUPERPOWER
Arab categories:
Israeli categories: — they cannot dictate to Egypt — they are less dependent
— the need for energy has made the Arabs more independent
— OPEC has made the Arabs more independent
— the Arabs are very independent when in unity
— with their enormous resources they are not
— less than Israel

What are the goals of the other side in the conflict?

BELLIGERENT
Arab categories:

ISRAEL IS EXPANSIONISTIC
— Israel now wants more land
— Israel wants to establish Greater Israel
— history proves that Israel is expansionistic
— the whole logic of Israel is expansion
— Israel wants economic expansion
— Zionism proves the real expansionistic character of Israel

ISRAEL WANTS TO BECOME A DOMINATING POWER
— Israel plans to dominate the Middle East militarily, politically and economically

174

— Israel wants to become a superpower in the area
— Israel wants to dominate the Middle East militarily on the basis of the notion that the Arabs can only be dealt with by force
— they want to dominate the world

CONSOLIDATION NOW BUT EXPANSION LATER
— peace for some years, then further expansion
— Israel wants to regain her confidence both internally and in relation to the USA
— Israel is not serious when she is talking of peace
— to maintain a permanent state of war in the area

ISRAEL WANTS TO CRUSH WHAT WE HAVE GAINED
— Israel wants to crush the Palestinian resistance movement
— Israel wants to split the Arabs and keep us weak
— Israel wants to split the Arab unity

Israeli categories: SYSTEM TRANSFORMATION
— the Arabs want to destroy us
— the Arabs want to establish a Palestinian state
— the Arabs want a Middle East without Israel
— the Arabs want a military solution of the conflict
— Libya and Iraq really teach us what the Arabs want
— want elimination of Israel politically
— get rid of Israel

MIXED
Arab categories: PEACE
— the young generation in Israel wants peace
— there are some peaceful elements in Israel
— minor groups in Israel want peace
— Oriental Jews are like the Arabs — they want to live in peace

CONSOLIDATION
— Israel wants security
— Israel wants maximum of security and believes that she has to keep territory to be secure
— Israel now wants status quo
— Israel now wants to keep as much territory as possible

CONSOLIDATION
— the Arabs want economic growth
— the Arabs want independence
— the Arabs want unity
— various, do not want to generalize
— Egypt wants a political solution
— Sadat's main concern is to keep himself in power
— different kind of goals, some will destroy us, some will not
— King Hussein wants to protect his kingdom
— the border states show a certain realism

175

THERE ARE DIFFERENT KINDS OF OPINIONS ON THE OTHER SIDE

ACCOMMODATIVE

Arab categories:
COMPROMISE NOW
— the most important thing for Israel is to be recognized as a sovereign state by her neighbors

Israeli categories:
THE OTHER SIDE WANTS TO GET A SOLUTION OF THE CONFLICT
— the other side wants to get back its territories
— do something for the Palestinians
— some evil elements do exist but I do not believe that they will turn into devils

Are there any differences concerning the goals and strategies of the other side?

NO DIFFERENCES

Arab categories:
— don't believe in distinction between Israeli hawks and doves — all Israelis are hawks

Israeli categories:
— what dominates Arab policy is the extermination of Israel and therefore there are no important differences

NEUTRAL (INSIGNIFICANT DIFFERENCES)

Arab categories:
— as in any other country there are in Israel differences concerning goals and strategies
— Jews in Israel and abroad have after the October war warned against following an aggressive and expansionistic policy, but these are still in the minority
— there is a growing revolutionary movement in Israel, this movement finds its main support among the Arabs in Israel
— there are differences within the ruling elite on how much to expand

Israeli categories:
— there are minor differences among the Arab states, especially between the confrontation states and the peripheral states
— basically they have the same goals, but there are differences, of course

SIGNIFICANT DIFFERENCES

Arab categories:
— the young generation in Israel disagrees with the elites
— the intellectuals oppose the ruling classes
— after the October war more people disagree with the government and want a peaceful solution
— there are differences between the founders of Israel and those settling afterwards
— many Jews, who are not Zionists, wish to live in peace with their neighbors
— the Israeli community is composed of two main sects: Jews and Zionists

176

Israeli categories:	— some states are more realistic than others
	— Egypt wants a political solution
	— the October war has lead to greater realism, they now understand that war is too costly
	— Jordan and Lebanon now want a political solution

What do you think are the basic good and bad aspects of the other side in the conflict?

THE OTHER SIDE IS GOOD

Arab categories: THE ISRAELIS ARE VERY EFFICIENT
— they have a technologically advanced society
— they have successful propaganda
— the Israelis have economic strength

THE ISRAELIS ARE UNITED
— they are united in goals and strategies

SOME GROUPS IN ISRAEL WORK FOR PEACE
— there is increased self-criticism after the October war
— there is opposition in Israel to the present policy (anti-Zionism)
— opposition in Israel has increased after the October war

THE ISRAELIS ARE JUSTIFIED IN ASKING FOR SECURITY
— the Israelis are dedicated to fighting for a secure existence
— I admire the Jewish people and their history

Israeli categories: — the Arabs are proud and self-confident
— the Arabs are hospitable
— the Arabs understand their own weakness
— the Arabs preserve their own culture
— Egypt wants a solution with Israel

MIXED (BALANCED: BOTH GOOD AND BAD)

Arab categories: — one cannot have an objective opinion on this
— the Israelis are neither good nor bad

Israeli categories: — I would not generalize, they are as any other people
— there are no permanent characteristics
— some good and some bad aspects

THE OTHER SIDE IS BAD

Arab categories: THE ISRAELIS ARE ZIONISTS
— they are aggressive and expansionistic
— they are racists
— they treat Arabs as secondary citizens
— they treat Palestinians as secondary citizens
— they discriminate between their own oriental Jews and European and American Jews
— they will not accept the legitimate rights of the Palestinians

PERSONALITY FACTORS
— the Israelis are militaristic

177

— the Israelis are arrogant
— they have a complex from the concentration camps
— the Israelis make the Arabs suffer because of their own background

THE ISRAELIS WILL NOT ACCEPT THE UN RESOLUTIONS
— the Israelis are not willing to compromise

THE ISRAELIS DESCRIBE THE ARABS AS ANTI-SEMITES

DON'T KNOW
— I don't know if the Israelis have any good aspects
— basically I can't see any good Israeli aspects
— if they have any good aspects, I hope to see them after Israel agrees on a peaceful solution
— the Israelis do not have any good aspects
— the injustice of the Israeli goals make any good aspects impossible
— the Israelis are like crazy capitalists caught in a dynamic process

Israeli categories:
— the Arabs refuse to negotiate with Israel
— they are against Israel and the Jews
— the Arabs distinguish between Jews and Zionism, this is false
— the Arab world lack democratic institutions
— they lack modernization
— the Arabs are fanatic because they are socially and economically backward
— they are afraid of Israeli dominance
— they do not appreciate the truth
— they do not have logic
— they lack imagination
— they are irrational
— they are fanatic
— they lack humanity
— they do not appreciate human life
— they are full of hatred
— they want to kill us

Do you see any elements on the other side working for peace?

NO ELEMENTS WORKING FOR PEACE
Arab categories:
— they say they want peace, but there is no effort or work for peace on the Israeli side
— Israel's expansionist intentions show that nobody is working for peace
— it is impossible to know what Israel really is doing/really wants
— because of the shock of the October war the Israelis seem to be more in favor of peace, but in reality the Israelis are not working for peace

178

— the Israelis keep talking about peace, but nobody is working for peace

Israeli categories: — there is nobody on the Arab side working for peace

NEUTRAL (INSIGNIFICANT ELEMENTS WORKING FOR PEACE)
Arab categories: — some elements working for peace, but their influence is marginal
— the October war has broken the Israeli myth of superiority and some groups are now working for peace
— some intellectuals and ideologists of the left are working for peace

Israeli categories: — some groups want peace, but they have no influence
— some groups want peace in their own interest, like the economic establishment in Egypt and Jordan
— maybe, but their peace is not my peace
— don't know (If there are, I should very much like to meet them)

SIGNIFICANT ELEMENTS WORKING FOR PEACE
Arab categories: — the young generation in Israel is working for paece
— increasing number of anti-Zionist Jews are working for peace
— after the October war the majority in Israel can accept a peaceful solution

Israeli categories: — there are certain groups now willing to make peace with Israel
— there are signs of change — some elements in the Arab establishment now want peace
— sometimes a person is identical to the policy of a whole nation: el Sadat has changed
— the Arab establishment fears radicalization
— economic elements in Egypt works for peace

Do you think that the other side believes that you are threatening them?

YES
Arab categories: THINK THE ISRAELIS FEEL THREATENED BECAUSE OF THE ARAB VICTORY
— the Israelis feel threatened because the Arabs have shown they are able to fight as well as the Israelis
— the Israelis feel threatened because of the October war
— the Israelis feel threatened because the Arabs for the first time in history have shown that they can act in unity

THE ISRAELIS HAVE REASON TO FEEL THREAT-ENED AS THEY CONSTITUTE A STRANGE ELEMENT IN THE AREA
— the Israelis have reason to feel threatened after occupying increasing areas of Arab land
— they must expect that the Arabs will make efforts to resist this

179

— naturally, since the Arabs and Muslims are determined to liberate the whole of Palestine

THE ISRAELIS' PREOCCUPATION WITH SECURITY SHOWS THAT THEY FEEL THREATENED
— all the wars have been started by Israel out of security reasons
— their pre-emptive strategy shows that they feel threatened

STUPID ARAB STATEMENTS HAVE MADE THE JEWS FEEL THREATENED
— extreme Arab propaganda has made the Israelis feel threatened

THE ISRAELIS GET CAUGHT IN THEIR OWN PROPAGANDA, THAT IS WHY THEY FEEL THREATENED
— the Israeli military has created a feeling of being threatened in the Israeli people because this is the best way to make the Jews sacrifice their lives for the sake of their country
— the Israelis feel threatened because they have been stupid
— the Israeli leaders have created a feeling of being threatened in the Israeli people through propaganda and indoctrination

THE ACTIONS OF TERRORISM FROM ISRAEL SHOW THAT THEY FEEL THREATENED

THEY FEEL THREATENED BECAUSE OF MUTUAL DISTRUST

Israeli categories:

THEY FEEL THREATENED BUT IT IS NOT RATIONAL
— there exist myths about Israel that they like to cultivate; it is not rational — population, territory and resources are much bigger in the Arab area so they should not feel threatened

THEY FEEL THREATENED BECAUSE OF THEIR RELIGION
— many cultures look upon the rest of the world as being barbarians
— the Arab religion accepts only Muslims

THEY THINK ISRAEL THREATENS THEM
— they believe Israel is expansionistic
— they believe Israel represents an economic threat
— feel threatened through the USA
— some definitely feel threatened — some speak about it because of propaganda
— they believe Israel represents a threat generally against Arab countries
— they have a fear of Israeli democracy
— they see Israel as a threat against Arab unity
— they look at Israel as an aggressive state
— Israel reminds them of their own weakness

180

MIXED (BOTH YES AND NO)

Arab categories:
— the Israeli elite does not feel threatened, but the common citizens do
— small groups feel threatened
— Israelis both feel and do not feel threatened because the Zionist ideology is an ideology of fear and superiority over others

Israeli categories:
— economically maybe, but expansion used as an excuse
— don't know, but maybe

NO

Arab categories:

THE ISRAELIS DO NOT FEEL THREATENED
— they say they are threatened, but they do not really feel that way
— they say they are threatened to attract goodwill internationally
— they tell the world that the Arabs are barbarians to gain sympathy
— they use experiences from Hitler's Germany to attract sympathy
— Israel's feeling of being threatened is a classical case of false consciousness
— they try to convince themselves that they are threatened
— they say they feel threatened in order to continue their unjust policy
— they use Arab declarations as excuses for going to war
— after all the wars we have lost, how can they feel threatened?

Israeli categories:

THE ARABS DO NOT FEEL THREATENED
— they do not feel threatened, but use it as a pretext to solve their own problems
— they use Israel to create unity
— they use Israel to mislead international opinion
— they have to say they feel threatened to justify the destruction of Israel
— use it to strengthen public opinion
— don't know — they talk that way, but we have no studies. Experts differ in views

In what way do you think the events in recent years have basically changed the conflict?

IMPROVED THE SITUATION OF OUR SIDE

Arab categories:

CHANGED THE BALANCE OF POWER IN THE AREA
— the Arabs proved in the October war they can inflict military losses on Israel
— the Arabs have shown they are equal in strength to Israel
— the October war reduced Israel's military superiority resulting from the 67 war
— the October war indicates military victory for the Arabs in the future

181

— the Arab military victory in the October war showed that the Arabs have become the stronger party in the conflict

THE OCTOBER WAR HAS RESTORED ARAB SELF-CONFIDENCE
— the Arabs have proved that they can fight
— the October war removed the myth that the Arabs were unable to fight
— the October war strengthened the Arabs' self-confidence

THE OCTOBER WAR OPENED NEW POSSIBILITIES FOR A SOLUTION OF THE CONFLICT
— the war broke the situation of no peace/no war/active work for peace
— the October war forced the superpowers to try to solve the conflict by diplomatic means
— the October war forced Israel to give up her policy of status quo
— the Arabs' progress/victory in the October war made it possible for Egypt to take new initiatives for a peaceful solution

THE OCTOBER WAR HAS LED TO INCREASED ARABIC UNITY
— President Sadat's leadership made Arabic unity possible
— the October war has made the Arabs more pragmatic

THE ISRAELIS HAVE BECOME MORE ISOLATED
— the October war changed the official US views on the conflict
— world public opinion has become more balanced
— world public opinion has become more pro-Arab

THE ISRAELIS HAVE LOST THEIR SELF-CONFIDENCE
— the October war ended the myth of Israel's cultural, technological and military superiority
— the October war showed that the Arabs possessed means to stop Israeli expansionism
— the October war ended the myth of secure borders through expansion of territory
— the October war proved to Israel that military power was unable to bring about a solution of the conflict

THE PALESTINIAN PROBLEM IS NOW MORE IN FOCUS
— because of the October war + the Oil Embargo the world has become more interested in solving the conflict and securing the rights of the Palestinians

Israeli categories:
— Palestinians on the West Bank are now far friendlier to us
— groups in Egypt and Jordan are now friendlier to us
— Israel's chance of survival is now better
— Israel has now territory, oil, and more water

182

     — there is increasing realism — particularly in Egypt
     — the Arabs can now agree to a compromise more easily without getting their pride hurt

NEUTRAL
Arab categories:
     — the conflict is essentially the same
     — the events have changed nothing — Israel will only change tactics
     — significant changes on both sides
     — basic nature has not changed

Israeli categories:
     — there is now more realism on both sides
     — the conflict has grown in size — more actors are involved — military activity has increased
     — the superpowers are getting more and more involved
     — conflict more acute, more advantageous to both sides
     — brought out new elements on both sides
     — the conflict is now in the hands of the superpowers (October war changed relations completely — no reference to what way.)
     — don't know in which direction — in whose favor
     — nature of conflict has not changed. Too early to analyze

WORSENED THE SITUATION OF OUR SIDE
Arab categories:

Israeli categories:
     — an Israeli military victory is now less likely
     — the Arabs have got their revenge
     — the Arabs are now stronger vis-à-vis the world
     — the Arabs are starting to gain power on Israel militarily
     — the situation could be drastic for Israel
     — the victory in 1967 intoxicated the Israelis — the infighting after the October war has strengthened this tendency
     — the Israelis now understand that they cannot always win a war
     — the Arabs are getting more and more hostile to Israel
     — the Arabs have been given new hope that they can beat Israel
     — Israeli Jews have been reactivated

In what way has the Civil war in Jordan influenced the conflict?

ADVANTAGEOUS TO OUR SIDE
Arab categories:
     — increased sympathy for the Palestinians in the Arab world
     — increased understanding for the Palestinian cause in world public opinion
     — the Palestinian problem more in focus
     — the world realized the Palestinians constitute a national entity and consequently are entitled to their own country
     — demonstrated the fallacy of overlooking the Palestinians as a source of power
     — demonstrated to the Jordanian regime the necessity of giving the Palestinians freedom to express their opinions
     — gave an opportunity to unmask Zionism
Israeli categories:
     — Hussein is stronger

NEUTRAL (ADVANTAGEOUS TO NOBODY)

Arab categories:
— the war had no influence on the conflict
— there was no civil war
— the hatred among the Palestinians increased
— no comments
— refused to answer

Israeli categories:
— advantages to nobody, mostly a local problem
— marginal importance
— raised tensions only
— superficial change, no basic change

ADVANTAGEOUS TO THE OPPONENT

Arab categories:

WEAKENED THE ARAB SIDE IN THE CONFLICT WITH ISRAEL
— the civil war resulted in increased disagreement in the Arab world
— the civil war stressed conflicting interests between Arab states
— the civil war made it difficult for the Arab states to act in unity
— created a bad 'image' of the Arabs abroad

WEAKENED THE PALESTINIANS
— made it more difficult for the Palestinians to promote their interests in the conflict with Israel
— deprived the Palestinians of an elective base in their fight with Israel
— resulted in decimation of the guerrillas and weakened the strength of the Palestinian resistance movement

Israeli categories:
— resulted in disagreement within the resistance movement

In what way have the activities of the guerrillas abroad influenced the conflict?

ADVANTAGEOUS TO OUR SIDE

Arab categories:
— it has brought the Palestinian problem into the focus of world attention
— international public opinion is now more conscious of the desperate situation of the Palestinian people
— it has made the goals of the Palestinians clear to the world
— it has shown that the Palestinians are determined to fight for their rights
— it has proved that peace is impossible without a solution of the Palestinian problem
— these actions have been bothersome to the Israelis

Israeli categories:
— it has discredited the cause of the Palestinians internationally

NEUTRAL (ADVANTAGEOUS TO NOBODY)

Arab categories:
— no effect, balanced effect, or effect that does not imply advantages to anybody
— unwilling to justify these actions, even though I understand the motives behind them

184

  — the guerrillas should fight on Israeli territory and fight against the military forces

  — the war has weakened the Arab cause abroad, but has brought the plight of the Palestinians to the world's attention

  — international stress

Israeli categories: — it has ruined initiatives for peace

  — it has led to an escalation of the conflict

  — not influenced the conflict — importance marginal

ADVANTAGEOUS TO THE OPPONENT

Arab categories: — these actions have weakened the cause of the Arabs abroad

  — the advantages have been less than the disadvantages

  — the world now sees the Arabs as aggressive and un-civilized people

  — the most violent actions have only given the Arabs enemies

  — these actions have weakened the Palestinians' cause

  — even through there are some good aspects, it has mainly been to the benefit of the enemy

Israeli categories: — they have made the Palestinian problem look like an international problem

  — it has focused world attention on the Palestinian problem

  — the Arab governments can profit by looking more moderate by comparing themselves with the Palestinians

  — Committed Arabs to the Palestinian problem

  — has made them a recognized element

In what way has the Oil Embargo influenced the conflict?

ADVANTAGEOUS TO OUR SIDE

Arab categories: IT HAS INFLUENCED USA AND WESTERN EUROPE

  — the West is now far more willing to support the Arabs

  — the West is now more objective

  — the Oil Embargo linked the conflict to the daily lives of Europeans and Americans

  — demonstrated Western Europe's and USA's dependence on the Arab countries

  — it forced the West to take initiatives

  — USA has become more pro-Arab

  STRENGTHENED ARAB UNITY

  — the Arabs appeared to constitute a unitary actor

  — proved that the Arabs were willing to sacrifice large incomes to stand united

  HELPED TO BREAK THE DEADLOCKED SITUATION IN THE AREA

  — forced the superpowers to take initiatives

  — increased the Arabs' diplomatic power

  — proved to be the Arabs' best (most effective) weapon

Israeli categories: — the embargo worked against its purpose
— it was a blow in the air
— other countries suffered rather than the ones the embargo was aimed at
— the Arabs really got international opinion against them

NEUTRAL (ADVANTAGEOUS TO NOBODY)
Arab categories: — the Oil Embargo could have been used far more intelligently
— the superpowers still work according to their own interest

Israeli categories: — it only served to ruin efforts toward peace
— effect will disappear in two-three years; it had both negative and positive effects for the Arabs
— it has had a considerable political impact
— weak influence because of US stand

ADVANTAGEOUS TO THE OPPONENT
Arab categories: — the embargo gave the impression that we are against the welfare of the rest of the world

Israeli categories: — it has isolated Israel internationally. Europe submitted to pressure
— it proves in times of crisis we can only trust ourselves
— the Arabs now have a lot more to buy weapons with
— it has strengthened Arab unity

What were the basic causes of the October war?

FAULT OF THE OPPONENT
Arab categories: OCTOBER WAR A RESULT OF ISRAELI OCCUPATION OF ARAB LAND
— the October war came because the Israelis refused to pull out of occupied territories
— the October war came as a result of the June war
— the October war was a result of Israeli expansionism

OCTOBER WAR A RESULT OF ISRAELI ARROGANCE
— Israel refused to respect the UN resolutions
— Israel worked actively to prevent a peaceful solution
— Israel arrogantly overlooked every initiative for peace from the Arab countries

OCTOBER WAR A RESULT OF A DEADLOCKED SITUATION
— Sadat did not succeed with diplomatic initiatives
— all peaceful efforts failed
— the war resulted from the Arabs' dedication to break the deadlocked situation

OCTOBER WAR A RESULT OF THE UNSOLVED PALESTINIAN PROBLEM
— only a war would convince Israel that the Palestinian problem had to be solved

186

OCTOBER WAR A RESULT OF ARAB HUMILIATION IN 1967
— the Arabs wanted to prove they were able to fight bravely

Israeli categories:
— since the Arabs were not willing to compromise the war came
— the war was just another attempt to eliminate Israel
— the war was just another expression of Arab aggression that needs outlet from time to time
— the Arabs did not accept the status quo
— there was a general frustration on the Arab side because of the deadlock, but negotiations were not possible
— no way could be found to return territories

FAULT OF OUR SIDE
Arab categories:

Israeli categories:
— both sides have their share in the responsibilities

FAULT OF OUTSIDE POWERS
Arab categories:
— the USA did nothing to pressure Israel
— had to launch a war to get the superpowers to do their duty
— the war resulted from the superpowers' decision to preserve status quo

Israeli categories:
— the SU has the responsibility
— the weapon deliveries from the SU
— the interest of the SU to keep the conflict boiling
— the SU encouraged the Arabs to go to war

As regards the political situation, what would you like to see happen in the Middle East in the near future?

SOLUTION OF CONFLICT (PEACE)
Arab categories:
HOPE TO SEE A LASTING PEACE IN THE AREA
— a peace agreement based on justice
— a peace agreement satisfying the demands of both the Israelis and the Arabs
— a peace agreement which will be a foundation for prosperity, security, and stability

HOPE TO SEE A JUST POLITICAL SOLUTION OF CONFLICT
— a solution based on the UN resolutions

HOPE TO SEE DEVELOPMENT OF A GOOD POLITICAL RELATIONSHIP BETWEEN THE COUNTRIES IN THE AREA AND THE REST OF THE WORLD
— a relationship where the actors regard each other as equal

Israeli categories:
— we want peace
— we want a process toward peace
— we want separation of forces

- we want serious peace negotiations
- we want various actions to initiate peace, such as increased communication (policy of open bridges), increased economic cooperation, research, transport
- cooperation desirable but not realistic presently
- we want disarmament

MIXED (SOLUTION BUT OUR DEMANDS MUST BE MET)
Arab categories: HOPE TO SEE A JUST POLITICAL SOLUTION
- a solution based on negotiations in which the Palestinians take part
- a solution based on the principle: no acquisition of territories by force

HOPE TO SEE SELF-DETERMINATION FOR THE PALESTINIANS
- that the Palestinians will be allowed to return to their land
- that the Palestinians will be given their legitimate rights
- that the Palestinians will be allowed to establish a democratic Palestinian state

HOPE TO SEE ISRAELI WITHDRAWAL FROM OCCUPIED TERRITORIES
- that the Arabs get their land bock, as this will permit a solution of the Palestine problem

Israeli categories:
- we want peace but this is a gradual process
- we want peace but this is dependent on the other side
- we hope the Arabs will recognize Israel
- we hope the Arabs will stop killing innocent Jews
- we want security guarantees

STRENGTHENING OF OUR SIDE
Arab categories: HOPE TO SEE CONTINUED ARAB UNITY
- that the tendencies to Arab unity witnessed during the October war will be preserved and strengthened
- increased Arab unity as this will solve the conflict
- a federation of Arab states

HOPE THE PEOPLES IN THE AREA WILL MERGE THEIR RESOURCES TO WORK FOR DEVELOPMENT
- hope the peoples will join forces to work for economic and material development

Israeli categories:
- Arabs stop worrying about Israel

Now speaking realistically, what would you actually expect to happen?

OPTIMISTIC
Arab categories: PEACEFUL SOLUTION OF THE CONFLICT
- disengagement agreements will be established
- Israel will withdraw from most of the occupied territories
- Israel will withdraw to 1967-borders

— the parties to the conflict will work out an agreement at the Geneva negotiations

PALESTINIAN STATE WILL BE ESTABLISHED
— a Palestinian state on the West Bank
— a Palestinian state on parts of the occupied territories
— a secular democratic state will be established
— creation of a Palestinian state and maybe a small confederation between a Palestinian state, Trans-Jordan, Syria and Lebanon

CULTURAL AND ECONOMIC INDEPENDENCE FOR THE ARABS.
INCREASED PRESSURE ON ISRAEL
— the Arabs will unite

Israeli categories: PEACEFUL SOLUTION OF THE CONFLICT
— in the long run I think there will be peace
— conflict can develop in both directions, but I see some real movements for peace now

MIXED
Arab categories:
— Geneva Conference takes place, but can't predict any solutions
— a very long period of negotiations
— lack of understanding from Zionism but in the end our own state
— dependent on the American role in solving the problems

Israeli categories: THE FUTURE WILL DEPEND ON SOME CONCRETE EVENTS
— Sadat accepts what Israel can offer
— it depends on how the Palestinians are dealt with
— it depends on whether or not the superpowers will cooperate or confront each other
— it depends on whether or not the USA can expand its influence
— there is an optimistic and a pessimistic trend. Progress on some issues — not on others

PESSIMISTIC
Arab categories: NO SOLUTION OF THE CONFLICT
— Israeli refusal to withdraw from the occupied territories
— a new deadlocked situation in the area
— Israel will refuse to accept a peaceful solution
— Jerusalem will be divided
— the revolution will continue
— I can only see continued destruction and death

Israeli categories: SOME AGREEMENTS WITH THE ENEMY BUT NO REAL PEACE
— even if Kissinger succeeds, the Arabs will continue toward their final aim
— after the October war the Arabs will be even more impatient

189

— the Arabs may agree to negotiate, but will break off and
attack again
— the question is not interesting because we will have to
prepare for the worst alternative
— maybe settlement after some fighting
— optimistic in the long run
— maybe some arrangements for a few years but then war
again

*Now realistically speaking, what would you actually expect to happen concerning
the new generation?*

WILL COMPROMISE
Arab categories: WILL BE MORE PEACE-MINDED
— the new generation has witnessed the cruelties of war
and wants a peaceful solution

WILL BE MORE REALISTIC

WILL GET USED TO THE EXISTENCE OF ISRAEL

Israeli categories: THE YOUNGER GENERATION IS MORE OPTIMISTIC
WHEN IT COMES TO THE POSSIBILITY OF PEACE

MIXED
Arab categories: HOPE THEY WILL OVERCOME THEIR BITTERNESS
WILL DO THEIR BEST TO DEVELOP THE COUNTRY
— they will build a strong new nation
— they understand Egypt is a poor country and will use all
resources to rebuild the country

Israeli categories: THERE IS NO DIFFERENCE BETWEEN THE
YOUNGER AND THE OLDER GENERATION
— there is no change

WILL NOT COMPROMISE
Arab categories: WILL NOT RELAX UNTIL A PEACEFUL SOLUTION
HAS BEEN REACHED
— will keep on fighting until the Palestinians are able to
return to their homes
— will continue the battle for a just solution

Israeli categories: THE YOUNGER GENERATION IS LESS OPTIMISTIC
WHEN IT COMES TO THE POSSIBILITY OF PEACE

*Now realistically speaking, what would you actually expect to happen concerning
the military situation?*

FAVORABLE TO OUR SIDE
Arab categories: THE ARABS WILL DOMINATE THE FUTURE
MILITARY SITUATION
— the October war gave a foretaste of the future Arab
dominance
— the only way to solve the conflict is to beat the opponent
by military means

    — the Arabs have learnt that they have to base their
     defences on military power
    — continue the battle until Arab rights have been achieved

Israeli categories: THE MILITARY SITUATION WILL DEVELOP MORE
       FAVORABLY FOR US
       — Israeli research and production will keep track with the
        development
       — the USA will not allow the military balance to tip in
        Israel's disfavor

MIXED
Arab categories: THE EXISTING MILITARY TENSION WILL BE
       REDUCED
       — a peaceful solution of the conflict will strongly reduce
        the military forces
       — the superpowers' interest in building peace will reduce
        military tension
       — prudent Israeli reactions to the changes caused by the
        October war will reduce military tension
       — military groups in Israel will try another war
       — a new deadlocked situation like the one between 1957
        and 1967
       — further military technification

Israeli categories: THERE WILL DEVELOP A BALANCE OF TERROR
       AND THE PARTIES WILL BE FACED WITH MUTUAL
       DESTRUCTION
       — technology will become more and more important
       THERE WILL NOT BE A BALANCE OF TERROR IN
       THE MIDDLE EAST BECAUSE OF CRAZY LEADERS
       — the military situation depends on the superpowers and
        is unpredictable

UNFAVORABLE TO OUR SIDE
Arab categories:

Israeli categories: THE MILITARY SITUATION WILL DEVELOP IN
       FAVOR OF THE ARABS
       Ex.: Sooner or later the Arabs will become stronger. As
       education in the Arab world increases, military ability will
       increase.
       — Modern technology makes the human factor less im-
        portant and that works in favor of the Arabs.
       — human factor will not be so important
       — the Russians worry me
       — may improve technologically but will not manage to win

*Now realistically speaking, what do you actually expect to happen concerning
international public opinion?*

FAVORABLE TO OUR SIDE
Arab categories: CHANGE IN FAVOR OF THE ARABS
       — it has already turned in favor of the Arabs as a result

of the Oil Embargo and the October war
— it will turn in favor of the Arabs in the future
— by seeking a peaceful solution of the conflict the Arabs can make international public opinion turn to their advantage
— by acting more realistically the Arabs can make international public opinion turn to their advantage
— by removing threatening aspects from Arab propaganda Israel would lose her support from international public opinion

MORE OBJECTIVE UNDERSTANDING OF THE ARABS' PROBLEMS
— will not base their opinions of the conflict only on Israeli propaganda
— will get more balanced understanding of the conflict

Israeli categories: INTERNATIONAL OPINION WILL STAY FRIENDLY TO US
BECOME MORE FRIENDLY TO ISRAEL

MIXED
Arab categories: WILL FORCE THE GOVERNMENTS TO END STATE OF WAR

Israeli categories:
— don't expect much change
— remain the same
— don't regard it as important
— not vital

UNFAVORABLE TO OUR SIDE
Arab categories: WILL NOT CHANGE IN FAVOR OF THE ARABS
— will continue to minimize the conflict
— the Arabs will not reach international public opinion with their views because of the negative images of the Arabs in Western culture
— because of lack of resources the Arab propaganda will be weak and unable to influence international public opinion

Israeli categories: INTERNATIONAL OPINION WILL NOT BECOME MORE FRIENDLY TO ISRAEL

Given what you would like to see happen in the Middle East in the near future, what do you think are the most effective ways to achieve these aims?

CONCILIATORY
Arab categories: MUTUAL UNDERSTANDING BETWEEN THE PEOPLES IN THE AREA
— better communication between the Arab countries and between the Arabs and the Israelis
— disengagement of military forces
— peace negotiations in Geneva
— peaceful solution based on restoration of the occupied areas

— by remembering that we are all human beings

INCREASED EFFORTS FROM THE SUPERPOWERS
— the superpowers — especially USA — have to apply pressure on Israel to change her position
— the superpowers must force Israel to accept UN resolution 242
— the superpowers must work together with the UN to achieve a peaceful solution

IMPLEMENTATION OF THE UN RESOLUTION
— the work for peace must be carried out within UN frameworks

ECONOMIC RECONSTRUCTION OF THE COUNTRIES IN THE AREA

Israeli categories: — the parties to the conflict should try to eliminate distrust by showing more understanding for each other

SHOULD TRY TO COOPERATE MORE WITH THE OPPONENT
— cooperate more, show diplomatic flexibility, attitude change

COMPROMISE ON ISSUES
— we should negotiate
— we should negotiate on certain conditions

OUTSIDE FORCES SHOULD TAKE ACTION
— the superpowers should try harder
— combine military force with mediation
— re-education of basic Israeli perceptions

NEUTRAL
Arab categories: ## SOLUTION OF THE PALESTINE PROBLEM
— by supporting the Palestinians in Lebanon, and then promoting negotiations between Palestinians and Israelis
— the Palestinians must take part in negotiations in Geneva
— Israel must be willing to solve the Palestine problem
— creation of mass institutions through democratic means

Israeli categories: — the other side should show more understanding
— the other side must change its attitude

REFRACTORY
Arab categories: ## UNITARY ARAB FRONT
— the Arab countries must join forces to beat Israel
— the liberation movements must act in unity
— the Arab states must force Israel to accept a peaceful solution — if necessary with military means
— an Israeli initiative to war will unite the Arabs

DECOLONIZATION OF PALESTINE
— the revolution must continue
— the Arabs and Muslims must embark on a war of liberation

Israeli categories: **WE SHOULD GET STRONGER VIS-A-VIS THE OPPONENT**
— we must become more united
— we must increase our military strength
— we must teach the opponent that we are stronger
— the parties should create peace themselves
— the other party has to change
— leadership
— we must need a lot of time
— direct negotiations
— Arabs must stop their hatred
— Arab regimes must be destroyed

How long do you think the conflict will last?

OPTIMISTIC
Arab categories: A FEW YEARS
— the conflict will be over by the end of the year
— the conflict will be over within a few years (1—5 years)
— the conflict will be over by the end of this decade (1980)
— it may remain 10, 20, or more years, but it will definitely result in Arab victory

Israeli categories: A FEW YEARS
MIXED
Arab categories: A GENERATION OR MORE
— the military and economic conflict will be solved fairly soon, but the psychological conflict will go on for generations
— the conflict will go on for generations

Israeli categories: A GENERATION OR MORE
— the military conflict will be solved in a few years from now, but the basic issues will not be solved for a generation or so
— It don't expect a solution for a least two generations/ several generations/ 200 years

PESSIMISTIC
Some good and bad trends — it depends

Arab categories: DO NOT SEE AN END TO IT
— the conflict will go on forever
— I can't see any end to it
— the conflict will not last in the present political or military form, but evolve into a cultural/ethnical conflict that will last forever
— for 50 or 100 years, maybe longer
— until the end of the century, if not solved then it will continue forever

Israeli categories: DO NOT SEE AN END TO IT
— I am basically pessimistic

194

— the enemy will be persistent
— it will take a long time
— I hope I will experience the end of it

DON'T KNOW

Arab categories:
— don't know how long the conflict will last
— it is impossible to try to guess when the conflict will be solved
— depends on the attitude of Israel: if this is changed it is impossible to say
— it is up to Israel how long the conflict will last: as long as Israel remains a pure Jewish state based on Zionism, the conflict will last
— depends on the attitude of the USA, as long as USA continues its one-sided support of Israel, the conflict will last
— as long as the immigration of Jews from the whole world continues, the conflict will last
— the conflict will last as long as Israel exists
— the conflict will last as long as the source of the conflict — the Palestinian problem — remains unsolved
— the conflict will last until the Arabs achieve cultural independence based on a strong economic foundation
— the conflict will last until the Israeli entity has become integrated in the Arab world

Israeli categories:
Ex.: This will depend on a lot of factors: internal conditions in the Arab world, the global development, especially the relation with the USA and SU

Some additional coding problems on stability

For coding the samples in 1970 and 1972 some additional instructions are necessary. The coding has to be somewhat more improvised here. First code the respondents on the questions that are relevant, using the same coding-rules as in 1974 and 1976.

For example, concerning 'the future' we do not have any questions in the first sample corresponding exactly to any of the questions that we had in the second and the third sample. All statements can be compared to the questions 'What do you actually expect to happen?' and 'How long do you think this conflict will last?' in the second and the third sample.

Concretely, when coding the answers from 1970 and 1972, you should proceed in the following way:

Distribute the statements in different categories, each category representing a particular dimension, as e. g. self-image/enemy-image, instrumental beliefs, etc. Then we go on to examine each category, trying to sort out statements that could be seen as answers to one of the questions posed in 1974 and 1976. Do not look at the name of the respondent, only the country to which he belongs. All statements referring to a question should be coded (theoretically then, one respondent could contribute several statements to one question, though this is not likely). Count the number of statements referring to each question. The question with the highest number of statements was used for comparison with the samples in 1974 and 1976.

When dealing with the respondents who were re-interviewed, proceed in the same way. But you should now take the name of the respondent into consideration.

After having done this coding, you are in a position to compare these results with the results in 1974 and 1976, both concerning respondents reappearing in two samples (1970/72 and 1974) and concerning the total samples.

What can be argued against quantifying is that the n's are very low, and consequently we cannot say anything about the generality of our results — how representative they are.

But we consider this testing a good basis for generating hypotheses on change. Even though we deal with a small number of respondents, it is nevertheless of interest to analyze isolated cases when dealing with the problem of change, especially since we are dealing with elites. Finding out, e.g., how a person in a high position has changed his beliefs over time is in itself interesting.

The kind of changes or stability of beliefs and attitudes we can find in the same persons over time will be relevant to the issue of how you trigger a change or what causes change. Any change that we can trace will be attributed to intervening events in the time period between the interviews. We will also examine whether change can be attributed to reliability, response validity, or inadequate representation of the universe of responses. There is also a possibility, of course, that changes in the respondents' attitudes and beliefs may be attributed to change of role, or changing political leaderships, but this we will not be able to control for.

We make the assumption that the respondents have the same role. The absence of a control group makes it impossible to control for random variances and for potential explanatory variables other than the intervening events.

A somewhat less exact measure of change is to make comparisons across different samples. The measures here are less exact, in that we will also have the variations from sample to sample. A sample is never identical to the universe, and there are bound to be variations from one sample to the other, even though good sampling procedure from a known universe rules out these variations to a great extent. We are not dealing with a known universe. Consequently we do not have representative samples. Furthermore, we did not pose the same questions in the first sample as we did in the second and the third.

Still we should be able to make some evaluations of change. When we obtain similar results, we take this result to be not only a rather good indication of high reliability — same results obtained by different interviewers over different time periods — but also a strong indication of the representativeness of the result.

The possibility that the result we have obtained in three different samples also applies to the whole universe is high.

Coding-Forms, 1974

Coder:
Interviewee: Country:
Year:

A₁ *If you should point out one single factor as the main cause of the Middle*
East conflict, which would you mention?
1. We are to blame   (   )   2. Mixed   (   )
3. They are to blame (   )   4. No reference   (   )

A₂ *If UN resolution 242 were implemented, who do you think would gain and*
lose?
1. Favorable   (   )   2. Mixed   (   )
3. Unfavorable   (   )   4. Don't know   (   )
5. No reference   (   )

B. *What parts of the territories occupied during the 1967 war do you consider*
most vital for you to keep (Israeli side)/to get back (Arab side)?
1. Uncompromising   (   )   2. Mixed   (   )
3. Compromising   (   )   4. Don't know   (   )
5. No reference   (   )

C. *What parts of the territories do you consider most vital for the other side*
to get back (Israeli side) / to keep (Arab side)?
1. Uncompromising   (   )   2. Mixed   T (   )
3. Compromising   (   )   4. Don't know   (   )
5. No reference   (   )

D. *How do you see the solution of the Palestinian problem?*
1. Uncompromising   (   )   2. Mixed   (   )
3. Compromising   (   )   4. Don't know   (   )
5. No reference   (   )

E. *What are the goals of your side in the conflict?*
1. Belligerent   (   )   2. Mixed   (   )
3. Accommodative   (   )   4. Don't know   (   )
5. No reference   (   )

F. *Are there any differences concerning goals and strategies on your side?*
1. No differences   (   )   2. Neutral
3. Significant   (insignificant
   differences   (   )   differences)   (   )
5. No reference   (   )   4. Don't know   (   )

198

G. *What do you think are the basic good and bad aspects of your side in the conflict?*
   1. We are good   (   )   2. Mixed   (   )
   3. We are bad   (   )   4. Don't know   (   )
   5. No reference   (   )

H. *Do you see any elements in your own country working against peace?*
   1. No elements working against peace   (   )
   2. Neutral (insignificant elements working against peace)   (   )
   3. Significant elements working against peace   (   )
   4. Don't know   (   )   5. No reference   (   )

I. *Do you think that the other side is threatening you?*
   1. Yes   (   )   2. Mixed   (   )
   3. No   (   )   4. Don't know   (   )
   5. No reference   (   )

J. *In what way and how much is your side dependent on the superpowers?*
   1. Dependent on both superpowers   (   )
   2. Dependent on the USA   (   )
   3. Dependent on the Soviet Union   (   )
   4. Not dependent on any of the superpowers   (   )
   5. Don't know   (   )   6. No reference   (   )

K. *In what way do you think the superpowers and the UN can influence a peace solution?*
   1. Favorable   (   )   2. Mixed   (   )
   3. Unfavorable   (   )   4. Don't know   (   )
   5. No reference   (   )

L. *In what way and how much is the other side dependent on the superpowers?*
   1. Dependent on both superpowers   (   )
   2. Dependent on the USA   (   )
   3. Dependent on the Soviet Union   (   )
   4. Not dependent on any superpower   (   )
   5. Don't know   (   )   6. No reference   (   )

M. *What are the goals of the other side in this conflict?*
   1. Belligerent   (   )   2. Mixed   (   )
   3. Accommodative   (   )   4. Don't know   (   )
   5. No reference   (   )

N. *Are there any differences concerning the goals and strategies of the other side?*
   1. No differences   (   )   2. Neutral
   3. Significant   (insignificant
      differences   (   )   differences)   (   )
   5. No reference   (   )   4. Don't know   (   )

O. *What do you think are the basic good and bad aspects of the other side in the conflict?*
   1. The other side is   2. Mixed   (   )
      good   (   )
   3. The other side is   4. Don't know   (   )
      bad   (   )
   5. No reference   (   )

P. *Do you see any elements on the other side working for peace?*
  1. No elements working for peace   (   )
  2. Neutral (insignificant elements working for peace)   (   )
  3. Significant elements working for peace   (   )
  4. Don't know   (   )   5. No reference   (   )

Q. *Do you think that the other side believes that you are threatening them?*
  1. Yes   (   )   2. Mixed   (   )
  3. No   (   )   4. Don't know   (   )
  5. No reference   (   )

R. *In what way do you think that the events in recent years have basically changed the conflict?*
  1. Improved the situation of our side   (   )
  2. Neutral   (   )
  3. Worsened the situation of our side   (   )
  4. Don't know   (   )   5. No reference   (   )

S. *In what way has the civil war in Jordan influenced the conflict?*
  1. Advantageous to   2. Neutral   (   )
     our side   (   )
  3. Advantageous to   4. Don't know   (   )
     the opponent   (   )
  5. No reference   (   )

T. *In what way have the activities of the guerrillas abroad influenced the conflict?*
  1. Advantageous to   2. Neutral   (   )
     our side   (   )
  3. Advantageous to   4. Don't know   (   )
     the opponent   (   )
  5. No reference   (   )

U. *In what way has the Oil Embargo influenced the conflict?*
  1. Advantageous to   2. Neutral   (   )
     our side   (   )
  3. Advantageous to   4. Don't know   (   )
     the opponent   (   )
  5. No reference   (   )

V. *What were the basic causes of the October war?*
  1. Fault of the   2. Fault of our side   (   )
     opponent   (   )   4. Fault of outside
  3. Fault of both sides   (   )   powers   (   )
  5. Don't know   (   )   6. No reference   (   )

W. *As regards the political situation, what would you like to see happen in the Middle East in the near future?*
  1. Solution of conflict (peace)   (   )
  2. Mixed (solution but our demands must be met)   (   )
  3. Strengthening of our side   (   )
  4. Don't know   (   )   5. No reference   (   )

X. *Now speaking realistically, what would you actually expect to happen?*
  1. Optimistic   (   )   2. Mixed   (   )
  3. Pessimistic   (   )   4. Don't know   (   )
  5. No reference   (   )

Y. *Now speaking realistically, what would you actually expect to happen concerning the new generation?*
1. Will compromise ( )   2. Mixed ( )
3. Will not com-   4. Don't know ( )
   promise ( )
5. No reference ( )

Z. *Now speaking realistically, what would you actually expect to happen concerning the military situation?*
1. Favorable to   2. Mixed ( )
   our side ( )
3. Unfavorable to   4. Don't know ( )
   our side ( )
5. No reference ( )

... *Now speaking realistically, what would you actually expect to happen concerning international public opinion?*
1. Favorable to   2. Mixed ( )
   our side ( )   4. Don't know ( )
3. Unfavorable to
   our side ( )
5. No reference ( )

Ö. *Given what you would like to see happen in the Middle East in the near future, what do you think are the most effective ways to achieve these aims?*
1. Conciliatory ( )   2. Neutral ( )
3. Refractory ( )   4. Don't know ( )
5. No reference ( )

Å. *How long do you think this conflict will last?*
1. Optimistic ( )   2. Mixed ( )
3. Pessimistic ( )   4. Don't know ( )
5. No reference ( )

Coding-Forms, 1976

Coder:
Interviewee: Country:
Year:

A. *Do you expect another war in the coming years?*
   1. Yes   (   )   2. Mixed   (   )
   3. No   (   )   4. Don't know   (   )
   5. No reference   (   )

B. *Are you in favor of a Palestinian state on the West Bank and the Gaza Strip?*
   1. Yes   (   )   2. Mixed   (   )
   3. No   (   )   4. Don't know   (   )
   5. No reference   (   )

C. *What are the goals of your side in the conflict?*
   1. Belligerent   (   )   2. Mixed   (   )
   3. Compromising   (   )   4. Don't know   (   )
   5. No reference   (   )

D. *Are there any differences concerning the goals and strategies on your side?*
   1. No differences   (   )   2. Neutral
   3. Significant   (insignificant
      differences   (   )   differences)   (   )
   4. Don't know   (   )   5. No reference   (   )

E. *Do you think that the other side is threatening you?*
   1. Yes   (   )   2. Mixed   (   )
   3. No   (   )   4. Don't know   (   )
   5. No reference   (   )

F. *What are the goals of the opponent in this conflict?*
   1. Belligerent   (   )   2. Mixed   (   )
   3. Accommodative   (   )   4. Don't know   (   )
   5. No reference   (   )

G. *Are there any differences concerning the goals and strategies of the other side?*
   1. No differences   (   )   2. Neutral
   3. Significant   (insignificant
      differences   (   )   differences)   (   )
   4. Don't know   (   )   5. No reference   (   )

H. *Do you think that the other side believes that you are threatening them?*
   1. Yes   (   )   2. Mixed   (   )
   3. No   (   )   4. Don't know   (   )
   5. No reference   (   )

I. *In what way do you think the events in recent years have basically changed the conflict?*
   1. Improved the situation of our side   (   )
   2. Neutral   (   )
   3. Worsened the situation of our side   (   )
   4. Don't know   (   )   5. No reference   (   )

J. *Do you think the Sinai Agreement has been favorable*
   1. To both sides   (   )   2. Only to your side   (   )
   3. Only to the   4. Has had no effect   (   )
       opponent   (   )
   5. Don't know   (   )

K. *In what way do you think the increased international recognition of the PLO has influenced the conflict?*
   1. Advantageous to   2. Neutral   (   )
       our side   (   )   4. Don't know   (   )
   3. Advantageous to
       the opponent   (   )
   5. No reference   (   )

L. *In what way has the civil war in Lebanon influenced the conflict?*
   1. Advantageous to   2. Neutral   (   )
       our side   (   )
   3. Advantageous to   4. Don't know   (   )
       the opponent   (   )
   5. No reference   (   )

M. *How do you see the solution of the Palestinian problem?*
   1. Uncompromising   (   )   2. Mixed   (   )
   3. Compromising   (   )   4. Don't know   (   )
   5. No reference   (   )

N. *As regards the political situation, what would you like to see happen in the Middle East in the near future?*
   1. Solution of the conflict (peace)   (   )
   2. Mixed (solution but our demands must be met)   (   )
   3. Strengthening of our side   (   )
   4. Don't know   (   )   5. No reference   (   )

O. *Now speaking realistically, what do you actually expect will happen?*
   1. Optimistic   (   )   2. Mixed   (   )
   3. Pessimistic   (   )   4. Don't know   (   )
   5. No reference   (   )

P. *Given what you would like to see happen in the Middle East in the near future, what do you think are the most effective ways to achieve these aims?*
   1. Conciliatory   (   )   2. Neutral   (   )
   3. Refractory   (   )   4. Don't know   (   )
   5. No reference   (   )

Q. *How long do you think this conflict will last?*

1. Optimistic ( )   2. Mixed ( )
3. Pessimistic ( )   4. Don't know ( )
5. No reference ( )

Appendix D

Tests of reliability

Intercoder reliability

Below are reported the tests of intercoder reliability. The coding procedures as such can be studied in the codebook.

First we will look at the ratio of coding agreement relative to the total number of coding decisions, using the well-known formula: $CR = \dfrac{2M}{N_1 + N_2}$

The results are: .86 in 1974, .88 in 1976.

This test does not, however, take into account the extent of intercoder agreement which may result from chance.

To cope with this problem, we use *Scott's Pi*.

We find it appropriate to report the score on every question.

1. *If UN resolution 242 were implemented, who do you think would gain and lose?* $Pi = .65$
2. *What parts of the territories occupied during the 1967 war do you consider most vital for you to keep (Israeli side) / to get back (Arab side)?* $Pi = .71$
3. *What parts of the territories do you consider most vital for the other side to get back (Israeli side) / to keep (Arab side)?* $Pi = .57$
4. *Do you expect another war in the coming years?* $Pi = .78$
5. *How do you see the solution of the Palestinian problem?* $Pi = .58$
6. *Are you in favor of a Palestinian state on the West Bank and the Gaza Strip?* $Pi = .86$
7. *What are the goals of your side in the conflict?* $Pi = .80$
8. *Are there any differences concerning goals and strategies on your side?* $Pi = .75$
9. *What do you think are the basic good and bad aspects of your side in the conflict?* $Pi = .57$
10. *Do you see any elements in your own country working against peace?*
11. *Do you think that the other side is threatening you?* $Pi = .83$
12. *In what way and how much is your side dependent on the superpowers?* $Pi = .80$
13. *In what way do you think the superpowers and the UN can influence a peace solution?* $Pi = .100$
14. *In what way and how much is the other side dependent on the superpowers?* $Pi = 1.00$
15. *What are the goals of the other side in this conflict?* $Pi = .68$
16. *Are there any difference concerning the goals and strategies of the other side?* $Pi = .85$
17. *What do you think are the basic good and bad aspects of the other side in the conflict?* $Pi = 1.00$

18. *Do you see any elements on the other side working for peace?*   Pi = .80
19. *Do you think that the other side believes that you are threatening them?*
                                                                  Pi = .74
20. *In what way do you think that the events in recent years have basically changed the conflict?*   Pi = .83
21. *In what way has the civil war in Jordan influenced the conflict?*   Pi = .57
22. *In what way have the activities of the guerrillas abroad influenced the conflict?*   Pi = .70
23. *In what way has the civil war in Lebanon influenced the conflict?*
                                                                  Pi = .78
24. *In what way has the Oil Embargo influenced the conflict?*   Pi = .84
25. *In what way do you think the increased international recognition of the PLO has influenced the conflict?*   Pi = 1.00
26. *What were the basic causes of the October war?*   Pi = 1.00
27. *Do you think the Sinai agreement has been favorable?*   Pi = 1.00
28. *As regards the political situation, what would you like to see happen in the Middle East in the near future?*   Pi = .80
29. *Now speaking realistically, what would you actually expect to happen?*
                                                                  Pi = .58
30. *Now speaking realistically, what would you actually expect to happen concerning the new generation?*   Pi = .68
31. *Now speaking realistically, what would you actually expect to happen concerning the military situation?*   Pi = .63
32. *Now speaking realistically, what would you actually expect to happen concerning international public opinion?*   Pi = .68
33. *Given what you would like to see happen in the Middle East in the near future, what do you think are the most effective ways to achieve these aims?*
                                                                  Pi = .84
34. *How long do you think this conflict will last?*   Pi = .81
Average Pi of total (34 questions): .78

Appendix E

Distribution of answers on all questions asked in 1974

		Favorable	Mixed	Unfavorable	
If UN resolution 242 were implemented, who do you think will gain and lose?	Israeli	51.6	12.9	35.5	n = 31
	Arab	58.1	16.7	32.3	n = 62

		Uncompro- mising	Mixed	Compro- mising	
What parts of the territories occupied during the 1967 war do you consider most vital for you to keep (Israeli side)/ to get back (Arab side)?	Israeli	58.3	16,7	25.0	n = 36
	Arab	72.6	1.6	25.8	n = 62

		Uncompro- mising	Mixed	Compro- mising	
What parts of the territories do you consider most vital for the other side to get back (Israeli side)/to keep (Arab side)?	Israeli	48.6	13.5	37.8	n = 37
	Arab	46.6	5.2	48.3	n = 58

		Uncompro- mising	Mixed	Compro- mising	
How do you see the solution of the Palestinian problem?	Israeli	69.4	0	30.6	n = 34
	Arab	55.4	6.2	38.5	n = 65

		Belligerent	Mixed	Accommo- dative	
What are the goals of your side in the conflict?	Israeli	22.9	5.7	71.4	n = 33
	Arab	45.2	21.0	33.9	n = 62

		No differences	Neutral	Significant differences	
Are there any differences concerning goals and strategies on your side?	Israeli	8.8	14.7	76.5	n = 32
	Arab	34.4	21.9	43.8	n = 64

		We are good	Mixed	We are bad	
What do you think are the basic good and bad aspects of your side in the conflict?	Israeli	45.2	54.8	0	n = 31
	Arab	70.0	30.0	0	n = 60
		No elements	Neutral	Significant elements	
Do you see any elements in your own country working against peace?	Israeli	43.8	21.9	34.3	n = 32
	Arab	63.1	23.1	13.8	n = 65
		Yes	Mixed	No	
Do you think that the other side believes that you are threatening them?	Israeli	66.7	3.3	30.0	n = 33
	Arab	66.7	7.9	25.4	n = 64
		Improved	Neutral	Worsened	
In what way do you think that the events in recent years have basically changed the conflict?	Israeli	26.7	50.0	23.3	n = 28
	Arab	98.4	1.6	0	n = 62
		Advantageous to our side	Neutral	Advantageous to the opponent	
In what way has the civil war in Jordan influenced the conflict?	Israeli	70.4	25.9	3.7	n = 27
	Arab	8.6	29.3	62.1	n = 58
		Advantageous to our side	Neutral	Advantageous to the opponent	
In what way have the activities of the guerrillas abroad influenced the conflict	Israeli	26.9	50.0	23.1	n = 26
	Arab	42.4	27.1	30.5	n = 59
		Advantageous to our side	Neutral	Advantageous to the opponent	
In what way has the Oil Embargo influenced the conflict?	Israeli	16.0	32.0	52.0	n = 25
	Arab	91.7	8.3	2.7	n = 60

		Favorable	Mixed	Unfavorable	
What were the basic causes of the October war?	Israeli	91.9	5.4	2,7	n = 37
	Arab	96.7	1.6	1.6	n = 61

		Solution of the conflict	Mixed	Strength-ening of our side	
As regards the political situation, what would you like to see happen in the Middle East in the near future?	Israeli	89.3	7.1	3.6	n = 26
	Arab	43.1	43.1	13.8	n = 65

		Yes	Mixed	No	
Do you think that the other side is threatening you?	Israeli	74.3	5.7	20.0	n = 33
	Arab	79.7	1.6	18.8	n = 64

		Dependent on both superpowers	Dependent on USA only	Dependent on the USSR only	
In what way and how much is your side dependent on the superpowers?	Israeli	11.4	77.1	11.4	n = 35
	Arab	65.1	6.3	28.6	n = 65

		Favorable	Mixed	Unfavorable	
In what way do you think the superpowers and the UN can influence a peace solution?	Israeli	78.8	9.1	12.1	n = 33
	Arab	87.5	1.6	10.9	n = 64

		Dependent on both superpowers	Dependent on the USA only	Dependent on the USSR only	
In what way and how much is the other side dependent on the superpowers?	Israeli	37.5	0	37.5	n = 32
	Arab	23.1	76.9	0	n = 65

		Belligerent	Mixed	Accom-modative	
What are the goals of the other side in this conflict?	Israeli	64.7	17.6	17.6	n = 32
	Arab	89.1	4.7	6.3	n = 64

		Differences	Neutral	Significant differences	
Are there any differences concerning the goals and strategies of the other side?	Israeli	12.1	9.1	78.8	n = 32
	Arab	17.5	33.3	49.2	n = 63

		Other side good	Mixed	Other side bad	
What do you think are the basic good and bad aspects of the other side in the conflict?	Israeli	7.4	29.6	63.0	n = 27
	Arab	0	23.8	76.2	n = 63

		No elements	Neutral	Significant elements	
Do you see any elements on the other side working for peace?	Israeli	26.7	16.7	56.7	n = 30
	Arab	24.2	43.5	32.3	n = 62

		Optimistic	Mixed	Pessimistic	
Now speaking realistically, what would you actually expect to happen?	Israeli	46.9	18.8	34.3	n = 30
	Arab	60.0	12.7	27.3	n = 55

		Will compromise	Mixed	Will not compromise	
Now speaking realistically, what would you actually expect to happen concerning the new generation?	Israeli	15.4	53.8	23.1	n = 13
	Arab	54.8	19.4	25.8	n = 31

		Favorable to our side	Mixed	Favorable to other side	
Now speaking realistically, what would you actually expect to happen concerning the military situation?	Israeli	25.0	33.3	41.7	n = 12
	Arab	60.9	39.1	0	n = 23

		Conciliatory	Neutral	Refractory	
Given what you would like to see happen in the Middle East in the near future, what do you think are the most effective ways to achieve these aims?	Israeli	66.7	0	33.3	n = 25
	Arab	62.5	4.7	32.8	n = 64

		Optimistic	Mixed	Pessimistic	
How long do you think this conflict will last?	Israeli	10.5	10.5	78.9	n = 17
	Arab	52.3	15.9	31.8	n = 44

		Favorable	Mixed	Unfavorable	
If you should point out one single factor as the main cause of the Middle East conflict, which would you mention?	Israeli	5.6	66.7	27.8	n = 36
	Arab	0	46.2	53.8	n = 65

The distribution of answers to all questions asked in 1976

		Yes	Mixed	No	
Do you expect another war in the coming years?	Israeli	57	27	16	n = 70
	Arab	52	33	15	n = 28

		Yes	Mixed	No	
Are you in favor of a Palestinian state on the West Bank, and the Gaza Strip?	Israeli	13	9	78	n = 77
	Arab	72	7	21	n = 29

		Belligerent	Mixed	Compromising	
What are the goals of your side in the conflict?	Israeli	11	27	61	n = 78
	Arab	71	4	25	n = 28

		No differences	Insignificant differences	Significant differences	
Are there any differences concerning the goals and strategies on your side?	Arab	0	33	67	n = 78
	Israeli	76	10	14	n = 29

		Yes	Mixed	No	
Do you think that the other side is threatening you?	Israeli	91	6	3	n = 78
	Arab	93	0	7	n = 29

		Belligerent	Mixed	Accommodative	
What are the goals of the opponent in this conflict?	Israeli	76	20	4	n = 78
	Arab	96	0	4	n = 28

		No differences	Neutral	Significant differences	
Are there any differences concerning the goals and strategies of the other side?	Israeli	1	41	58	n = 76
	Arab	29	43	29	n = 28
		Yes	Mixed	No	
Do you think that the other side believes you are threatening them?	Israeli	69	19	12	n = 78
	Arab	45	21	35	n = 29
		Favorable	Neutral	Unfavorable	
In what way do you think that the events in recent years have basically changed the conflict?	Israeli	26	49	25	n = 77
	Arab	83	10	7	n = 29
		to both sides?	to your side?	only to opponent?	
Do you think the Sinai agreement has been favorable	Israeli	84	1	15	n = 76
	Arab	60	0	40	n = 20
		Advantageous to our side	Neutral	Advantageous to opponent	
In what way do you think the increased international recognition of the PLO has influenced the conflict?	Israeli	8	15	77	n = 78
	Arab	90	10	0	n = 29
		Advantageous to our side	Neutral	Advantageous to opponent	
In what way has the civil war in Lebanon influenced the conflict?	Israeli	65	29	6	n = 68
	Arab	4	18	79	n = 28
		Uncompromising	Mixed	Compromising	
How do you see the solution of the Palestinian problem?	Israeli	72	10	18	n = 78
	Arab	62	0	38	n = 29

		Peace	Mixed	Strengthening of our side	
As regards the political situation, what would you like to see happen in the Middle East in the near future?	Israeli	58	35	7	n = 77
	Arab	41	35	24	n = 29
		Optimistic	Mixed	Pessimistic	
Now speaking realistically, what do you actually expect will happen?	Israeli	24	28	48	n = 67
	Arab	56	4	41	n = 27
		Conciliatory	Neutral	Refractory	
Given what you would like to see happen in the Middle East in the near future, what do you think are the most effective ways to achieve these aims?	Israeli	46	20	34	n = 76
	Arab	31	7	62	n = 29
		Optimistic	Mixed	Pessimistic	
How long do you think this conflict will last?	Israeli	16	25	59	n = 61
	Arab	5	38	57	n = 21

Notes

CHAPTER II

1 See Heradstveit, Daniel: *Arab and Israeli Elite Perceptions*, pp. 110—111.
Bronebakk, Jørg Willy: *Supermakter og påvirkning*. Mimeo, Norwegian Institute of International Affairs. Tørum, Harald: *Konfliktforestillinger i Egypt. En intervjuundersøkelse om eliteoppfatninger*. Mimeo, Norwegian Institute of International Affairs. Oslo. Øvrevik, Geir: *Konflikt-forestillinger i Jordan og Libanon*, Mimeo, Institute of Political Science, University of Oslo, Oslo, 1975.
Other examples of this type of research are:
Bronfenbrenner, U.: 'The Mirror-image in Soviet-American Relations', *Journal of Social Issues*, 17 (3), 45—56, 1961.
Harkabi, Y.: *Arab Attitudes to Israel*. Jerusalem: Israel Universities Press, 1971.
Suliman, Michael W.: 'Attitudes of the Arab Elite Toward Palestine and Israel' in *American Political Science Review*. Vol. LXVII, No. 2, 482—489, 1973.
White, Ralph K.: 'Misperception in the Arab-Israeli Conflict' in *Journal of Social Issues*, Vol. 33, No. 1, 190—221, 1977.

2 George, Alexander L.: 'The Operational Code: A Neglected Approach to the Study of Political Leaders and Decision-Making', *International Studies Quarterly*, XIII, 190—222, 1969.
A discussion of various approaches to prediction that serve to clarify the operational code can be found in:
Singer, J. David: 'The Peace Research and Foreign Policy Prediction' in *The Papers of the Peace Science Society (International)* Vol. 21, 1973, and Bell, Daniel: 'Twelve Modes of Prediction', *Dædulus*, Vol. 193, 1964.

3 Leites, Nathan: *The Operational Code of the Politburo*. New York: McGraw-Hill, 1951.
Leites, Nathan: *A Study of Bolshevism*. Glencoe, III: The Free Press, 1953.
On the more general problem of relating beliefs to behavior, see for example:
Miller, George A., Galanter, Eugene and Pribraen, Karl H.: *Plans and the Structure of Behavior*, ch. 1, New York, 1960.

4 George, Alexander L., et al.: *Toward a More Soundly Based Foreign Policy: Making Better Use of Information*. Appendix D of the Report of the Commission on the Organization of the Government for the Conduct of Foreign Policy, Vol. 2, p. 2, 1975.

5 Holsti, Ole R.: 'The "Operational Code" as an Approach to the Analysis of Belief System'. Final Report to the National Science Foundation. Mimeo, Duke University 1977.
Holsti, Ole R.: 'The "Operational Code" Approach to the Study of Political Leaders: John Foster Dulles: Philosophical and Instrumental Beliefs' in *Canadian Journal of Political Science*, No. 1, 123—157, 1970.

Ashby, Ned: *Schumacher and Brandt: The Divergent 'Operational Codes' of two German Socialist Leaders.* Stanford University, mimeo, 1969.

Johnson, Loch: 'Operational Codes and the Prediction of Leadership Behavior: Senator Frank Church at Mid-Career'. Paper prepared for the 1973 Annual Meeting of the American Political Science Association, New Orleans, September 1973, 54, chap. 1.

McLellan, David S.: 'Study of Political Leaders: Dean Acheson's Philosophical and Instrumental Beliefs'. *Canadian Journal of Political Science,* Vol. IV. No. 1, 52—75, 1971.

Walker, Stephen G.: 'The Interface Between Beliefs and Behavior: Henry Kissinger's Operational Code and the Vietnam War'. *The Journal of Conflict Resolution,* Vol. XXI, No. 1, 129—168, 1977.

A complete listing of operational code studies to date is to be found in Holsti, 77, op. cit.

6 Discussion of centrality appears in a number of studies, see for example:

Steinbruner, John D.: *'The Cybernetic Theory of Decision',* p. 113 in *New Dimensions of Political Analysis.* Princeton University Press, 1974.

Bem, Daryl J.: *Beliefs, Attitudes and Human Affairs,* p. 12. Brooks/Cole Publishing Company, Belmont, California, 1970.

7 For a discussion of this, see:

George, Alexander L. and Holsti, Ole R.: 'Operational Code Belief Systems and Foreign Policy Decision-Making', Research Proposal submitted to and funded by the National Science Foundation, 1974.

A review of the research on cognitive approaches and the various methodological problems involved has recently been done by Ole R. Holsti, see:

Bonham, Matthew and Shapiro, Michael (eds.): *Thought and Action in Foreign Policy,* ch. 2. Basel and Stuttgart: Birkhäuser Verlag, 1977.

8 Bonham, Matthew G., Shapiro, Michael J. and Trumble, Thomas L.: 'The October War: Changes in Cognitive Orientation Toward the Middle East Conflict', *International Studies Quarterly,* 1979, (forthcoming).

9 For a recent review of theories on attribution, see:

Ross, L.: *Distortion in the Social Perception Process: The Production and Perseverance of Attributional Biases and Errors.* Mimeo, Stanford University, 1975.

10 See Bem, op. cit. ch. 2, for a discussion of how this can be explained.

11 Abelson, Robert P., Aronson, Elliot, McGuire, William J., Newcomb, Theodore M., Rosenberg, Milton J. and Tannenbaum, Percy H. (eds.), *Theories of Cognitive Consistency: A Source Book.* Chicago: Rand McNally and Co., 1968.

For a more recent discussion on this, see for example:

Gerard, Harold B., Connolley, Edward S. and Wilhelmy, Roland A.: 'Compliance, Justification and Cognitive Change', pp. 217—246 in Leonard Berkowitz (ed.) *Advances in Experimental Social Psychology,* Vol. 7. Academic Press, New York and London, 1974.

12 For a discussion of relationships between intentions and behavior, see:

Fishbein, Martin and Ajzen, Icek: *Belief, Attitude, Intention and Behavior: An Introduction to Theory and Research,* pp. 368—381. Addison-Wesley, London 1975.

13 For introductory works, see:

Heider, Fritz: *The Psychology of Interpersonal Relations.* John Wiley & Sons, Inc., New York, Chapman & Hall Limited, London, 1958.

Festinger, Leon: *A Theory of Cognitive Dissonance.* Stanford University Press, 1957.

Bannister, D. and Mair, J. M. M.: *The Evaluation of Personal Constructs.* New York: Academic Press, 1968.

14 Cited from: Bem, op. cit. (70), p. 4.
15 Steinbruner, op. cit., p. 113.
16 Bem, op. cit. (70) p. 5.
17 For a discussion of centrality and change, see:
Jervis, Robert: *Perception and Misperception in International Politics*, p. 297. Princeton, N. J.: Princeton University Press, 1976.
18 About processes of change, see also:
Etzioni, Amitai: 'Social-Psychological Aspects of International Relations' in Lindsey, Gardner and Aronson, Elliot (eds.) *The Handbook of Social Psychology*. 2nd edn., Vol. 5, ch. 43, 549—550. Addison-Wesley Publishing Company, Menlo Park California, 1968.
19 Bem, op. cit., p. 8.
Axelrod, Robert: 'Schema Theory: An Information Processing Model of Perception and Cognition', *American Political Science Review*, LXVII, 1248—1266, 1973.
20 Converse, Philip E.: 'The Nature of Belief Systems in Mass Publics' p. 214 in David Apter (ed.) *Ideology and Discontent*. New York, The Free Press, 1964.
21 George, Alexander L.: 'The Causal Nexus Between Cognitive Beliefs and Decision-Making Behavior: The "Operational Code" Belief System', in Lawrence Falkowski (ed.) *Psychological Models in International Politics*. Boulder, Colorado: Westview Press, 1979, (forthcoming).
22 For a general review, see, for example:
Zajonc, Robert: 'Cognitive Theories in Social Psychology', *Handbook of Social Psychology*, 2nd edn., Vol. 1, 1968. Jervis op. cit. chapter II.
23 George op. cit., (75) p. 31.
Jervis op. cit., pp. 117—120.
24 George (75), p. 31.
25 Bonham, Matthew G., in *Simulation and Games*, June 1976, p. 128.
26 Ross, op. cit., p. 2.
27 Ibid.
28 Berkowitz, Leonard (ed.) *Advances in Experimental Social Psychology*, Vol. 6, p. 6. New York and London, 1972.
29 Bem, Daryl J.: 'Self-Perception Theory', pp. 2—57 in Leonard Berkowitz (ed.) *Advances in Experimental Social Psychology*, Vol. 6. New York and London, 1972.
30 Bem, Ibid.
31 This idea was first put forward in the field by Fritz Heider. At the beginning, however, only his ideas on consistency generated further research, while his ideas on attribution have only in later years received increasing attention, see,
Heider, Fritz: *The Psychology of Interpersonal Relations*. John Wiley & Sons, Inc., New York, Chapman & Hall Limited, London, 1958.
32 Kelly, Harold H.: 'The Process of Causal Attribution', p. 107 in *The American Psychologist*, 1973.
33 For a good general discussion of the logical schemata in information processing, see:
Kelley, Harold H. 'Attribution in Social Interaction' in Jones, Edward R., Kanouse, David E. et al. *Attribution: Perceiving the Causes of Behavior*. Morristown, N. J., Greater Learning Press, 1971.
34 Jones, E. and Nisbett, R.: 'The Actor and the Observer: Divergent Perceptions of the Behavior', p. 93 in Jones, E. E. et al. (eds.), *Attribution: Perceiving the Causes of Behavior*. New Jersey, General Learning Press, 1971.
35 For a recent study of how attributions vary along the scale of attractiveness — unattractiveness, see:

Eagly, Alice H. and Chaiken, Shelley: 'An Attribution Analysis of the Effect of Communication Characteristics on Opinion Change: The Case of Communicator Attractiveness', pp. 136—144 in *Journal of Personality and Social Psychology,* Vol. 32, No. 1, 1975.

36 Shapiro, Michael J. and Bonham, B. Matthew: 'Cognitive Process and Foreign Policy Decision-Making', p. 149 in *International Studies Quarterly,* Vol. 17, No. 2, June 1973.

37 Ross op. cit., p. 17.

38 The hypothesis is stated as follows:
'..... There is a pervasive tendency for actors to attribute their actions to situational requirements, whereas observers tend to attribute the same actions to stable personal dispositions.' In Jones and Nisbett, op. cit., p. 80.

39 Fishbein op. cit., pp. 202—213.

40 Jones and Nisbett op. cit., p. 93.

41 Ross op. cit., p. 22.

42 Jones and Nisbett, op. cit., p. 87.

43 For a discussion on this, see:
Rokeach, Milton: 'Attitude Change and Behavioural Change', *Public Opinion Quarterly,* 30, 4, 529—550, 1966.

44 Finley, David J. and Fagen, Richard R.: *Enemies in Politics,* ch. 1. Chicago 1967.

45 See, Deutsch, Karl W. and Meritt, Richard L.: 'Effects of Events on National and International Images', in Kelman, Herbert C. (ed.), *International Behavior: A Social-Psychological Analysis.* New York: Holt, Reinehart and Winston, 1965.

46 Jervis op. cit., p. 298.

47 Kelman, Herbert C.: 'Attitudes Are Alive and Well and Gainfully Employed in the Sphere of Action', *American Psychologist,* Vol. 29, No. 5, 312, 1974.
Jessor, Richard and Jessor, Sherley L.: 'The Perceived Environment in Behavioral Science: Some Conceptual Issues and Some Illustrated Data'. *American Behavioral Scientist,* Vol. 16, No. 6, 801—822, 1973.
Ehrlich, Howard J.: 'Attitudes, Behavior, and the Intervening Variables'. *American Sociologist,* Vol. 4, No. 1, 29—34, 1969.

48 The recent study by Bonham et al., op. cit., serves to validate our tentative conclusions on thie issue.

49 Holsti, Ole R., articulates this problem in: Bonham and Shapiro (77) chapter 2.

50 This point is brought forward most clearly in the study by Ashby, Ned.: *Schumacher and Brandt: The Divergent 'Operational Codes' of Two German Socialist Leaders.* Stanford University, mimeo, 1969.

51 A study that may illustrate this, is:
Holsti, Ole R.: 'The "Operational Code" Approach to the Study of Political Leaders: John Foster Dulles' Philosophical and Instrumental Beliefs', *Canadian Journal of Political Science,* III, 123—157, 1970.

52 For a general review, see Zajonc, op. cit.,
and
Abelson et al., op. cit.

53 The first elaborate statement of the theory is to be found in Festinger, Leon: *A Theory of Cognitive Dissonance.* Stanford: Stanford University Press, 1957.

54 Shaw, Marvin E. and Constanzo, Philip R.: *Theories of Social Psychology,* p. 191. McGraw-Hill Book Company, 1970.

55 See, McGuire, William J.: 'The Nature of Attitudes and Attitude Change', in Lindsey, G. and Aronson, E.: *The Handbook of Social Psychology,* 2nd edn., Vol. III, ch. 21. Menlo Park, California, 1968.

56 Bem (70) op. cit., p. 29.

57 Gerard et al., op. cit., p. 240.
58 Converse, Phillip E.: 'The Nature of Belief Systems in Mass Publics', p. 209 in David Apter (ed.), *Ideology and Discontent*. New York: The Free Press, 1964.
59 Zajonc, op. cit., p. 325.
60 This also depends on the cognitive complexity; an empirical illustration of this is: Bonham and Shapiro (73), op. cit.
61 Converse, op. cit., p. 212.
62 Fishbein, op. cit., pp. 170—174.
63 McGuire in Abelson et al., op. cit., p. 150.
64 Converse, op. cit., p. 207.
65 Converse, op. cit., p. 207.

CHAPTER III

1 Stabell, Charles B.: *Individual Differences in Managerial Decision-Making Processes: A Study of Conversational Computer System Usage*, p. 62. PhD Thesis, MIT, Mimeo 1974.
2 An additional problem is presented by the fact that an elite member may not know the basis for his own actions; this is discussed in Axelrod, Robert (ed.) *The Structure of Decision*, p. 255. Princeton N. J.: Princeton University, 1976.
3 McCloskey, Herbert: *Political Inquiry: The Nature and Uses of Survey Research*, p. 21. The MacMillan Company, London, 1969.
4 Kahn, Roberg L. and Cannell, Charles F.: *The Dynamics of Interviewing*, p. 4. John Wiley and Sons, Inc., New York, 1957.
5 Kahn et al., op. cit., p. 46.
6 Robert D. Putnam reported to me in a personal conversation that he had similar experiences in interviewing Italian and English elites.
   See also, Putnam, Robert D.: *The Beliefs of Politicians. Ideology, Conflict and Democracy in Britain and Italy*, p. 241. New Haven and London, 1973.
7 Brown, Roger: *Social Psychology*, p. 480. The Free Press, New York, Collier-MacMillan, London, 1965.
8 Bonham, Matthew and Shapiro, Michael (eds.) *Thought and Action in Foreign Policy*, ch. 10. Basel and Stuttgart: Birkhäuser Verlag, 1977.
   Useful experiences in interviewing in sensitive international conflicts are also reported in:
   Elliot, R. S. P. and Hickie, John: *Ulster. A Case Study in Conflict Theory*, ch. 4. London, 1971.
9 About one-third of the interviews were conducted by the author, Harald Tørum, Nils Butenschøn, and Jørg Willy Bronebakk, and Nils Butenschøn did another third, while the final interviews were conducted by Gunnar Lunde and Steven R. David.
10 Kahn et al., op. cit., p. 11.
11 An exellent discussion of this problem is provided in: Aberbach, Joel D., Chesney, James D. and Rockman, Bert A.: *Exploring Elite Political Attitudes. Some Methodological Lessons*, p. 4. The University of Michigan, 1975.
12 La Piere: 'Attitudes vs Action', *Social Forces*, 13, 237, 1934.
13 See Harriel Zuekerman cited in:
   Aberbach et al., op. cit., p. 9.
14 McCloskey, op. cit., p. 4.
15 La Piere, op. cit., p. 237.
16 The unit of analysis is really the individual, even though I am looking at different countries. I am trying to illustrate notions derived from theories about individual psychological processes. Therefore, I am not interested in generalizing to other individuals, e.g. the Arab elite.

17 In other words, we tried to get the most influential officials and persons within each major foreign policy elite. It is a sampling plan without random selection of R's. For an example of another study of international conflict applying chain sampling, see, Elliot and Hickie, op. cit., p. 91.

18 List of re-interviewed respondents appear in appendix A.

19 McCloskey, op. cit., p. 21.

20 Putman, op. cit., pp. 241—245.

21 Aberbach, et al., op. cit., pp. 4—13.

22 Holsti, Ole R.: *Content Analysis for the Social Sciences and Humanities,* p. 94, Addison-Wesley, London 1969.

23 Cf. Putnam, op. cit., p. 24 'halo effect'.

24 Holsti, Ole R. (69), op. cit., pp. 116—119.

CHAPTER IV

1 Bem (70), op. cit.

2 Ross, op. cit., p. 15.

3 Jones and Nisbett, op. cit., p. 92.

4 Ibid., p. 93.

5 Heradstveit (74) op. cit., pp. 101—111.

6 The results are being validated by a recent study on attribution, see:
Rosenberg, Shawn, W. and Wolfsfeld Gary: 'International Conflict and the Problem of Attribution', *The Journal of Conflict Resolution,* Vol. XXI, No. 1, 1977.

7 For a discussion on perceived freedom, see:
Steiner, Ivan D.: 'Perceived Freedom'. *Advances in Experimental Social Psychology,* No. 5, 208—216, 1970.

8 See: Rosenberg/Wolfsfeld, op. cit.

9 A recent study along these lines is Joann Horai: 'Attribution Conflict', in *Journal of Social Issues,* Vol. 33, No. 1, 1977.

CHAPTER VIII

1 Heradstveit (74), op. cit., p. 126.

2 Ibid., pp. 111—134.

3 This point is elaborated in Larson, Deborah: *Cognitive Processes and Foreign Policy Decision-Making: An Information Processing Model.* Stanford University, mimeo, 1976.

4 Heradstveit (74), op. cit., p. 110.

5 Ibid., p. 121.

6 Ibid., pp. 101—111.

7 See, for example, Jervis, op. cit., pp. 306—308.

8 Kelman, Herbert C.: *Israelis and Palestinians: Psychological Prerequisites for Mutual Acceptance,* p. 33, mimeo, Harvard University, 1977.

9 The results are supported by previous studies, see:
Lampton, David M.: 'The U. S. Image of Peking in Three International Crises', *The Western Political Quarterly,* Vol. XXVI, No. 1, 1973.
Fagen, Richard et al. (eds.) *Enemies in Politics,* p. 14. Chicago: Rand McNally, 1967.
Osgood, Charles E. et al.: *The Measurement of Meaning.* Urbana: University of Illinois Press, 1957.
Holsti, Ole R.: 'Cognitive Dynamics and Images of the Enemy: Dulles and Russia', Fagen (ed.), op. cit.
Pruitt, Dean: 'Definition of the Situation as a Determinant of International Action', in Kelman, Herbert (ed.). *International Behavior, A Social Psychological Analysis.* New York: Holt, Rinehart and Winston, 1966.

Zimmerman, William: *Soviet Perspectives on International Relations, 1956—67.* Princeton: Princeton University Press, 1969.

Gamson, William A. and Modigliani, Andre: *Untangling the Cold War.* Boston: Little, Brown, 1971.

10 The principles of this type of approach are outlined in:

Merrit, Richard L. (ed.) *Communication in International Politics,* ch. 7.

Kelman, Herbert C.: *The Problem-Solving Workshop in Conflict Resolution.* University of Illinois Press, 1972.

For a report on a recent attempt to apply this approach to the Arab-Israeli Conflict: see Cohen, Stephen P., Kelman, Herbert C., Miller, Fredrick D. and Smith, Bruce L.: 'Evolving Intergroup Techniques for Conflict Resolution: An Israeli-Palestinian Pilot Workshop'. *Journal of Social Issues,* Vol. 33, No. 1, 165—188, 1977.

Bibliography

Abelson, Robert P., Aronson, Elliot, McGuire, William J., Newcomb, Theodore M., Rosenberg, Milton J., and Tannenbaum, Percy H. (eds.), *Theories of Cognitive Consistency: A Source Book*. Chicago: Rand McNally and Co., 1968.

Abelson, Robert P.: 'The Ideology Machine', Paper prepared for the Annual Meeting of the American Political Science Association, Chicago, Sept. 1971.

Abelson, Robert P.: 'Script Processing in Attitude Formation and Decision-making', in J. S. Carroll and J. W. Payne (eds). *Cognition and Social Behavior*, 1976.

Aberbach, Joel D., Chesney, James D., and Rockman, Bert A.: *Exploring Elite Political Attitudes. Some Methodological Lessons*. P. 4. The University of Michigan, 1975.

Ajzen, Icek: 'Attributions of Dispositions to an Actor: Effects of Perceived Decision Freedom and Behavioral Utilities', *Journal of Personality and Social Psychology*, Vol. 18, No. 2, 144—156, 1971.

Allison, Graham T.: *Essence of Decision: Explaining the Cuban Missile Crisis*, Little, Brown and Company, Boston, 1971.

Anderson, Joel E. Jr.: *The 'Operational Code' Belief System of Senator Arthur Vandenberg: An Application of the George Construct*. University of Michigan, unpublished Ph. D. dissertation, 1973 B.

Ashby, Ned: *Schumacher and Brandt: The Divergent 'Operational Codes' of two German Socialist Leaders*. Stanford University mimeo, 1969.

Axelrod, Robert: 'Schema Theory: An Information Processing Mode of Perception and Cognition', *American Political Science Review*, LXVII, 1248—1266, 1973.

Axelrod, Robert: *The Structure of Decision*, Princeton, N. J. Princeton University Press, 1976.

Bannister, D. and Mair, J. M.: *The Evaluation of Personal Constructs*, New York: Academic Press, 1968.

Bauer, Raymond: 'Problem of Perception and the Relations between the United States and Soviet Union', *Journal of Conflict Resolution 5*, 1961.

Beckman, Linda: 'Effects of Students' Performance on Teachers and Observers' Attributions of Causality', *Journal of Educational Psychology*, Vol. 51, No. 1, 76—82, 1970.

Belden, Thomas G.: 'Indications, Warnings and Crisis Operations' *International Studies Quarterly*. Vol. 21, No. 1, 1977.

Bell, Daniel: 'Twelve Modes of Prediction — A Preliminary Sorting of Approaches in the Social Sciences' in *Daedulus*, Vol. 93, 1964.

Bem, Daryl, J.: *Beliefs, Attitudes and Human Affairs*, Brooks/Cole Publishing Company, Belmont, California, 1970.

Bem, Daryl J.: 'Self-Perception Theory' pp. 2—57 in Leonard Berkowitz (ed). *Advances in Experimental Social Psychology*, Vol. 6. New York and London, 1972.

Berkowitz, Leonard, (ed.) p. 6 in *Advances in Experimental Social Psychology*,

Vol. 6, New York and London, 1972.

Bloomfield, Lincoln P.: *The Foreign Policy Process: Making Theory Relevant*, Vincent Davis and Maurice A. East (eds), Sage Publications, University of Kentucky, Vol. 3.

Bonham, Matthew G. and Shapiro, Michael J.: 'Explanation of the Unexpected: of a Theory of Foreign Policy Decision-Making', in Patrick J. McGowan (ed), *Sage International Yearbook of Foreign Policy Studies*, Vol. 1, 1973.

Bonham, Matthew G. and Shapiro, Michael J.: 'Explanation of the Unexpected: The Syrian Intervention in Jordan in 1970', in Robert Axelrod (ed), *The Structure of Decision*, Princeton, N. J. Princeton University Press, 1976.

Bonham, Matthew G. and Shapiro, Michael J.: 'Foreign Policy Decision-Making in Finland and Austria: The Application of a Cognitive Process Model' in M. G. Bonham and M. J. Shapiro (eds.) *Thought and Action in Foreign Policy*, Basel: Birkhäuser Verlag, 1977.

Bonham, Matthew, G., Heradstveit, Daniel, Narvesen, Ove and Shapiro, Michael J.: 'A Cognitive Model of Decision-making: Application to Norwegian Oil Policy, *Cooperaction and Conflict*, Nordic Journal of International Politics, Oslo University Press, Vol. 2, 1978.

Bonham, G. Matthew and Shapiro Michael J. (eds.) *Thought and Actions in Foreign Policy*, Basel and Stuttgart: Birkhäuser Verlag, 1977.

Bonham, G. Matthew and Shapiro, Michael J. and Trumble, Thomas L. 'The October War: Changes in Cognitive Orientation Toward the Middle East Conflict', *International Studies Quarterly*, 1979. (forthcoming).

Bonoma, Thomas V., and Milburn, Thomas W. (eds.): 'Social Conflict', *Journal of Social Issues*, Vol. 33, No. 1, 1977.

Boulding, Kenneth E.: 'National Images and International Systems' *Journal of Conflict Resolution 3*, 1959.

Boulding, Kenneth E.: *The Image; Knowledge in Life and Society*, The University of Michigan Press, 1956.

Bowers, Kenneth: 'Situationism in Psychology' *Psychological Review*, 1973.

Brecher, Michael: *The Foreign Policy System of Israel; Setting, Images, Process*, London, Oxford University Press, 1972.

Brecher, Michael: *Decisions in Israel's Foreign Policy*, London, Oxford University Press, 1974, Vol. 1.

Brodin, Katarina, Goldman, Kjell and Lange, Christian, 'Belief Systems, Doctrines and Foreign Policy, *Conflict and Cooperation*. VIII, 97—112, 1972.

Bronebakk, Jørg Willy: *Supermakter og påvirkning*. Mimeo, Norwegian Institute of International Affairs.

Bronfenbrenner, U. 'The Mirror-image in Soviet-American Relations'. *Journal of Social Issues*, 17 (3), 45—56, 1961.

Brown, Roger, *Social Psychology*. The Free Press, New York, Collier-MacMillan, London, 1965.

Burgess, Philip M., *Elite Images and Foreign Policy Outcomes*, Columbus: Ohio State University Press, 1967.

Burton, John W.: *Conflict and Communication: The Use of Controlled Communication in International Relations*, The Free Press, New York, 1969.

Caldwell, Dan: 'Bureaucratic Foreign Policy-Making' *American Behavioral Scientist*, Vol. 21, No. 1, 1977.

Cohen, Stephen P., Kelman, Herbert C., Miller, Fredrick D. and Smith, Bruce L.: 'Evolving Intergroup Techniques for Conflict Resolution: An Israeli-Palestinian Pilot Workshop'. *Journal of Social Issues*, Vol. 33, No. 1, 1977.

Converse, Philip E.: 'The Nature of Belief System in Mass Publics' in David Apter (ed.) *Ideology and Discontent*. New York: The Free Press, 1964.

Coser, Lewis A.: *Continuities in the Study of Social Conflict*, The Free Press, New York, 1970.

222

Crespi, Irving: 'What Kinds of Attitudes Measures are Predictive of Behavior?'. *Public Opinion Quarterly*, Vol. 35, No. 3., 327—334, 1971.

Deutsch, Karl and Merritt, Richard: 'Effects of Events on National and International Images' in Herbert Kelman (ed.) *International Behavior*. New York: Holt, Reinhart and Winston, 1965.

Diesing, Paul: *Patterns of Discovery in the Social Sciences*. Chicago and New York: Aldine-Atherton, 1971.

Eagly, Alice H. and Chaiken, Shelley: 'An Attribution Analysis of the Effect of Communication Characteristics on Opinion Change: The Case of Communicator Attractiveness' in *Journal of Personality and Social Psychology*, Vol. 32, No. 1, 136—144, 1975.

Eckstein, Harry: 'Case Study and Theory in Political Science' Ch. 3, Vol. 7, in Greenstein, F. I. and Polsby, N. W. (eds.) *Handbook of Political Science*. Reading, Mass. 1975.

Ehrlich, Howard J.: 'Attitudes, Behavior and the Intervening Variables. *American Sociologist*, Vol. 4, No. 1, 29—34, 1969.

Elliot, R. S. P. and Hickie, John: *Ulster. A Case Study in Conflict Theory*, ch. 4., London, 1971.

Etheredge, Lloyd: *A World of Men. The Private Sources of American Foreign Policy*. Yale University, unpublished Ph. D. dissertation, 1974.

Etzioni, Amitai: 'Social-Psychological Aspects of International Relations' in Lindsey, Gardner and Aronson, Elliot (eds.) *The Handbook of Social Psychology*. 2nd. edn. Vol. 5, ch. 43, Addison-Wesley Publishing Company, Menlo Park California 1968.

Even-Zohar, Chaim: *The Image of the Enemy: An Exploration of Some Psychological Aspects of the Arab-Israeli Conflict as They Affect Policy*.

Fagen, Richard, et al. (ed.) *Enemies in Politics*, Chicago: Rand McNally, 1967.

Festinger, Leon: *A Theory of Cognitive Dissonance*, Stanford University Press, 1957.

Finley, David J. and Fagen, Richard R.: *Enemies in Politics*, Chicago, 1967.

Fishbein, Martin and Ajzen, Icek: *Belief, Attitude, Intention and Behavior: An Introduction to Theory and Research*, Addison-Wesley, London 1975. 1975.

Fisher, Roger: *International Conflict for Beginners*, Herper and Row, Inc., New York, 1970.

Fox, William T. R.: 'The Causes of Peace and Conditions of War' *Annals of the American Academy*, No. 392, 1—13.

Gamson, William A. and Modigliani, Andre: *Untangling the Cold War*. Boston: Little, Brown & Co., 1971.

George, Alexander L., *Propaganda Analysis*. Evanston, Illinois, Row, Peterson, 1959 A.

George, Alexander L.: 'Quantitative and Qualitative Approaches to Content Analysis' in Ithiel de Sola Pool (ed.) *Trends in Current Analysis*. Urbana, Illinois: University of Illinois Press, 1959 B.

George, Alexandre L.: 'The "Operational Code": A Neglected Approach to the Study of Political Leaders and Decision-Making', *International Studies Quarterly*, XIII, 190—222, 1969.

George, Alexander L.: 'Adaptation to Stress in Political Decision-Making', in G. V. Coelho, D. A. Hamburg, and J. Adams (eds.). *Coping and Adaptation*, New York: Basic Books, 1974.

George, Alexander L. and Holsti, Ole R.: 'Operational Code Belief System and Foreign Policy Decision-Making'. Research Proposal submitted to and funded by the National Science Foundation, 1974.

George, Alexander L. and Smoke, Richard, *Deterrence in American Foreign Policy: Theory and Practice*, New York: Columbia University, 1974.

George, Alexander L., et al.: *Toward a More Soundly Based Foreign Policy: Making Better Use of Information.* Appendix D of the Report of the Commission on the Organization of the Government for the Conduct of Foreign Policy, Vol. 2, 1975.

George, Alexander L.: 'The Causal Nexus between Cognitive Beliefs and Decision-Making Behavior: The "Operational Code" Belief System', in Lawrence Falkowski (ed.) *Psychological Models in International Politics.* Boulder, Colorado: Westview Press, 1979, (forthcoming).

George, Alexander L.: 'Case Studies and Theory Development: The Method of Structured, Focussed Comparison', in Lauren P. G. (ed.) *Diplomatic History: New Approaches,* forthcoming 1979.

Gerard, Harold B., Conolley, Edward S. and Wilhelmy, Roland A. 'Compliance Justification and Cognitive Change', in Leonard Berkowitz (ed.) *Advances in Experimental Social Psychology,* Vol. 7, Academic Press, New York and London 1974.

Glenn, Edmund S., Johnson, Robert H., Kimmel, Paul R. and Wedge, Bryant: 'A Cognitive Interaction Model to Analyze Culture Conflict in International Relations' *Journal of Conflict Resolution,* Vol. 14, No. 1. 35—48, 1970.

Gutierrez, G. G., 'Dean Rusk and Southeast Asia: An Operational Code Analysis'. Paper prepared for the Annual Meeting of the American Political Science Association, New Orleans, Sept., 1973.

Harkabi, Y.: *Arab Attitudes to Israel.* Jerusalem: Israel University Press, 1971.

Hart, Thomas G.: *The Cognitive World of Swedish Security Elites.* Scandinavian University Press, Sweden, 1976.

Hart, Jeffrey A.: 'Cognitive Maps of Three Latin American Policy Makers', *World Politics,* XXX, 115—140, 1977.

Heider, Fritz: *The Psychology of Interpersonal Relations.* John Wiley & Sons, Inc., New York, Chapman & Hall Limited, London, 1958.

Heradstveit, Daniel: *Nahost-Guerillas: Eine politologische Studie,* Berlin Verlag, 1973.

Herastveit, Daniel: *Arab and Israeli Elite Perceptions,* Oslo University Press and Humanities Press, 1974.

Heradstveit, Daniel: *The Outline of a Cumulative Research Strategy for the Study of Conflict Resolution in the Middle East,* NUPI-report, No. 20, 1974.

Heradstveit, Daniel and Narvesen, Ove: 'Psychological Constraints on Decision-making. A Discussion of Cognitive Approaches: Operational Code and Cognitive Map', *Cooperation and Conflict,* Nordic Journal of International Politics, Oslo University Press, Vol. 2, 1978.

Heradstveit, Daniel and Torstensen, Karl A.: *Frykt og Forventning i Midt-Østen,* Dreyers Forlag, Oslo, 1975.

Herman, Charles F.: *International Crises: Insight from Behavioral Research.* The Free Press, New York, 1972.

Herman, Margaret C. and Milburn, Thomas W. (eds.): *A Psychological Examination of Political Leaders.* The Free Press, New York, 1977.

Hochberg, Julian E.: *Perception.* Englewood Cliffs, N. J.: Prentice-Hall, 1964.

Holsti, Ole R.: *The Belief System and National Images. John Foster Dulles and the Soviet Union.* Stanford University, unpublished Ph. D. dissertation, 1962.

Holsti, Ole R.: 'Cognitive Dynamics and Images of the Enemy' in David J. Finlay, Ole R. Holsti, and Richard R. Fagen, *Enemies in Politics,* pp. 25—96. Chicago: Rand McNally, 1967.

Holsti, Ole R., North, Robert, and Brody, Richard: 'Perception and Action in the 1914 Crisis' in J. David Singer (ed.) *Quantitative International Politics,* New York: Free Press, 1968.

Holsti, Ole R.: *Content Analysis for the Social Sciences and Humanities.* Addison-Wesley, London 1969.

Holsti, Ole R.: 'The "Operational Code" Approach to the Study of Political Leaders: John Foster Dulles. Philosophical and Instrumental Beliefs', *Canadian Journal of Political Science*, III, 123—157, 1970.

Holsti, Ole R.: *Crisis, Escalation, War*. Monteral and London, McGill-Queen's University Press, 1972.

Holsti, Ole R., and George, Alexander L.: 'The Effects of Stress on the Performance of Foreign Policy-Makers', in C. P. Cotter (ed.) *Political Science Annual: Individual Decision-Making*. Indianapolis: Boobs-Merrill, 1975.

Holsti, Ole R.: 'Foreign Policy Formation Viewed Cognitively' Ch. 2 in Robert Axelrod (ed.), *Structure of Decision*. Princeton University Press, 1976.

Holsti, Ole R.: The *'Operational Code as an Approach to the Analysis of Belief Systems,* Final Report to the National Science Foundation. (Grant No. SOC75-15368), Dec. 1977.

Holsti, Ole R., and Rosenau, James N.: 'Vietnam, Consensus, and the Belief Systems of American Leaders'. Paper delivered at the 1977 Hendricks Symposium on American Politics and World Order, University of Nebraska, Oct. 6—7, 1977.

Holsti, Ole R.: 'Foreign Policy Decision-Makers Viewed Psychologically: Cognitive Process Approaches' in M. G. Bonham and M. J. Shapiro (eds.) *Thought and Action in Foreign Policy*. Basel: Birkhäuser Verlag, 1977.

Horai, Joann: 'Attribution Conflict', in *Journal of Social Issues*, Vol. 33, No. 1, 1977.

Hovland, Carl I., Janis, Irving L. and Kelly, Harold H.: *Communication and Persuasion. Psychological Studies of Opinion Change*. New Haven and London, Yale University Press, 1953.

Iklë, Fred Charles: *Every War Must End,* Columbia University Press. New York and London, 1970.

Insko, Chester, *Theories of Attitude Change*. New York: Appleton-Century-Crofts, 1967.

Janis, Irving L.: *Victims of Groupthink*. Boston, Houghton, Mifflin Co., 1972.

Jervis, Robert: *Perception and Misperception in International Politics*. Princeton, N. J.: Princeton University Press, 1976.

Jessor, Richard and Jessor, Sherley L.: 'The Percieved Environment in Behavioral Science: Some Conceptual Issues and some Illustrated Data'. *American Behavioral Scientist,* Vol. 16, No. 6, 801—822, 1973.

Johnson, Loch: 'Operational Codes and the Prediction of Leadership: Senator Franck Church at Midcareer', in Margaret G. Herman (ed.), *A Psychological Examination of Political Leaders*, New York: The Free Press, 1977.

Jones, Edward, and Davis, Keith: 'From Acts to Dispositions: The Attribution Process in Person Perception', in Leonard Berkowitz (ed.) *Advances in Experimental Social Psychology 2*, New York: Academic Press, 1965.

Jones, Edward E. (ed.), *Attribution: Perceiving the Causes of Behavior*. Morristown, N. J.: General Learning Press, 1971.

Jones, Edward and Nisbett, Richard: *The Actor and the Observer: Divergent Perception of the Causes of Behavior*. New York: General Learning Press, 1971.

Jones, Russell A. and Brehm, Jack A.: 'Attitudinal Effects of Communicator Attractiveness When One Chooses to Listen' *Journal of Personality and Social Psychology,* Vol. 6, No. 1. 64—70, 1967.

Kahn, Robert L. and Cannell, Charles F.: *The Dynamics of Interviewing*. John Wiley and Sons, Inc., New York, 1957.

Kaplowitz, N.: *Psychopolitical dimensions of international relations: The case of the Middle East Conflict*. Unpublished manuscript, Department of Political Science, UCLA, 1975.

Kavanagh, Dennis, *The Operational Code' of Ramsay McDonald*, Stanford University, mimeo, 1970.

Kelly, George A., *The Psychology of Personal Constructs*. Vol. I and II, New York, Norton, 1955.

Kelly, Harold H.: *Attribution Theory in Social Psychology*, Nebraska Symposium on Motivation, 1967.

Kelly, Harold H.: 'Attribution in Social Interaction' in Edward R. Jones, David E. Kanouse et al., *Attribution: Perceiving the Causes of Behavior*. Morristown. N. J. Greater Learning Press, 1971.

Kelly, Harold H.: *Causal Schemata and the Attribution Process*, Morristown, N. J.: General Learning Press, 1972.

Kelly, Harold H.: 'The Process of Causal Attribution'. *The American Psychologist*, 1973.

Kelman, Herbert C. (ed.) *International Behavior: A Social-Psychological Analysis*. New York: Holt, Reinhart and Winston, 1965.

Kelman, Herbert C.: *The Problem-Solving Workshop in Conflict Resolution*. University of Illinois Press, 1972.

Kelman, Herbert C.: 'Attitudes Are Alive and Well and Gainfully Employed in the Sphere of Action', *American Psychologist*, Vol. 29, No. 5, 1974.

Kelman, Herbert C.: *Israelis and Palestinians: Psychological Prerequisites for Mutual Acceptance*, pp. 162—187, International Security, Summer 1978, Vol. 3, No. 1.

Kuhn, Thomas, *The Structure of Scientific Revolutions*, Chicago: University of Chicago Press, 1962, 2nd. ed. 1970.

Lane, Robert E.: *Political Man*, The Free Press, New York, 1972.

Lampton, David M., 'The U. S. Image of Peking in Three International Crises', *Western Political Quarterly*, XXVI, 28—50, 1973.

La Piere, 'Attitudes vs Action'. *Social Forces 13*, 237, 1934.

Larson, Deborah, *Cognitive Processes and Foreign Policy Decision-Making: An Information Processing Model*. Stanford University, mimeo, 1976.

Latour, Stephen, Houlden, Pauline, Walker, Lawrence and Thibaut, John: 'Some Determinations of Preference for Modes of Conflict Resolution'. *Journal of Conflict Resolution*. Vol. XX, No. 2, 1976.

Leites, Nathan, *The Operational Code of the Politburo*. New York: McGraw-Hill, 1951.

Leites, Nathan, *A Study of Bolshevism*, Glencoe, Ill.: The Free Press, 1953.

Lewin, Kurt: *Resolving Social Conflicts: Selected Papers on Group Dynamics*, ed. by Gertrud Weiss Lewin. Souvenir Press, Ltd., 1948.

Malone, Craig S., *The Operational Code of Lyndon Baines Johnson*. Stanford University, mimeo, 1971.

McArthur, Leslie Ann. 'The How and What of Why: Some Determinants and Consequences of Causal Attribution'. *Journal of Personality and Social Psychology*. Vol. 22, No. 2, 171—193, 1972.

McCloskey, Herbert: *Political Inquiry: The Nature and Uses of Survey Research*, The MacMillan Company, London, 1969.

McGuire, William J.: 'The Nature of Attitudes and Attitude Change' in Gardner Lindzey and Elliot Aronson (eds.) *The Handbook of Social Psychology 3*, 2nd. ed., Reading, Mass.: Addison-Wesley, 1968.

McGuire, William J.: 'Theory of the Structure of Human Thought' in Abelson et. al.: *Theories of Cognitive Consistency: A Sourcebook*.

McLellan, David, 'The "Operational Code" Approach to the Study of Political Leaders: Dean Acheson's Philosophical and Instrumental Beliefs', *Canadian Journal of Political Science*, IV, 52—75, 1971.

Merrit, Richard L. (ed.) *Communication in International Politics*, Ch. 7. London, University of Illinois Press, 1972.

Merton, Robert K. and Kendall, Patricia: 'The Focused Interview' *The American Journal of Sociology.* Vol. 51, No. 6, 1946.

Miller, George A., Galanter, Eugene, and Pribraen, Karl H.: *Plans and the Structure of Behavior,* New York, 1960.

van Nievwenhuijze, V. C. A. O.: 'Some Thoughts on the Present State of the Sociology of the Middle East', *Der Islam Band 41,* 1965.

Osgood, Charles E. et. al. *The Measurement of Meaning.* University of Illinois Press, 1957.

Øvrevik, Geir: *Konflikt-forestillinger i Jordan og Libanon.* Mimeo, Institute of Political Science, University of Oslo, Oslo 1975.

Pruitt, Dean G. and Snyder, Richard C. *Theory and Research on the Causes of War.* Prentice Hall Inc., 1969.

Pruitt, Dean G., 'Definition of the Situation as a Determinant of International Action, in Herbert Kelman (ed.) *International Behavior,* New York: Holt, Rinehart and Wiston, 1965.

Putnam, Robert D.: *The Beliefs of Politicians. Ideology, Conflict, and Democracy in Britain and Italy.* New Haven, and London, 1973.

Randel, Robert F.: *The Origins of Peace. A Study of Peacemaking and the Structure of Peace Settlement.* The Free Press, New York, 1973.

Rokeach, Milton, 'Attitude Change and Behavior Change', *Public Opinion Quarterly,* 30, No. 4, 529—550, 1966.

Rokeach, Milton, *The Open and Closed Mind,* Basic Books, Inc., New York, 1960.

Rosenberg, Shawn and Wolfsfeld, Gary, 'International Conflict and the Problem of Attribution'. *Journal of Conflict Resolution,* Vol. XXI, No. 1, 1977.

Ross, L.: *Distortion in the Social Perception Process: The Production and Perseverance of Attributional Biases and Errors.* Mimeo, Stanford University, 1975.

Ruble, Thomas L.: 'Effects of Actor and Observer Roles on Attributions of Causality in Situations of Success and Failure'. *The Journal of Social Psychology,* No. 90, 41—44, 1973.

Shapiro, Michael J., and Bonham, Matthew G.: 'Cognitive Processes and Foreign Policy Decision-Making', *International Studies Quarterly,* XVII, 1973.

Shaw, Marvin E., and Constanzo, Philip R.: *Theories of Social Psychology,* McGraw Hill Book Company, New York, 1970.

Sherwin, Ronald G. 'Decision Making and Information Processing: Changing Patterns of Cognition in Egypt and Israel, 1967 and 1973'. Institute of International Studies, University of California, Berkeley, Paper presented at International Studies Association — West, 10. May, 1973. Berkeley, California.

Shlaim, Avi: 'Failures in National Intelligence Estimates: The Case of the Yom Kippur War. *World Politics,* Vol. XXVIII, No. 3, 1976.

Singer, David J.: 'The Peace Research and Foreign Policy Prediction' in *The Paper of the Peace Science Society (International),* Vol. 21, 1973.

Siverson, Randolph M.: 'A Research Note on Cognitive Balance and International Conflict: Egypt and Israel in the Suez Crisis', *Western Political Quarterly,* Vol. XXVII, No. 2, 1974.

Stabell, Charles B.: *Individual Differences in Managerial Decision-Making Processs: A Study of Conversational Computer System Usage'.* Ph. D. Thesis, MIT, Mimeo, 1974.

Stagner, Ross: *Psychological Aspects of International Conflict.* Belmont, California, Brooks/Cole, 1976.

Steinbruner, John D.: *The Cybernetic Theory of Decision,* Princeton, N. J. Princeton University Press, 1974.

Steiner, Ivan D.: 'Perceived Freedom'. *Advances in Experimental Social Psychology,* No. 5, 1970.

227

Stuart, Douglas, *The Operational Code of John F. Kennedy.* University of Southern California, Ph. D. dissertation.

Suleiman, Michael W.: 'Attitudes of the Arab Elite Toward Palestine and Israel' in *American Political Science Review,* Vol. LXVII, No. 2, 482—489, 1973.

Thordarson, Bruce: *Trudeau and Foreign Policy: A Study in Decision-Making.* Toronto: Oxford University Press, 1972.

Tørum, Harald: *Konfliktforestillinger i Egypt. En intervjuundersøkelse om eliteoppfatninger.* Mimeo, Norwegian Institute of International Affairs.

Tweraser, Kurt: 'Changing Patterns of Political Beliefs: The Foreign Policy Operational Code of J. William Fulbright' *Sage Professional Papers in American Politics,* Number 04-016, 1974.

Walker, Stephen G. 'The Interface Between Beliefs and Behavior: Henry Kissinger's Operational Code and the Vietnam War'. *Journal of Conflict Resolution 21,* 129—168, 1977.

White, Gordon: *A Comparison of the Operational Codes of Mao Tse-tung and Liu Shao-chi.* Stanford University, mimeo, 1969.

White, Ralph K.: 'Misperception in the Arab-Israeli Conflict'. *Journal of Social Issues,* Vol. 33, No. 1. 190—221, 1977.

Wrightson, Margaret: 'The Documentary Method' in R. Axelrod (ed.) *The Structure of Decision.* Princeton, N. J.: Princeton University Press, 1976.

Yaniv, Avner: 'Conflict Theory and the Arab-Israeli Conflict'. *The Jerusalem Journal of International Relations,* Vol. 3, No. 1, 1977.

Zajonc, Robert: 'Cognitive Theories in Social Psychology', in Gardner Lindzey and Elliot Aronson (eds.) *The Handbook of Social Psychology 1,* 2nd. ed. Reading, Mass.: Addison-Wesley, 1968.

Zimmerman, William: *Soviet Perspectives on International Relations.* Princeton, University Press, 1969.

Subject Index

230

Reinforcement psychologist, 49
Relationship, 13, 16—17, 20, 22, 26, 41, 94, 111, 113, 116—117, 119, 129, 132; actor-observer, 55; hypothesized, 56, 93; means-ends, 66, 73; of beliefs, 28; political, 67; predicted, 54
Relevance, 29, 128
Reliability, 33, 39, 44—46, 83, 93; intercoder, 46
Representativeness, 30, 40, 43, 83
Research, 9, 10, 12, 15, 16, 26, 28—29, 32, 35, 40—41, 43—45, 75, 79 102, 122, 125, 136; cumulative; 130; political, 19
Researcher, 32, 35, 44, 77, 136
Resolution of the conflict, 23, 24, 67, 71, 102, 122, 128
Resources, 10, 40, 90
Respondents, 20, 31, 51, 53, 55—57, 60—61, 67—69, 77—78, 80, 82—83, 88, 90—96, 98, 101, 107, 110—111, 113, 117, 118, 128—129, 132—133, 134; Arab, 52, 54, 58, 59, 60, 65—66, 68—69, 80—81, 86—87, 90, 95, 104—105, 112; consistent, 91—95, 98, 100—101, 103, 105, 116—117, 119, 133—34; consistently compromising, 101, 103, 105; Egyptian, 94, 104; inconsistent, 92—95, 97—100, 103—105, 116; Israeli, 52, 58—59, 62, 64, 66, 68, 81, 83, 87, 93—94, 99, 104—105, 112; Jordanian, 104—105; Libanese, 104; moderately consistent 92—95, 98—100; purely consistent 92—95, 98—100
Response, 25, 37, 45, 48, 58, 66, 73, 83—85, 93, 124, 135; behavioral, 26, 27; response consistency, 88, 89, 101, 104, 105, 113
Resposibility, 54, 57, 60, 75—76, 125
Results, 9—10, 15, 32, 37, 41—43, 45—47, 50—51, 53—57, 63—66, 68, 72—75, 83, 86, 93, 95—96, 98, 104—105, 107, 110, 112, 116—118, 121, 127, 129, 131, 133—134, 136
Rewards, 35—36

Sample, 12, 33, 40—45, 47, 49, 55, 63, 77, 80—82, 86—87, 100, 103, 107, 121, 127—128; representative, 41, 77, 136
Sampling procedure, 41, 42, 47
Sanctions, 33—35

Self-attitudes, 43; -attribution, 23, 72; -determination, 67; -esteem, 23, 70, 72, 73; -image, 31, 78, 81, 92, 108, 109, 110, 112, 115, 117, 118, 119, 120, 131, 132, 133; -perception, 22, 23, 72; -protection, 64
Settlement, 10, 13, 79, 91, 113, 114, 123; of the conflict, 93, 122
Situational attribution, 50, 51, 52, 53, 54, 55, 56, 58, 59, 60, 61, 63, 64, 66, 68, 69, 70, 74, 127; constraints, 13, 14, 27, 52, 61, 62, 65, 67, 125; factors, 22, 25, 51; tendency, 63; variables, 24, 49, 54, 56, 59, 69, 74, 123, 126, 128
Social force, 49; psychologist, 19, 135—136; psychology, 19, 70
Society, 116, 130, 131
Solution, 50, 84—85, 90, 95, 100, 102, 121; of conflict, 66, 69, 86, 130, 132; military, 79, 95, 123; political, 123
Soviet policies, 27
Stability, 12, 15, 17, 21, 25—26, 80, 83, 86, 88, 101, 133
Statements, conciliatory, 91—92, 96, 98—99, 102—103, 124, 131—133; non-, 91—92, 96, 99, 102—103, 131—133
Stereotypes, 21
Stimulus, 23, 26—27, 49, 72, 74, 127
Stimulus-response model, 49
Strain, 28
Strategy, 10, 17, 44—45, 51, 75, 78, 89, 96, 98—99, 108, 132, 135
Students, 42—43
Study, 9—10, 12—15, 17, 20, 22, 24—25, 30—32, 37—40, 43—44, 47, 74—75, 88, 107, 113—114, 121, 124—126
Subject, 47, 88
Subjective insider, 34
Superpowers, 9, 37, 50, 60, 61, 69, 78, 108, 109; influence of, 68
Syria, 32, 33
System, 17, 19, 21, 30, 45, 122, 133; linkage, 19

Tel Aviv, 34
Tension, 28—29
Theory, 9, 13—15, 17, 19, 22, 24, 28, 44, 48, 66, 70, 75, 88
Traditionalist, 129—132, 135
Trait psychologist, 49
Typology, 19, 130

233